Legends in Marketing
CHRISTIAN GRÖNROOS

Legends in Marketing
CHRISTIAN GRÖNROOS

Series Editor
Jagdish N. Sheth, Ph.D.

Volume 5

RELATIONSHIP MARKETING

Volume Editor
David Ballantyne, Ph.D.

Contributors
Adrian Payne, Ph.D.
Michael Saren, Ph.D.
Richard Varey, Ph.D.

⑤SAGE www.sagepublications.com
Los Angeles • London • New Delhi • Singapore • Washington DC

First published in 2013 by

SAGE Publications India Pvt Ltd
B1/I-1 Mohan Cooperative Industrial Area
Mathura Road, New Delhi 110 044, India
www.sagepub.in

SAGE Publications Inc
2455 Teller Road
Thousand Oaks, California 91320, USA

SAGE Publications Ltd
1 Oliver's Yard, 55 City Road
London EC1Y 1SP, United Kingdom

SAGE Publications Asia-Pacific Pte Ltd
33 Pekin Street
#02-01 Far East Square
Singapore 048763

Published by Vivek Mehra for SAGE Publications India Pvt Ltd, typeset in 11/13 pt Adobe Garamond Pro by Diligent Typesetter, Delhi and printed at Saurabh Printers Pvt Ltd, New Delhi.

Library of Congress Cataloging-in-Publication Data

Grönroos, Christian, 1947–
    Legends in marketing. Christian Grönroos / series editor, Jagdish N. Sheth, Ph.D.
        8 volumes; cm. — (Legends in marketing)
    Includes bibliographical references.
    1. Marketing. 2. Marketing research. 3. Communication in marketing. 4. Grönroos, Christian, 1947– I. Sheth, Jagdish N. II. Title. III. Title: Christian Grönroos.
    HF5415.G756   658.80092—dc23   2013   2013037200

ISBN: 978-81-321-1002-6 (HB) (set of 8 volumes)

The SAGE Team: Shambhu Sahu, Shreya Lall, Archita Mandal, Rajib Chatterjee, and Umesh Kashyap

VOLUMES IN THIS SET

Thank you for choosing a SAGE product! If you have any comment,
observation or feedback, I would like to personally hear from you.
Please write to me at <u>contactceo@sagepub.in</u>

—Vivek Mehra, Managing Director and CEO,
SAGE Publications India Pvt Ltd, New Delhi

Bulk Sales

SAGE India offers special discounts for purchase of books in bulk.
We also make available special imprints and excerpts from our
books on demand.

For orders and enquiries, write to us at

Marketing Department
SAGE Publications India Pvt Ltd
B1/I-1, Mohan Cooperative Industrial Area
Mathura Road, Post Bag 7
New Delhi 110044, India
E-mail us at <u>marketing@sagepub.in</u>

Get to know more about SAGE, be invited to SAGE events, get on
our mailing list. Write today to <u>marketing@sagepub.in</u>

————————ನಿ ೦ೞ————————

Contents

Perspectives of Other Scholars

David Ballantyne Interviews Christian Grönroos

Appendix of Sources

All articles and chapters have been reproduced exactly as they were first published. All cross-references can be found in the original source of publication.

Grateful acknowledgment is made to the following sources for permission to reproduce material for this volume:

1. "Return on Relationships: Conceptual Understanding and Measurement of Mutual Gains from Relational Business Engagements," Christian Grönroos and Pekka Helle
    Journal of Business & Industrial Marketing, Vol. 27, No. 5, 2012: 344–359.
    Published by Emerald Group Publishing Limited. Reprinted with permission.

2. "A Service Perspective on Business Relationships: The Value Creation, Interaction and Marketing Interface," Christian Grönroos
    Industrial Marketing Management, Vol. 40, No. 2, 2011: 240–247.
    © 2010 Elsevier Inc. All rights reserved. Reprinted with permission from Elsevier via Copyright Clearance Center's RightsLink service.

3. "Relationship Marketing as Promise Management," Christian Grönroos
    Pauline Maclaran, Michael Saren, Barbara Stern, and Mark Tadajewski (eds), *The SAGE Handbook of Marketing Theory*, SAGE (London), 2009, pp. 397–412.
    Published by SAGE Publications Ltd. Reprinted with permission.

4. "Love at First Sight or a Long-Term Affair? Different Relationship Levels as Predictors of Customer Commitment," Maria Sääksjärvi, Katarina Hellén, Johanna Gummerus, and Christian Grönroos
    Journal of Relationship Marketing, Vol. 6, No. 1, 2007: 45–61.
    © 2007 by The Haworth Press, Inc. All rights reserved. Reprinted by permission of Taylor & Francis (http://www.tandfonline.com).

5. "Taking a Customer Focus Back into the Boardroom: Can Relationship Marketing Do It?" Christian Grönroos
    Marketing Theory, Vol. 3, No. 1, 2003: 171–173.
    Published by SAGE Publications Ltd. Reprinted with permission.

CHRISTIAN GRÖNROOS

Christian Grönroos is Professor of Service and Relationship Marketing (from 1999 to present; prior to that, he was Professor of International and Industrial Marketing from 1984 to 1999) at Hanken School of Economics, Finland (Svenska handelshögskolan) and Initiator and Past Chair of the Board of the research and knowledge center, Centre for Relationship Marketing and Service Management (CERS), of this business university. He is Honorary Professor at Nankai University and Tianjin Normal University, People's Republic of China and at Oslo School of Management, Norway. From 2002 to 2007, he served as Guest Professor of Service Management at Lund University (Campus Helsingborg), Sweden. In 1988 and 1992 he was Visiting Professor at Arizona State University, USA, where its centre for services marketing (now Centre for Service Leadership) was pioneering research in this field. He has also been a scholar at several universities world wide.

He is a pioneer and leading scholar developing modern service marketing and service logic as well as relationship marketing and customer relationship management, and one of the earliest proponents of the term service management to describe customer- or market-oriented management based on a service logic in service and manufacturing firms. He is one of the fathers of the school of service marketing and management that has been internationally labeled The Nordic School of thought.

He is CSL Distinguished Faculty at Center for Services Leadership, Arizona State University, USA and International Fellow at Service Research Center (Centrum för tjänsteforskning), Karlstad University, Sweden. In Finland, he is scholarly affiliated (docent) with Åbo Academy University, Helsinki University of Technology (now part of Aalto University) and University of Tampere. He is also an honorary member of the Italian Marketing Association and a guest professor at Marketing Research Center of China.

He is a distinguished member of the Finnish Society of Sciences and Letters and a member of the board of the society since 2008.

Among his current academic administrative positions are member and chair of the University Council as well as member of the Academic Council of Hanken School of Economics, Finland.

He has published extensively in several languages on service marketing and management and relationship marketing issues as well as on contemporary views on marketing theory. His most recent books on the service and relationship perspective in business are *Service Management and Marketing*; *Customer Management in Service Competition* (2007) and *In Search of a New Logic for Marketing—Foundations of Contemporary Theory* (2007).

In two separate studies of the academic and societal impact of professors in business administration in Finland in 2007, Christian Grönroos came out as the professor with the highest impact. In 2009 he was again found to top this list. In 2012, he was elected one of the most influential professors for the business community in Finland.

In a study of the academic impact of scholars who had published in the top-tier *Journal of Business Research* in 2000, one of his articles ("Relationship Approach to Marketing in Service Contexts: The Marketing and Organizational Behavior Interface," *Journal of Business Research*, Vol. 20, No. 1, 1990: 3–11) came out as the one with the highest impact.

In a citation index study from 1994 comparing Finnish scholars in business administration with those in sociology, political science, and public law, Christian Grönroos was internationally by far the most cited scholar in business administration, and in terms of citations, on the same level as the most prominent scholars in sociology and political science in Finland (the reference disciplines in the study). Quoting from the study, "In business administration Grönroos comes first, then no one, then no one, and then the rest."

His article "From Marketing Mix to Relationship Marketing: Towards a Paradigm Shift in Marketing" (*Management Decision*, Vol. 32, No. 2, 1994: 4–20; lead article; Award for Literary Excellence, 1994) is still the most downloaded article of all scientific articles published in an Emerald journal.

In 2003, he was awarded the most prestigious prize for scholarly achievements of the Finnish Society for Sciences and Letters (The Professor E. J. Nyström's Prize). In 1999, he received the American Marketing Association's Services Special Interest Group (SERVSIG) Career Contributions to Services Discipline Award, as the first scholar ever from outside North America to receive this award. In 2002 he was awarded the Pro Oeconomia Prize for the best business book published in Finland. In Scandinavia he has been awarded for his service management research: The Ahlsell Award for outstanding research into marketing and distribution, and the Erik Kempe Award for his textbooks on service management and marketing.

From 1999 to 2008 he served as the chair of the jury for the CERS Award for Excellence in Relationship Marketing and Management. From 2008 to 2011 he served as a member of the jury for the Finnish Quality Award.

In addition to his academic career he frequently lectures on service management and marketing and service business logic as well as customer relationship management and relationship marketing in university-level executive programs as well as in in-house seminars in service and manufacturing firms in Europe, North America (USA), Latin America (Brazil), Asia (China, Singapore, and Thailand), Africa (South Africa), and Oceania (Australia and New Zealand).

His family consists of his wife Viveca Ramstedt, two children from a previous marriage, and four grandchildren.

VOLUME 5 ARTICLE TIMELINE

• Return on Relationships: Conceptual Understanding and Measurement of Mutual Gains from Relational Business Engagements, **2012**

2012

• A Service Perspective on Business Relationships: The Value Creation, Interaction and Marketing Interface, **2011**

• Relationship Marketing as Promise Management, **2009**

2008: Guest Professor, Oslo School of Management, Norway
2008: Honorary Guest Professor, Tianjin Normal University, China

• Love at First Sight or a Long-Term Affair? Different Relationship Levels as Predictors of Customer Commitment, **2007**

2005: Visiting Scholar: The University of Auckland, New Zealand, December 2005
2003: Receiver of Emerald Literati Club's Lifetime Achievement Award "for his contribution to the field of marketing"

• Taking a Customer Focus Back into the Boardroom: Can Relationship Marketing Do It?, **2003**

• Creating a Relationship Dialogue: Communication, Interaction and Value, **2000**

2002: Honorary Guest Professor, Nankai University, Tianjin, China
2002: Guest Professor of Service Management, Lund University/Campus Helsingborg, part time 2002–2007

2000

• Relationship Marketing: The Nordic School Perspective, **1999**
• Relationship Marketing: Challenges for the Organization, **1999**

• Value-Driven Relational Marketing: From Products to Resources and Competencies, **1997**

1999: Receiver of the American Marketing Association's (Servsig Service Special Interest Group) Contribution to the Service Discipline Award (first receiver from outside North America)
1999: Professor of Service and Relationship Marketing, Hanken School of Economics, Finland, 1999–Present

• Relationship Marketing: Strategic and Tactical Implications, **1996**

• Relationship Marketing: The Strategy Continuum, **1995**

• From Marketing Mix to Relationship Marketing: Towards a Paradigm Shift in Marketing, **1994** (republished **1997**)

1994 (April), 1995 (October), 1996 (October), 1999 (May): Visiting Professor of Marketing, Nankai University, Tianjin, China

• Relationship Approach to Marketing in Service Contexts: The Marketing and Organizational Behavior Interface, **1990**
• Marketing Redefined, **1990**

1990

1988: Visiting Professor, Department of Marketing, Arizona State University, USA, July 1988–January 1989

1986: Selected as Distinguished Member of the Finnish Society of Sciences and Letters

1984: Professor of International and Industrial Marketing, Hanken School of Economics, Finland, 1984–1999
1983: Associate Professor, Marketing, Hanken School of Economics, Finland, 1983–1984

1980

1979: Ph.D. (Economic sciences), Hanken School of Economics, Finland

1970

Legends in Marketing

As a post doc Research Fellow at Columbia University while writing the book *The Theory of Buyer Behavior* (Wiley, 1969) with my mentor and professor, John A. Howard, I had spent two full years in the stacks of Columbia University Library, reading in awe, classic books in psychology, philosophy, economics, sociology, and anthropology. I was always fascinated with history since my undergraduate days and especially with the biographies of philosophers, scholars, and advisors to kings and monarchs. I was curious about how they developed their thoughts; what made them challenge existing wisdom; and the context or circumstances which made them propose alternative perspectives or explanations.

What impressed me the most through this experience was the realization that knowledge is recursive: what we discover today was also discovered yesterday but forgotten just like the ancient civilizations in Machu Picchu, Egypt, India, and China. The old monuments and ruins were overrun by vegetation and buried in forests or swallowed by floods, only to be rediscovered by archeologists and anthropologists. Just as we are in awe of ancient civilizations and marvel at how advanced our ancestors were in organizing civic societies and synthesizing extant knowledge in either scriptures or in mythologies, I am always in awe of insightful concepts, discoveries, experiments, and synthesis of knowledge by well respected scholars. Furthermore, often their best writings are not just in top-tier journals but also in symposia, monographs, and chapters in specialized books. Often their books become textbooks for graduate students because of their unique perspectives or research findings. In fact, most of the best-known scholars are more remembered by their books and not for their papers.

The breadth and depth of knowledge I gained in those two years at Columbia University was simply invaluable in writing *The Theory of Buyer Behavior*. This was also the case in my other academic books including *Marketing Theory: Evolution and Evaluation* (Wiley, 1988) and *Consumption Values and Market Choices* (Southwestern, 1991).

I followed that tradition in my doctoral seminars at the University of Illinois in Consumer Behavior, Marketing Theory and Multivariate Methods, by assigning and encouraging doctoral students to read classic writings, many of them out of print and therefore not easily accessible, unlike today. Similarly, I continue to encourage doctoral students to read and review old literature to gain perspectives for their doctoral dissertations and research papers.

The genesis of *Legends in Marketing* comes from these experiences as a doctoral student, post-doc Fellow, and doctoral seminar leader. There are world class thinkers and researchers in marketing, who, over their four to five decades of scholarship, have generated knowledge which is both deep and broad. However, it is scattered in different publications, some of them out of print and not digitized. What if we could assemble and organize this knowledge into volumes and make them available both in print and online? Hence, this series is called *Legends in Marketing*.

The mission of *Legends in Marketing* is to:

1. Compile and organize decades of published academic research of a world renowned marketing scholar into six to ten volumes.
2. Ensure that his or her legacy is widely disseminated to the next generation of marketing scholars especially from emerging markets such as Africa, China, and India as well as from the transition economies of ex-Soviet Union including Russia, Eastern Europe, and Central Asia.
3. Preserve this knowledge as a Legacy in marketing.

Each Legend selected compiles and organizes his or her published works from academic journals, conference proceedings, chapters of books and any other source of publication. While this is not a census of all the Legend's writings, it includes a vast majority of his or her lifelong contributions over several decades which can be organized into six to ten volumes.

For each volume, the Legend selects a Volume Editor (VE) who is familiar with the Legend's publications in that specific area. The VE in collaboration with the Legend organizes the selected publications into a Table of Contents with thematic sections of the Volume. The VE also writes an Introduction to the Volume which traces the origins of the focal area, how the Legend has impacted that area, and how the field is likely to evolve in the future.

The VE also invites three contributors who comment on how the Legend's work has impacted the field and them personally. Finally, the VE interviews the Legend to get his or her latest views and reflections on the published works.

I went through this process for my own writings with the extraordinary assistance from Balaji C. Krishnan, who agreed to be the Set Editor, resulting in eight volumes which SAGE (India) published in early 2010.

The first set of nine Legends who have agreed to be featured are:

Shelby D. Hunt	Kent B. Monroe	Naresh K. Malhotra
Richard P. Bagozzi	Philip Kotler	Yoram Wind
Paul Green	V. Kumar	Gerald Zaltman

Both SAGE (India) and I are very pleased with the strong interest and enthusiasm about the *Legends in Marketing* Series from faculty, doctoral students, and academic libraries, especially from emerging markets. I am especially pleased that each Legend is also passionate about this project. Our plan is to continue the Series each year by adding five to six additional Legends in Marketing. This is a very gratifying labor of love.

Jagdish N. Sheth, Series Editor
Emory University

Legends in Marketing:
Christian Grönroos

Unlike other Legends in Marketing, I met Christian Grönroos much later in his life. In fact, it was in the mid-1990s at a conference on Relationship Marketing that we had organized at Emory University. Of course, we have been in touch with each other ever since, although we do not meet as often as we used to.

Christian Grönroos started his academic career in business administration and economics. He found economics a rigorous discipline, but too abstract and limited to explain management problems properly. His interest in marketing began through his research on demand for automobiles. He was invited to speak about the marketing of services at an executive meeting, and this led to his lifelong research in service industries. Also, he was asked to be a teaching assistant for a marketing class which further motivated him to specialize in marketing.

Today, there is no better European known scholar than Christian Grönroos in the services marketing industry. Indeed, he is considered one of the fathers of the Nordic School of Thought in Service Marketing and Management. What is unique about Christian's research is that it has been, from its inception, cross disciplinary between marketing, operations, and human resource management. I think this has enabled him to conceptualize concepts in marketing which are both enriching and at the same time practical. They often force us to think that internal marketing is a necessary first step before a company should engage in external marketing.

Like all other Legends in Marketing, Christian Grönroos always wanted to be an academic scholar. Going to college was natural because his older brother went to college and his father was an engineer for the paper and pulp industry. What he finds most satisfying is making an impact on managerial practice and transforming their mindset from an engineering-centric to customer-centric perspective. Christian Grönroos has stayed in Finland all his life, even though he could have easily migrated to the United States. This is due to family reasons and personal preferences.

I asked him what advice he has for young scholars. His answer was: Believe in what you do and do not allow others to talk you out of it. Be stubborn. He agrees that it was easier to be stubborn 40 years ago than it is today. In his view, this is sad for the advancement of knowledge and for the discipline's growth. Today, it is too much a "publish or perish" world and consequently, it often loses sight of what is correct and what is not.

He also suggests that as a young scholar, you need to increase your visibility by attending international conferences, where you meet scholars from other cultures and traditions.

Unfortunately, academic career opportunities are limited in Scandinavia. Therefore, you have to make a mark and thereby enhance your opportunities all over the world and especially in the United States.

I asked Christian Grönroos about his future areas of research. He has focused on service and relationship marketing all his life. Now, he would like to focus on understanding a service—centred logic thoroughly, and an exploring the implications of marketing theory of such a business and marketing perspective, and how it can benefit the development of business strategies and marketing in the manufacturing sector.

I am very pleased to invite Christian Grönroos as one of the Legends in Marketing. His contribution to the discipline, as you will see from his publications, is invaluable and evergreen.

Jagdish N. Sheth, Series Editor
Emory University

Volume Introduction: The Changing Domain of Relationship Marketing— An Introductory Commentary

David Ballantyne
Associate Professor of Marketing
University of Otago, New Zealand

A good place to begin is with the term *relationship marketing*. It was contributed to a conference paper by Len Berry in 1983 as a new rubric for services marketing. In the same year as Berry's paper, in a seminal *Harvard Business Review* article, Theodore Levitt (1983a) recommended that firms and their managers would do well to treat long-standing connections with key customers as if they were marriages. The idea was that the sale "consummates courtship" as part of a process "to build relationships and bonds that last." The marriage metaphor was useful but in many respects it was a simplification of business realities (Tynan, 1997). Nevertheless, it prompted a rethink among many marketing scholars and practitioners about the implicit assumptions guiding marketing practices.

Cooperation in business had been overlooked in the competitive emphasis of the times, with the *4Ps marketing mix* being the prevailing mind-set. The 4Ps related to the pursuit of business transactions but had nothing to say about developing cooperative business relationships. Some scholars today resolve conceptual contradictions between "cooperating" and "competing" by treating both as interrelated parts of the business relationship, rather than two irreconcilable contradictory logics (Bengtsson and Kock, 2000).

In the 1980s, the new relationship orientation was emerging in Europe and especially in the Scandinavian countries. Christian Grönroos at the Hanken School of Economics in Finland, together with Evert Gummesson at Stockholm University, had established what they called the *Nordic School of Services*. Much of the early foundations for relationship marketing were conceived within this Nordic branded context. Important relationship insights were developed from the *interactive* nature of service. Grönroos (1983) introduced the idea of customer relationship "risk points" in what he called the *customer life cycle*. Gummesson (1987) showed how interaction between service providers and customers contributed to long-term relationships. In other words, firms risk loss of customers to competitors whenever a narrow transactional orientation dominates. This and the contribution of other early thought leaders gave a temporal framing for the development of relationship marketing strategies. For the Nordic School community and a whole generation of Ph.D. students since then, a *service orientation* contributed to a shift in mainstream marketing's emphasis on the value of a *single* transaction to the mutual value of a relationship containing *many* transactions.

Nordic school service and relationship mindedness has not faltered to this day. As will be seen in the articles by Professor Christian Grönroos selected for this special volume, and in supporting commentaries by three notable marketing scholars, Grönroos's unique contribution to the development of relationship marketing is made clear.

Contemporary with the evolution of the Nordic School service perspective a new business network perspective was emerging at Uppsala University in Sweden and more broadly in Europe. Those involved became known as the Industrial Marketing and Purchasing (IMP) group. The first large-scale IMP research study (reported by Turnbull and Cunningham, 1981; also Håkansson, 1982) led the group to formulate their *interaction approach* to industrial marketing and purchasing. This set up a base for later work on a *network approach* to understanding business relationships (Håkansson and Snehota, 1995) and the sharing of both streams of research through journal articles and annual IMP conference proceedings. For IMP researchers, business interactions always occur within the context of business relationships, whether weak or strong, long or short, harmonious or conflictual. Furthermore, the nature of a business relationship is not the choice of one party, but a consequence of the interactions between all parties. Thus, both Nordic School and IMP recognized marketing as a multisided activity, where interactions are episodes in the life of a relationship.

This relationship-oriented challenge to mainstream marketing was initially slow to gain support in spite of wake-up calls from marketing thought leaders in the 1980s. Theodore Levitt (1983b) communicated his vision succinctly: "The purpose of a business is to create *and* keep a customer." Jackson (1985) emphasized relationship marketing in business markets, making a clear distinction between transactional and relationship orientations. New relationship-oriented marketing channels' perspectives were introduced, especially in the United States of America (e.g., Dwyer et al., 1987; Anderson and Narus, 1990). Also, major innovations in *direct marketing* practice took hold, with a move from mail list delivery mechanisms to interactive database-enabled mechanisms. Yet mainstream marketing continued its competitive quest for new customers, with strategies for customer service and quality management usually delegated down to service operations departments. At the same time, continuous quality improvement of internal business processes (known as Total Quality Management, or TQM) reached fan-craze status among business practitioners. Marketing academics were hesitant and mostly not involved, in spite of early conceptual formulations for *internal marketing* by Len Berry and Christian Grönroos in 1981.

In the 1990s, relationship marketing came into its own as a rubric, and as a field of marketing inquiry. Webster (1992), Normann and Ramirez (1993) and Sheth and Parvatiyar (1995) contributed influential articles. Operational insights for managing interaction episodes were absorbed from services marketing and from TQM. This led to greater marketing involvement in keeping customers, not just getting them, as had been recommended earlier by Levitt (1983b). Jag Sheth and colleagues at Emory University (USA) established a biannual International Relationship Marketing Conference. At Monash University (Australia) in the following year I initiated the first *International Colloquium in Relationship Marketing (ICRM)*, now held annually at different host universities. New, broader strategic frameworks were proposed for scoping out and developing the stakeholder relationships of the firm (see, e.g., Christopher et al., 1991; Gummesson, 1999a; Morgan and Hunt, 1994).

At this time one-to-one relationship marketing opportunities were "rediscovered." This was partly a consequence of improvements to database information and communication technologies (ICT), which set in motion a tsunami of technology-driven *customer relationship management (CRM)* and *loyalty program* activity (see, e.g., Peppers and Rogers, 1993; Reichheld, 1996). CRM in many cases since has departed from the mutually beneficial relationship concepts proposed by Christian Grönroos and other thought leaders of the 1980s, adopting instead the retro-logic that customer relationships can and should be managed and controlled by supplier firms.

One important issue under critical discussion around the turn of the millennium was the meaning given to the term "relationship," especially in a network context. Wilkinson and Young (2002) argued that there was no single basis for understanding the degree of cooperativeness or competitiveness between B2B customers and their suppliers. Consumer marketers on the other hand tended to take for granted that the worth of customer relationships could be calculated and strategies appropriate to each relationship segment determined. Under an expanding spread of ideas and assumptions, Harker (1999) reported finding 26 definitions of relationship marketing in the academic literature. And O'Malley and Tynan (2000) felt the need to ask: "Is relationship marketing rhetoric or reality?"

With a growing diversity of ideas and assumptions, some sorting out was needed. Two Scandinavian researchers, Möller and Halinen (2000), set out to analyze the historical sources of relationship marketing. They saw four streams: business marketing, services marketing, marketing channels, and database marketing/direct marketing. Each, they argued, had its own agenda and relationship perspectives. In other words, the relationship marketing agenda was categorically divided and contested. Not so unusual in the evolution of ideas! Especially insightful in my view was the contribution of Egan (2003). He argued that relationship marketing was divided not so much by historical antecedents but between proponents who see relationship marketing as focused one-to-one management of customer relationships, and those who hold a more holistic network view of markets and marketing.

Can these perspectives be reconciled? Relationship marketing increased in popularity in the 1990s with a challenging agenda emphasizing gaining customers through positive word of mouth, not just through advertising and promotion, and retaining them through quality and service-based offerings (see, e.g., Grönroos, 2009). This called for customer–supplier strategies and processes that positioned marketing activity between firms as potentially collaborative, and within the firm as cross-functional and relational. These normative requirements are well developed in my view, except for one link, which is the skillfulness needed to achieve cross functional coordination between business actors *within* the firm, under conditions where leaders often face a lack of employee trust and suspicion as to their motives (Ballantyne, 2003; Varey, 1995). The agenda hidden and not adequately realized in relationship marketing is *internal marketing*, first raised in 1981 in separate articles by Berry and Grönroos. For me, internal marketing is how customer value creation begins.

According to Grönroos (2000), internal marketing is an organizational strategy involving marketing, operations, and human resource management (HRM) specialists working together. This is likely why it is not "owned" by any particular specialist group. At the same time, its realization depends on cooperation between these groups. As a consequence of the firm-centric excesses unraveling during the global financial meltdown of 2008–09, the social and economic macro-climate supporting the development of such positive internal relationships may be better now than at any other time in the last 30 years.

There is also the emergence of the digital social network to consider, where *economic* relationships are best thought of as embedded in networks of *social* relationships. This is not a new idea, nor is it currently the dominant business logic. The crucial point is that if marketing is viewed as interactions within networks of relationships of many kinds, and if these are systemically connected (Gummesson, 1999b), then the managerial logic of absolute firm-level control is not sustainable, at least not in the manner to which we have become accustomed (Håkansson and Ford, 2002). Understandably, firms may be keen to make new "friends" in the new digital social contexts but the idea of a focal firm attempting to manage and control a captive network of relationships, to draw value to itself from customers, does not fit well with a still emerging new socioeconomic logic.

The global financial perturbations of the 2010s have exposed the weakness at the heart of macro-level laissez-faire capitalism. In my view what is needed is a more inclusive societal and ecological approach to economic development, where people are placed at the center of economic models. New ideas are emerging which acknowledge the work of the relationship marketing pioneers (e.g., Vargo and Lusch, 2004; Lusch and Vargo, 2006). Christian Grönroos has often stressed in his published work and conference presentations that marketing relationships begin with interaction between people and a mutual exchange of promises (e.g., Grönroos, 1990). In spite of the changes and challenges to relationship marketing over the last 30 years, these fundamentals seem to be holding up very well indeed.

References

Anderson, J.C. and J.A. Narus. 1990. "A Model of Distributor Firm and Manufacturer Firm Working Partnerships," *Journal of Marketing*, 54 (January): 42–58.

Ballantyne, D. 2003. "A Relationship Mediated Theory of Internal Marketing," *European Journal of Marketing*, 37 (9): 1242–60.

Bengtsson, M. and S. Kock. 2000. "Co-opetition in Business Networks—to Cooperate and Compete Simultaneously," *Industrial Marketing Management*, 29: 411–26.

Berry, L.L. 1981. "The Employee as Customer," *Journal of Retail Banking*, 3 (March): 25–28.

———. 1983. "Relationship Marketing," in L.L. Berry, G.L. Shostack, and G.D. Upah (eds), *Emerging Perspectives of Services Marketing*, pp. 25–28. Chicago, Il: American Marketing Association.

Christopher, M., A. Payne, and D. Ballantyne. 1991. *Relationship Marketing: Bringing Quality, Customer Service and Marketing Together.* Oxford: Butterworth-Heinemann.

Dwyer, F.R., P.H. Schurr, and S. Oh. 1987. "Developing Buyer-Seller Relationships," *Journal of Marketing*, 51 (April): 11–27.

Egan, J. 2003. "Back to the Future: Divergence in Relationship Marketing Research," *Marketing Theory*, 3 (1): 145–57.

Grönroos, C. 1981. "Internal Marketing: An Integral Part of Marketing Theory," in J.H. Donnelly and W.R. George (eds), *Marketing of Services*, pp. 236–38. Chicago, Il: American Marketing Association.

———. 1983. *Strategic Management and Marketing in the Service Sector.* Cambridge, Massachusetts: Marketing Science Institute.

———. 1990. "Relationship Approach to Marketing in Service Contexts: The Marketing and Organizational Behavior Interface," *Journal of Business Research*, 20 (1): 3–11.

———. 2000. *Service Management and Marketing. A Customer Relationship Management Approach.* 2nd edn. Chichester: Wiley & Sons.

———. 2009. "Relationship Marketing as Promise Management," in P. Maclaran, M. Saren, B. Stern, and M. Tadajewski (eds), *The SAGE Handbook of Marketing Theory*, pp. 397–412. Los Angeles, CA: SAGE Publications.

Gummesson, E. 1987. "The New Marketing: Developing Long Term Interactive Relationships," *Long Range Planning*, 20 (4): 10–20.

———. 1999a. *Total Relationship Marketing: Rethinking Marketing Management from 4Ps to 30Rs.* Oxford: Butterworth-Heinemann.

———. 1999b. "Total Relationship Marketing: Experimenting with a Synthesis of Research Frontiers," *Australasian Marketing Journal*, 7(1): 72–85.

Håkansson, H., (ed.). 1982. *International Marketing and Purchasing of Industrial Goods.* New York: Wiley.

Håkansson, H. and D. Ford. 2002. "How Should Companies Interact in Business Networks," *Journal of Business Research*, 55: 133–39.

Håkansson, H. and I. Snehota. 1995. *Developing Relationships in Business Networks.* London: Routledge.

Harker, M.J. 1999. "Relationship Marketing Defined? An Examination of Current Relationship Marketing Definitions," *Marketing Intelligence and Planning*, 17(1): 13–20.

Jackson, B.B. 1985. *Winning and Keeping Industrial Customers.* Lexington, MA: Lexington Books.

Levitt, T. 1983a. "After the Sale Is Over," *Harvard Business Review*, 62 (1): 87–93.

———. 1983b. *The Marketing Imagination.* New York/London: Free Press.

Lusch, R.F. and S.L. Vargo. 2006. "Service-Dominant Logic: Reactions, Reflections and Refinements," *Marketing Theory*, 6 (3): 281–88.

Möller, K. and A. Halinen. 2000. "Relationship Marketing Theory: Its Roots and Direction," *Journal of Marketing Management*, 16: 29–54.

Morgan, R.M. and S.D. Hunt. 1994. "The Commitment-Trust Theory of Relationship Marketing," *Journal of Marketing*, 58 (July): 20–38.

Normann, R. and R. Ramirez. 1993. "From Value Chain to Value Constellation: Designing Interactive Strategy," *Harvard Business Review*, July–August: 65–77.

O'Malley, L. and C. Tynan. 2000. "Relationship Marketing in Consumer Markets: Rhetoric or Reality?" *European Journal of Marketing*, 34(7): 797–815.

Peppers, D. and M. Rogers. 1993. *The One to One Future: Building Relationships One Customer at a Time*. New York: Currency/Doubleday.

Reichheld, Frederick F. 1996. *The Loyalty Effect*. Boston, MA: Harvard Business School Press.

Sheth, J.N. and A. Parvatiyar. 1995. "Relationship Marketing in Consumer Markets: Antecedents and Consequences," *Journal of the Academy of Marketing Science*, 23 (4): 255–71.

Turnbull, P.W. and M.T. Cunningham (eds). 1981. *International Marketing and Purchasing: A Survey among Marketing and Purchasing Executives in Five European Countries*. London: Macmillan.

Tynan, C. 1997. "A Review of the Marriage Analogy in Relationship Marketing," *Journal of Marketing Management*, 13 (7): 695–703.

Varey, R.J. 1995. "Internal Marketing: A Review and Some Inter-Disciplinary Research Challenges," *International Journal of Service Industry Management*, 6 (1): 40–63.

Vargo, S.L. and R.F. Lusch. 2004. "Evolving to a new Dominant Logic for Marketing," *Journal of Marketing*, 68 (1, January): 1–17.

Webster, F.E., Jr. 1992. "The Changing Role of Marketing in the Corporation," *Journal of Marketing*, 56 (October): 1–17.

Wilkinson, I.F. and L.C. Young. 2002. "On Cooperating: Firms, Relations and Networks," *Journal of Business Research*, 55: 123–32.

1

Return on Relationships: Conceptual Understanding and Measurement of Mutual Gains from Relational Business Engagements

Journal of Business & Industrial Marketing
Vol. 27, No. 5, 2012
pp. 344–359

Christian Grönroos

Pekka Helle

Purpose—*Relationship is based on the idea of creating a win-win situation for parties involved in a business engagement. The purpose of the article is to develop a model of mutual value creation and reciprocal return on relationships (ROR_R) assessment, which enables calculation of joint and separate gains from a relational business engagement.*

Design/methodology/approach—*The approach takes the form of a conceptual analysis, which is tested empirically through a real-life case. The empirical part is based on a longitudinal empirical study including several empirical cases.*

Findings—*Following a practice matching process, resulting in mutual innovation and aligning of their processes, resources and competencies, the parties in a business engagement make investments in the relationship. This enables the creation of joint productivity gains. Valuation of joint productivity gains produces an incremental value, which can be shared between the parties through a price mechanism. Finally, based on this shared value and costs of investments in the relationship by the parties, a reciprocal return on the relationship can be assessed and split between the business parties.*

Research limitations/implications—*The study addresses dyadic business engagements only. The findings enable calculation of reciprocal return on relationships (ROR_R) and form a basis of further development of marketing metrics and financial contribution of marketing, and of developing financial measures of intangible assets called for by the finance and investor communities.*

Practical implications—*Using the conceptual model and corresponding metrics, the financial outcome of the development of customer relationships as well as an assessment of the return on relationships with customers can be established.*

Originality/value—*The approach to assess the value of customer relationships as a two-sided endeavor is novel, as well as the joint productivity construct and the value sharing approach, and the way of assessing ROR as a reciprocal measure that can be split between the business parties.*

Introduction

The relationship marketing approach is based on a thought that two (or several) parties establish a business engagement that enables both (or all) parties to gain something. In other words, it is assumed that a win-win situation can be achieved (see Christopher *et al.*, 1991; Grönroos, 1994; Gummesson, 1987 and, 2008; Morgan and Hunt, 1994; Sheth and Parvatiyar, 1995; Storbacka and Lehtinen, 2001; Little and Marandi, 2003; Tzokas and Saren, 2004). The parties may have differing and even conflicting ambitions and goals, but nevertheless, according to relationship marketing the possibilities to achieve mutual gains exist. Furthermore, relationship marketing can be considered "investing in customers ... (and having) an opportunity to make marketing relevant for shareholders, top management, (and) customers" (Grönroos, 2003, p. 172). Although benefits for customers of relationship marketing exist, in spite of this studies on relationship marketing normally look at this marketing approach from the supplier side only (see the criticism of relationship marketing in practice in Fournier *et al.*, 1998), and as spending a budget instead of as an investment. In this way the win-win assumption is either implicitly taken for granted, or neglected.

However, relationships are two-sided. It takes two for a relationship to exist, and this has to be true for a relationship-based approach to marketing as well. Hence, in the present article we take as a starting point that possible benefits to be gained from a relational business engagement between two parties, established through a relationship marketing approach, have to be mutually perceived as beneficial (compare Grönroos and Helle, 2010). In this sense, our work relates to the studies of "pie extension" by Jap (1999, 2001), where she analyzed cooperation between firms in dyadic relationships which "... are designed to expand the size of the joint benefit pie and give each party a share" (Jap, 1999, p. 461). In her study she showed that, according to the respondents, the "pie" indeed could be grown, and that the returns on investments in this "pie extension" for both parties in a dyad "... are products of the idiosyncratic contribution and effort of the specific partners together", and that these incremental returns "... could not have been generated by either firm in isolation" (Jap, 1999, p. 461).

In order to establish the outcome of collaboratively made investments in a relationship, the benefits that mutually can be created have to be calculated in some way. The purpose of the present article is to develop a conceptual understanding and model of how mutual gains in a business engagement are created, and to develop metrics for measuring the corresponding returns for the business partners in this relational engagement. Although supplier-customer relationships frequently exist in networks of other relationships, where the outcome of business conducted in a dyad may be influenced by how other relationships in the network function (Gummesson, 2006), for clarity we focus on a dyadic situation only in this study.

Larger firms engaged in close and on-going relationships with customers will probably benefit the most from the model and metrics developed in the present article. Additionally, providers that become intertwined with their customers in terms of roles, activities, and risks are likely to benefit from the model and metrics. Such a situation is frequently occurring when customers move ahead in their industry value chain, and by so doing open up opportunities for providers to re-define existing arrangements for division of labor. Another example of companies that may find the model and metrics useful is industry innovators. These are companies that do not limit their strategies to dyadic make-or-buy decisions, but that aim to re-configure the surrounding value system in ways that make it more effective for all involved parties. Furthermore, dynamic and uncertain environments as well as rising demands may increase firms' willingness to engage in the collaborative relational efforts required. On the other hand, perceived risk of opportunistic behavior by the other party in the dyad, or of decreased flexibility to act on the marketplace may make firms less inclined to engage in this type of business (compare Jap, 1999).

Return on Relationships

Marketing accountability has become an important focus for marketing research, and marketing's failure to demonstrate its financial accountability has been pointed out (McGovern et al., 2004; Rust, Ambler, Carpenter, Kumar and Srivastava, 2004; Stewart, 2009). In the literature the complex and multi-faceted process leading to customer relationship profitability has also been discussed (see, for example, the rather elaborate conceptual customer relationship profitability model in Storbacka et al., 1994). The notion that customers or customer relationships are valuable assets is not new (e.g. Bursk, 1966, Levitt, 1983; Wayland and Cole, 1994; Cravens et al., 1997). Customer relationships have been considered examples of firms' market-based assets (Srivastava et al., 1998) and strategic assets (Amit and Shoemaker, 1993). However, the discussion about how financial effects of marketing can be calculated, in relational and non-relational contexts, is based on a one-sided view only. What returns from customers marketing can create for the firm is in focus, and considered interesting. For example, studies of customer asset management and customers as investments using customer life time value (Gupta and Lehman, 2003; Gupta et al., 2006) and customer portfolio approaches (Venkatesan and Kumar, 2004; Kumar and George, 2007) are based on such one-sided views. The same goes for analyses of customer equity relating to current customers (Blattberg and Deighton, 1996; Blattberg et al., 2001) as well as future potentials (Rust, Lemon and Zeithaml, 2004), where the customer side is included implicitly only, if at all.

Moreover, because portfolio models are based on models for analyzing financial instruments, customers are treated as soulless assets that can be included in a portfolio or disposed of more or less as financial assets, without taking into account the fact that unlike such assets, customers do their own calculations and have their own rational and less rational decision-making criteria (Dhar and Glazer, 2003). Furthermore, the existence of interconnectedness between customers is neglected. Clearly, it is not realistic to use such models for calculating the value of customers as assets, and to treat customers in this way (compare Devinney *et al.*, 1985).

The effects of the other side of the coin, what a firm can do for its customers in terms of benefits for them, is left to traditional marketing measurements to cover, for example applying customer satisfaction and brand awareness studies. In addition to sales volumes and similar marketing information very little information exists about the supplier as an asset for its customer. If relationship marketing is to aim at helping the firm to create a win-win situation with its customers, conceptual models and metrics geared towards one-sided measurements only are not theoretically sound, nor are they helpful for business practice. Two-sided models and corresponding metrics are needed.

In the relationship marketing literature the concept return on relationships, or ROR, is used (e.g. Gummesson, 2004, 2008). Although there are other, non-monetary gains to be obtained as well, such as favorable word-of-mouth behavior and references (e.g. Ryals, 2002; Kumar *et al.*, 2007), usually return on relationships refers to monetary gains only. Gummesson (2008) defines it in the following way: *"ROR is the long-term net financial outcome caused by the establishment and maintenance of an organization's network of relationships"* (p. 257; italics added). According to this definition, return on relationships is a financial outcome over time, attributable to the fact that a relational business engagement has been established and functions. The definition also points out that an organization's relationships exist in a network. However, the reciprocal nature of ROR is only implicitly accounted for in this definition. Therefore, we suggest the following definition of return on relationships as a mutual and reciprocal construct:

> Return on relationships (ROR) is the long term net financial outcome emerging for all parties resulting from the establishment and mutual maintenance of a relational business engagement (Reciprocal ROR or ROR_R).

This definition implies that return on relationships is an outcome of a mutual reciprocal process, and can be assessed on a relationship level as well as separately for the parties in the relationship. In the present article, we develop a conceptual model and metrics for dyadic relationships only. However, in principle the model and the metrics can be extended to cover more complex relationships as well.

In a discussion of the challenge of calculating the return on investments in customer relationships, Ang and Buttle (2002) emphasize problems associated with developing the metrics needed. Basically, as they observe, return on investments (ROI) is a simple and straightforward idea. However, calculating returns on investments in customer relationships is complicated by four issues: defining the boundaries of a customer relationship and relationship marketing, establishing what an investment in customer relationships includes, deciding what is considered a return on such an investment, and choosing an appropriate time frame to use in assessing the return (Ang and Buttle, 2002). Although they discuss return on relationships in the traditional way as a one-sided issue, the requirements they address are equally valid for developing a reciprocal ROR assessment model. In subsequent sections when developing our model and related metrics, solutions to these requirements are suggested.

In principle, the financial outcome can be calculated either as returns on assets developed through the relational engagement based on the calculation of the net present value of future earnings from customers (e.g. customer portfolios or customers as assets), or based on changes in revenue and cost levels caused by the established engagement. Due to the two-sided nature of ROR adopted here—return-and-relationships as a reciprocal construct ROR_R—the first alternative would require not only calculating the value of the customers as asset for the supplier, but also calculating the value of the supplier as asset for the customer.

Due to the obvious complexity involved in such calculations, for our measurement approach we have chosen to use effects on revenues and costs for the supplier and customer in a relational dyad caused by the changes taking place in the way the relationship is developing. Cost effects for the parties in the relationship relate to investments in the mutual relationship made by them. This way of calculating financial outcomes minimizes the need to base financial effects on estimates of future returns from customers, which always are projections and not real figures. Normally, such estimates only implicitly take costs of serving customers into account. Overall, in marketing research there has been a limited interest in cost effects, and in studies of customer lifetime value, typically only assumptions about costs are made (Gupta, 2009). Customer-related costs effects are important and need to be taken into account (Ryals, 2005). However, normally the interest in cost effects is focused on acquisition, whereas costs of service are neglected. For that reason analyzing costs caused by how customers interact with suppliers is lacking in marketing research (for exceptions, see Niraj *et al.*, 2001; Van Raaij *et al.*, 2003).

In our study, cost and revenue effects of how a relationship develops are calculated separately. Changes in the cost level, for the customer and supplier, respectively, can be calculated as real cost effects, using activity-based costing, whereas only calculations of revenue effects for the customer are based on estimates. The revenue effect for the supplier is calculated through a price mechanism, determining the possible price increase made possible by the way the business engagement develops. Moreover, this approach makes it possible to combine financial effects caused for both sides in the relationship. In order to do win-win calculations in a transparent way, this is a necessity. This way of calculating the cost and revenue effects for both parties enables us to establish a measurement of the engagement between the business parties as an asset for the mutual relationship.

A Service and Value Approach to Calculating ROR$_R$

Because relationship marketing requires that the supplier aims at supporting its customers' processes, it has been claimed that a win-win oriented relational approach must be based on a service perspective (Grönroos, 2000). In the discussion of service as a perspective on business and marketing (service logic, service-dominant logic), it has been claimed that service is inherently relational (Grönroos, 2000; Vargo and Lusch, 2008). Logically, this means that understanding the underpinning logic of relationship marketing, and of relational business engagements, requires a service perspective. Therefore, we develop our conceptual model for understanding how return on relationships emerges, and the corresponding measurement model, in accordance with such a perspective.

Following Grönroos (2011), we understand a service business perspective (service logic) from the supplier's side as follows:

> *A service logic (service business perspective) means that a supplier does not provide resources for the customer's use only, but instead it provides support to its customers' business processes through value-supporting ways of assisting the customers' practices relevant to their business (business effectiveness instead of operational efficiency only)* (Grönroos, 2011, p. 241; italics added).

This means that the supplier gears its activities not only towards supporting the customer's various processes (e.g. order-making, warehousing, manufacturing, cost control), thereby creating operational efficiency. In addition, they are also geared towards directly supporting the customer's business outcome through how efficiently operational processes are supported. In this way the supplier also directly aims at having a favorable impact on its customer's business effectiveness. By taking this approach, it will be possible to track down both the cost effects and the revenue effects of the way the supplier serves its customers. The expression "serve a customer" means influencing the customer's business outcome favorably through support provided to customer practices relevant to the business outcome. In a business context, a practice is a process or activity performed by the customer or by the supplier, such as operational, administrative, financial, purchasing, or sales and marketing processes and activities (about practice theory, see, for example, Schatzki, 2001).

The win-win notion of relational business engagements, and the need for the supplier and customer to mutually maintain the relationship, means that both parties may need to work in favor of the relationship. Hence, although it is the supplier's task to support its customer, the latter party may also need to change some of its practices in order to improve the possibilities for mutual value creation (about mutual value creation, see Grönroos and Helle, 2010). The service perspective in a relational context emphasizes the value-in-use construct as a key indicator of value created for customers.

Value creation is a key concept in a service business perspective (cf. Grönroos, 2008; Vargo and Lusch, 2008). Taking a service perspective approach, it is only natural that we use value creation as a basis for calculating mutual returns on a relationship. In a value creation context, Gupta and Lehman (2005) observed that in a business engagement there are two sides to value, namely, value for the supplier and value for the customer. In the present article, we take this into account in the conceptual model as well as in the measurement model. In this way the need to incorporate the mutuality of a business relationship into ROR metrics is observed. Value is defined as a function of revenues and costs, and therefore, incremental value created in a business relationship is measured as changes in costs and revenues that are caused by activities in the relationship. Other value aspects, such as trust in the other party, are not included in the model, but they do of course exist and influence the relationship. Earlier indicators of value for customers used in net present value calculations of customers as assets are based on a value-in-exchange construct, and thus geared towards a transactional view of the business engagement. The service perspective and the value-in-use orientation enable calculations of value, and therefore also of return of relationships, which are relationally grounded. Thus, we get indicators which are truly relational.

Following the principles developed by Helle (2009; 2011) value is treated as a productivity gain enabling the creation of incremental value. Moreover, because value for the parties in a relationship is created from the same business engagement, improvements in productivity effects enjoyed by the supplier and the customer are pooled and treated as joint productivity gains. This leads to joint incremental value gain to be shared between the parties through a price mechanism. In order to be able to measure productivity in this way, an integration of productivity measurements for both the supplier and the customer is needed. For this the concept joint productivity is used (Helle, 2009; 2010; see also Grönroos and Helle, 2010).[1] This concept, and the relationship between value created for the business parties on one hand and joint productivity on the other hand are discussed in subsequent sections of the article.

Practice Matching and Mutual Value Creation

The service perspective means that the supplier supports all necessary customer practices (processes and activities) required to have a favorable impact on the customer's business outcome (business effectiveness). As MacMillan and McGrath (1997) observe, it is not enough for a firm to take well car of one, or even a few customer processes, for example with good product quality and fast deliveries. In order to distinguish itself from competitors it has to define all relevant customer processes and activities, and serve them well. In Figure 1 a typical flow of customer and supplier processes are illustrated in a schematic way. As can be seen from the figure, customer processes and activities have corresponding processes and activities on the supplier side. Corresponding practices, at least the ones which are important to the customer's business outcome, should function so that the supplier process supports the corresponding customer process. In this way the supplier does not only deliver resources, but serves its customer by supporting its performance. Sales and marketing corresponds to purchasing,

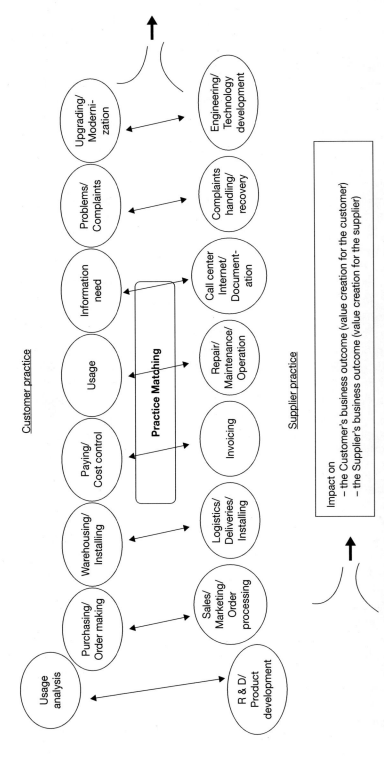

Figure 1. Customer and Supplier Practices and their Impact on the Business Outcome

Sources: Grönroos and Helle (2010); see also Grönroos (2011, p. 241)

order-taking and processing correspond to order-making, the supplier's outbound logistics and deliveries correspond to the customer's inbound logistics and warehousing, invoicing corresponds to the customer's need for cost control, repair and maintenance services correspond to the customer's need to keep its operational processes running in a smooth way, and so on.

In order to serve its customer well, and to effectively support its business outcome, the supplier must align its resources, competencies and processes with the corresponding customer resources, competencies and processes. At least those which are important for the customer's business outcome need to be aligned. However, as a business relationship is a mutual engagement, such development processes may be needed on both sides. Hence, it is a matter of mutually innovating and aligning ways of operating, and of resources and competencies used in various processes. This mutual process of innovating and aligning relevant processes, resources and competencies is called practice matching.

The practice matching concept, introduced by Grönroos and Helle (2010), is based on the notion of adaptation between business partners (Håkansson, 1982; Hallén et al., 1991; Brennan and Turnbull, 1999). Brennan et al. (2003, p. 1639) define adaptation as "... a behavioural or organizational modification at the individual, group or corporate level, carried out by one organization, which is designed to meet the specific needs of one other organization". In Brennan and Turnbull's (1999, p. 486) categorization of adaptation options, practice matching mainly corresponds to what they call strategic adaptation involving formal decision making. Both suppliers and customers may adapt, for example, their products and production methods, delivery, pricing, information routines and needs, and even the orgnization itself (Håkansson, 1982, p. 18). Hence, when firms adapt to their business counterparts in relational contexts, both interfirm and intrafirm adaptation have been found to be of importance (Brennan and Turnbull, 1999). Costs may arise in both the supplier and customer ends of the relationship (Axelsson and Wynstra, 2002), but calculations of costs and benefits stemming from an adaptive process have been found to be rarely occurring (Schmidt et al., 2007). According to Brennan and Canning (2002), adaptations seem to take place primarily for the benefit of the customer. However, from a relationship marketing perspective, potentially both parties could benefit from adaptive processes. Moreover, in addition to financial effects, interfirm adaptation may also have positive effects on trust and commitment in a business engagement (Brennan and Turnbull, 1999).

Practice matching as an interfirm and intrafirm adaptive process is the starting point for implementing mutual value creation, and for how to subsequently measure return on relationships. In Figure 2 the model of mutual value creation is illustrated.[2]

In the figure, the box in the center represents the actual practices (processes and activities) performed by the supplier and the customer, respectively. In essence, this part of the figure is similar to what was illustrated by Figure 1. In the final analysis,

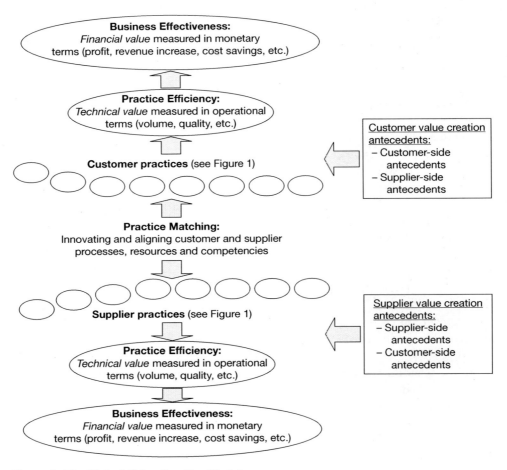

Figure 2. The Mutual Value Creation Model

the objective of performing these practices by the two parties is to create a favorable impact on the business outcome of the parties involved in the business engagement. The upper side of the figure illustrates how this value creation process progresses for the customer. The lower side shows how the process progresses for the supplier. The two processes are mirror picture of each other. As research into interfirm adaptation indicates, adaptation by suppliers may be more frequently occurring than adaption by customers (Brennan *et al.*, 2003), probably because it is more difficult for customers to decide what aspects of the supplier's processes to adapt to, and how to do it (Boddy *et al.*, 1999). However, in principle a practice matching process can be initiated by any party in an on-going or potentially developing business engagement, and it can result in changes in the supplier's or in the customer's, or in both parties' processes.

By developing and if necessary inventing processes, resources and competencies on either side of the relationship, or when found appropriate on both sides, the supplier and customer flows of practices are aligned. The goal of this practice matching process is to improve the technical effects of the customer's and supplier's corresponding processes, i.e. to have a positive effect on the practice efficiency of the two parties' processes and activities. In the mutual value creation model this effect is labeled technical value (Grönroos and Helle, 2010). This value dimension can be measured in various operational terms, such as volume and quality.

However, to be able measure the effects on business outcomes, and subsequently on return on relationships, one has to be able to transform this technical, operational effect into a financial value effect measured in monetary terms. For the customer (on the upper side of the model), such monetary measures are additional revenues created through possibilities to capture growth opportunities, or through premium pricing, and cost level changes. For the supplier (on the lower side of the model), such monetary measures are revenue increases through re-sales, up-sales and cross-sales possibilities and premium pricing opportunities, and cost level changes. If the first-stage effect on operational practices—technical value/practice efficiency effects—in a second stage can be calculated as financial value of the business engagement, a measurement of the business effectiveness in terms of value gains, or incremental value, for each party in the relationship can be established. This incremental value created is due to the implementation of the practice matching process, which in turn is based a service perspective on the business engagement.

For practice matching to work, the business parties need to open their books for each other, at least to some extent. This, of course, requires a substantial amount of trust. However, due to the nature of practice matching, an analysis of joint productivity gains, i.e. a combined and integrated improvement in both party's practices following the relationship development process, is made possible. Consequently, the incremental value, in the model for illustrative reasons depicted as separate financial value outcomes for the customer and supplier, respectively, emerges as a combined increase in the financial value of the business engagement achievable through the practice matching-based developmental process. Hence, we have a solid base for sharing this value gain through a price mechanism, and thereby also for assessing the return on the relationship for the parties involved as well as the value for the parties of the whole relationship as an asset.[3]

As Figure 2 illustrates the mutual value creation model, the logic of the total process for assessing ROR in a relational business engagement and for establishing the value of the relationship as an asset for the parties in this engagement is schematically summarized in Figure 3. By adopting a service perspective on business (a service logic), a mutual support of both parties in a relationship to be developed is made possible, which in turn triggers a practice matching process. This process aims at aligning the customer's and supplier's processes, resources and competencies, for the sake of establishing combined cost effects for the parties and revenue effects for the customer (the revenue effect for the supplier is established through a price mechanism in the value sharing phase). This combined effect equals a productivity gain, in this process

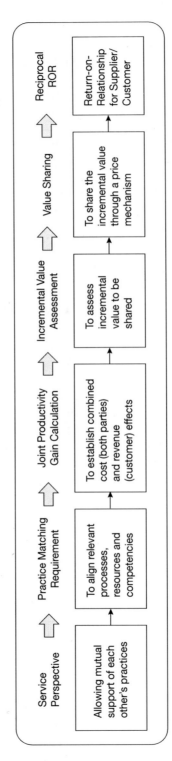

Figure 3. The Logic of the Return-on-Relationship Assessment Process

treated not as separate productivity measures for the supplier and customer, but instead as an integrated joint productivity gain attributable to the relationship itself. This is in line with the underpinning logic of relationship marketing, and enables an assessment of the incremental value in the relationship gained through the developmental process. In the next stage, this incremental value can be shared[4] between the supplier and customer through a price mechanism, whereby the supplier gets its share of the increased value as a premium price. The outcome of this phase of the process cannot be calculated, but is due to a negotiation process.

Finally, the value share of the two parties can be related to the investment in the relationship development process, i.e. the possible additional cost required to establish and implement this relational business engagement, and thereby a return on the relationship (ROR_R) as it has been developed can be assessed, and subsequently split into ROR for the supplier (ROR_S) and the customer (ROR_C). In subsequent chapters the calculation model and the metrics required as well as the constructs required are developed and illustrated with a real-life case.

Conceptual Model of Mutual Value Creation

To understand and estimate return on relationships (ROR), we build on a recent approach to value creation in a relational business context (Helle, 2009; 2011), called mutual value creation (Grönroos and Helle, 2010). We posit that the framework for mutual value creation has the capacity to provide the missing link that connects investments associated with a relational business engagement and the financial consequences that accrue to the involved parties. In so doing, the framework contributes to ongoing efforts to provide an answer to the question: Does relationship marketing pay off? (Gummesson, 2004).

The framework conceptualizes mutual value creation as the driver of return on relationships (ROR). In so doing, the framework expands previous indicators of return on relationships, which delimit themselves to treating only some aspects of exchange value as the underlying source of relationship returns. Instead, the framework claims that return on relationships depends on the involved actors' relational competence rather than their ability to advance each others' separate strategies for well-being. The article argues that doing so will align the concept of relationship return more closely with the basic tenets of relationship marketing. In Figure 4 the process flow illustrated in Figure 3 is further developed for the purpose of assessing mutual value and creating the ROR metrics.

First Facet of Mutual Value Creation—Practice Matching

Following Helle (2009, 2011; also Grönroos and Helle, 2010), the paper defines mutual value creation as an integration of two distinct, yet closely intertwined facets. The first facet of value creation comprises practice matching (Grönroos and Helle, 2010).

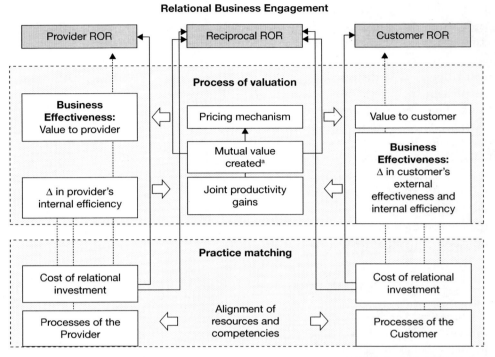

Figure 4. Mutual Value Creation and Return On Relationships (ROR): Calculation Model

Note: [a]Mutual value created denotes also the value of the relationship as an asset

Within the literature on relationship marketing, the role of comparing and aligning resources in value creation—and the interactive resource alignment it entails—is well established (Gummesson, 1995). It implies that customers and suppliers engage in interactions during which they learn from each other, which in turn may help them align their respective resources and competencies for the purpose of creating win-win outcomes (Berry, 1995; Morgan and Hunt, 1994; Gummesson, 2004).

However, practice matching is only half the value equation. That is, although practice matching does involve processes in which performance benefits are created, it does not in itself imply value creation. Whereas practice matching denotes a process of creating a new way of operating as the underlying source of value—or utility—a process of valuation determines whether the performance gains *de facto* imply value creation for the involved parties (Helle, 2009, 2011).

Second Facet of Mutual Value Creation—Valuation

The second aspect of value creation involves a process of some form of valuation. Examining value creation from the point of view of valuation implies looking at how the monetary results of practice matching, when shared through price accrue as value to the involved parties (Helle, 2009; 2011). Put differently, valuation determines whether the monetary worth of the performance gains actually exceeds the costs of resource inputs (the investment in the relationship), when shared through a price mechanism. Thus, value is a measure of the profitability of the practice matching.

This view of value is conceptually in line with many—if not most—value concepts that treat customer value as some form of assessment, evaluation, or outcome of value creating activities (Zeithaml, 1988; Cravens *et al.*, 1988; Monroe, 1990). Underscoring the supplier view, Porter (1985) seems to intimate a similar view when he suggests that value to the supplier is the difference between the price the customer pays and the cost of serving that customer.

The Interplay between Productivity and Value—Key to Mutual Value Creation

How does the conceptual framework presented here help understand mutual value creation, and consequently return on relationships (ROR)? The framework illustrates that mutual value creation—and ROR—is an outcome of the interplay between practice matching and valuation. Through practice matching, involved actors create performance joint gains. When these performance gains are shared through a pricing mechanism, their monetary worth accrues to the involved parties as value.

Following Davis (1955), the framework posits that the concept that captures these performance changes and translates them into monetized joint-gains is productivity. In a process of valuation, the monetary worth of those joint gains is shared through a price mechanism as value to the involved parties.

But how are productivity and value related? Put simply, value is a measure of the profitability of practice matching (Davis, 1955; Courbois and Temple, 1975; Gollop, 1979; Kurosawa, 1975; Pineda, 1990). That is, whereas productivity captures the success of practice matching, value captures the effects of practice matching in the involved actors' monetary process. To understand how relational investments associated with practice matching generate financial consequences for the involved parties, we must understand the interplay of productivity and value and the interplay between productivity outcomes for the parties in the business engagement. In the article the outcome of this interplay has been termed joint productivity.

The framework also highlights an interesting—and all-out crucial—dynamics between practice matching and the business effectiveness of the involved parties. For the customer, the business effectiveness is a direct consequence of practice matching. Whatever performance benefits that the practice matching process creates for the customer directly impact the customer's external effectiveness (additional revenues) and internal efficiency (changes in cost level), and thus its value-in-use. For the supplier, however, the link between practice matching and business effectiveness is more indirect. This means that the supplier's business effectiveness can only be determined once the joint productivity gains are shared through a pricing mechanism as value to the supplier and customer. That is, the supplier's business effectiveness is a function not only of its own success, but also the success of the customer. In investment terms, therefore, value to the customer is the supplier's investment and must come first. Value to supplier then becomes the return on that original investment, and must naturally come second.

Based on the above, the framework defines mutual value creation as an interactive process of creating and sharing joint productivity gains (Helle, 2009; 2011; also Grönroos and Helle, 2010). Mutual value is created when the monetary worth of the gains from practice matching exceeds the costs of resource inputs incurred during that process. How that value accrues to the involved actors depends on how the joint productivity gains are shared through a price mechanism as value to the involved parties.

Return on Relationships (ROR)

The framework posits that return on relationships (ROR) is driven by three factors: the cost associated with each party's relational investment following from the practice matching process, the capacity of the actors to create joint productivity gains, as well as their ability to negotiate a share of the joint productivity gain through price as value.

The framework expands previous indicators of return on relationships (ROR). It shifts the focus from exchange value and supplier earnings to the process of mutual value creation as the underlying basis of ROR. This means that ROR is not driven by the involved actors' separate strategies for success and well-being—as is suggested by transactional marketing—but their joint effort to make both parties better off.

The framework presented here also illustrates that the value of the relationship as an asset can be understood in terms of the mutual value created. The higher the worth of the mutual value created, the higher the value of the relationship for the involved parties. Mutual value that is created thus reflects the involved actors' relational competence. Hence, return on relationships can be understood, and assessed, as a joint, reciprocal ROR (ROR_R) relating to the relationship that has been developed as such, and as individual RORs for the parties in the relationship.

Metrics for Reciprocal Return on Relationships (ROR_R) Based on Mutual Value Creation

This section illustrates metrics that enable estimating return on relationships (ROR) based on mutual value creation (Helle, 2009, 2011; also Grönroos and Helle, 2010). As illustrated by the conceptual framework, estimating mutual value creation is a process that takes place through two phases. First, we need to quantify and monetize joint productivity gains that are created through practice matching. Second, we need to share the joint productivity gains through price as value to the involved parties. Both phases are illustrated below.

Determining Joint Productivity Gains

Joint productivity gain is determined in two steps as follows:

$$JPG = f(\Delta \text{ External Effectiveness Customer } [\Delta \text{ EE}_C],$$
$$\Delta \text{ Internal Efficiency Customer } [\Delta \text{ IE}_C],$$
$$\Delta \text{ Internal Efficiency Supplier } [\Delta \text{ E}_S])$$

such that:

$$JPG = (\Delta \text{ EEC}_C - \Delta \text{ IE}_C) - \Delta \text{ IE}_S$$

where:

JPG	=	Joint productivity gain.
$(\Delta \text{ EE}_C - \Delta \text{ IE}_C)$	=	A change in customer's value-in-use.
$\Delta \text{ EE}_C$	=	(Customer revenue Proposed − Customer revenue Current).
$\Delta \text{ IE}_C$	=	(Customer costs Proposed − Customer costs Current).
$\Delta \text{ IE}_S$	=	(Supplier costs Proposed − Supplier costs Current).

The first step involves examining whether the practice matching leads to a change in the customer's revenue-generating capacity that exceeds the change in customer's costs. The net difference between the two concepts corresponds to a net change in customer's value-in-use. The second step involves determining whether the net change in customer's revenues and costs exceeds the change in costs that the supplier incurs, when following the practice matching process, it helps the customer create more value-in-use. When the net change in customer revenues and costs more than compensates the change in costs that the supplier may have incurred in the practice matching process, a joint productivity gain (JPG) is created. Inversely, when the net change in customer revenues and costs does not exceed the change in costs that the supplier has incurred in the practice matching process, a joint productivity loss is created (JPL).

Sharing Joint Productivity Gains Through Price as Value

The second phase in estimating mutual value creation involves sharing the joint productivity gains through a price mechanism as value to the customer and the supplier. That is, value simply denotes the share of the joint productivity gain that the involved parties obtain, once the gains are shared through a price mechanism. Thus, pricing denotes a means of distributing the fruits of practice matching among the involved parties.

Customer Value

Sharing joint productivity gain through price as value to the customer is determined as follows:

$$CVC = ((\Delta EE_C - \Delta IE_C) - \Delta IE_S) \times (1 - P)$$

where:

CVC	=	Customer value creation
$(\Delta EE_C - \Delta IE_C)$	=	A change in customer's value-in-use
$(\Delta EE_C - \Delta IE_C) - \Delta IE_S$	=	Joint productivity gain
$(1-P)$	=	The share of the joint productivity gain that accrues to the customer when shared through price. "P" in (1–P) denotes here the relative share of the joint productivity gain that accrues to the provider. This means that the remainder of the joint productivity gain accrues to the customer; i.e. (1–P).[5]

As illustrated by the equation, customer value (CVC) is created when the difference between joint productivity gain and the share of the joint productivity gain that accrues to customer when shared through price is larger than zero. Inversely, negative customer value—effectively a loss—is created when the difference between joint productivity gain, and the share of the joint productivity gain that accrues to customer when shared through price is smaller than zero.

Supplier Value

Sharing joint productivity gain as value to the supplier is determined as follows:

$$PVC = ((\Delta EE_C - \Delta IE_C) - \Delta IE_S) \times P$$

where:

PVC	=	Supplier value creation.
$(\Delta EE_C - \Delta IE_C)$	=	A change in customer's value-in-use.
$(\Delta EE_C - \Delta IE_C) - \Delta IE_S$	=	Joint productivity gain.
ΔIE_S	=	A change in supplier costs.
P	=	Supplier's share of the joint productivity gain once the gain is shared through price.

As illustrated by the equation, supplier value creation takes place when the share of the joint productivity gain that accrues to the supplier when shared through price exceeds zero. Inversely, negative supplier value—a loss—is created when the difference between joint productivity gain and the share of the joint productivity gain that accrues to the supplier when shared through price is smaller than zero.

Return on Relationships (ROR)

In a very basic sense, return on relationships (ROR) denotes the extent to which a relational business engagement leaves an involved party better off. Thus, it answers the question: "Does it pay off to engage in a relational business engagement—and if yes, to what extent"? More technically, ROR denotes the ratio of money gained or lost on an investment in a relationship relative to the amount of money invested. ROR thus captures whether investments in time, knowledge building, and efforts in reconfiguring joint processes generate a pay-off that more than compensates for the costs incurred by the involved parties. To that end, this section illustrates metrics that enable estimating return on relationships based on mutual value creation.

Reciprocal Return on Relationship (ROR$_R$)

The reciprocal return on relationships (ROR$_R$) denotes the joint return that the involved parties can expect from the relationship. As both parties contribute towards this return, it is a reciprocal construct. It is determined as follows:

$$ROR_R = \frac{((\Delta EE_C - \Delta IE_C) - \Delta IE_S)}{\Delta C_C + \Delta C_P} \times 100$$

where:

ROR$_R$ = Reciprocal return on relationship.
JPG = Joint productivity gain, defined as: JPG = $((\Delta EE_C - \Delta IE_C) - \Delta IE_S)$.
ΔCc = Cost of customer's relational investment.
ΔCs = Cost of supplier's relational investment.

Return on Relationship (ROR) for the Customer

Return on relationship for the customer (ROR$_C$) is determined as follows:

$$ROR_C = \frac{CV_C}{\Delta C_C} \times 100$$

where:
CV$_C$ = Customer value; defined as $((\Delta EE_C - \Delta IE_C) - \Delta IE_S) \times (1 - P)$.
ΔCc = Cost of customer's relational investment.

Substituting the equation for customer value for CV_C gives:

$$ROR_C = \frac{((\Delta EE_C - \Delta IE_C) - \Delta IE_S) \times (1 - P)}{\Delta C_C} \times 100$$

Thus, return on relationship for the customer is a function of customer value; i.e. the share of the joint productivity gain (JPG) that accrues to the customer once that gain is shared through a price mechanism, and the cost of customer's relational investment. There is a positive return on the customer's relational investment when the ratio between the value that accrues to the customer and the cost of customer's relational investment is larger than 1. Expressed as a percentage, there is a positive return on the customer's relational investment when the ratio between the value that accrues to the customer and the cost of investment is larger than 100. In very basic terms, positive return on a relationship for a customer implies that the customer has become better off by participating in the relational business engagement.

Return on Relationship (ROR$_S$) for the Supplier

Return on relationship for the supplier (ROR$_S$) is determined as follows:

$$ROR_S = \frac{CV_S}{\Delta C_S} \times 100$$

where:
CV_S = Supplier value; defined as $((\Delta EE_C - \Delta IE_C) - \Delta IE_S) \times P$.
ΔC_S = Cost of supplier's relational investment.

Substituting the equation for supplier value for CV_S gives:

$$ROR_S = \frac{((\Delta EE_C - \Delta IE_C) - \Delta IE_S) \times (P)}{\Delta C_S} \times 100$$

Similarly, return on relationship for the supplier is a function of the value that accrues to the customer once joint productivity gains (JPG) are shared through a price mechanism, and the cost of supplier's relational investment. There is a positive return on the supplier's relational investment when the ratio between the value that accrues to the supplier and the cost of supplier's investment is larger than 1. Expressed as a percentage, there is a positive return on the supplier's relational investment when the ratio between the value that accrues to the supplier and the cost of investment is larger than 100. In very basic terms, positive return on a relationship

(ROR) for a supplier implies that the supplier has become better off by participating in the relational business engagement.

Determining Return on Relationships (ROR): Case Industrial Dyad

In this section, the process of determining return on relationships (ROR) is illustrated through a real-life case example.[6] The case example involves an industrial dyad with years' worth of common history. The customer is a leading supplier of water, air, and liquid measurement services that buys technology platforms, equipment, and spares to keep its measurement systems running smoothly. The supplier is a technology and product supplier with a long history of manufacturing and technology excellence.

The challenge facing the customer and the supplier is as follows. The supplier has suggested the customer a joint business opportunity where the supplier would take over the operational management of customer's measurement processes through an outsourcing agreement. According to the supplier, doing so would help the customer move ahead in the value chain and, in so doing, save operating expenses. The proposal also involves the supplier launching a new data processing technology to help the customer create additional revenue. Although the proposal seems promising, one question remains: does the relationship strategy pay off? To that end, the supplier and customer deploy a new approach that helps them understand the financial consequences of the practice matching.

Step 1 Identifying and Monetizing Operational Changes Associated with the Practice Matching

The first step is to identify the operational changes for the customer and the supplier that would be caused by re-aligning buyer and supplier resources. While the proposal implies work time savings and additional revenues for the customer, both parties are required to invest in relationship development as shown in Table I.

Step 2 Putting the Figures Together for Joint Productivity Gain

With all the changes in costs and revenues identified for both parties, the next step involves putting the figures together to determine the joint productivity gain. As the focus here lied on understanding the value-creating effects, all figures during the three-year analysis period were treated as real figures, and only in subsequent sales negotiations were the annual cash flows discounted with a proper discount factor. The analysis illustrated that the outsourcing initiative would generate a joint productivity

Table I

Customer Changes	Supplier Changes
Relational investment. The customer's relational investment consists of a one-off project cost of 45,000 required to carry out the necessary changes in operating processes, a one-off development cost of 50,000 to make use of the supplier's new data processing technology, and final investment of 25,000 required to train the involved workers. In total, the cost of these relational investments amounts to 120,000	*Relational investment in outsourcing capacity.* Carrying out the outsourcing initiative would require that the supplier invest 85,000 up-front in additional measurement capacity. Hiring three new measurement operators to run the automated measurement process would cost 135,000 yearly during the three years. Reconfiguring the data delivery to match the quality requirements of the customer would set the supplier back with a one-off cost of 70,000 *R&D investment.* For the supplier, launching the new data processing technology would require a one off R&D investment of some 25,000 the first year
Reduced work time. Outsourcing former core measurement activities to the supplier would reduce an amount of work equivalent to 15 man-years of labor for the customer. The monetary worth of these savings are estimated to amount to 900,000 yearly during the three years	
Revenue increase. Deploying the supplier's new data processing technology would help the customer to launch its existing measurement services into three new usage areas, thus creating an estimated revenue increase of some five per cent annually. All in all, the monetary worth of the additional revenue is estimated at 325,000 yearly for the customer	

gain of some 2,970,000 to be shared between the customer and the supplier during the three-year period (Table II).

Step 3 Sharing the Joint Productivity Gains Through Price

The next step involves sharing the joint productivity gains through a price mechanism as value to the buyer and value to the supplier. Through a series of iterations, the buyer and supplier agree to share the joint productivity gain during the three years so that the supplier obtained 30 percent ($p = 0.30$) of the documented gains while the customer obtained its share of the joint productivity gain as value 70 percent ($1-P = 1 - 0.30 = 0.70$). The process of sharing the joint productivity gains through price can be seen in Table III.

Step 4 Determining the Return on Relationship (ROR)

Determining the return on relationship (ROR) is carried out in two steps. First, the customer and the supplier estimate the total return on relationship for the whole business

Table II

A. Change in customer's use value

Formula	Δ Customer's value-in-use: $(\Delta EE_C - \Delta IE_C)$

where:

ΔEE_C = change in external effectiveness for the customer; ΔIE_C = a change in internal efficiency for the customer (includes the customer's relational investment of 120,000 for the first year)

Inserting values *Year 1:*

$\Delta EEC = 325,000 - 0^a = 325,000$

$\Delta EEC = -900,000 + 120,000 = -780,000$

Year 2:

$\Delta EEC = 325,000 - 0^a = 325,000$

$\Delta IEC = -900,00$

Year 3:

$\Delta EE_C = 325,000 - 0^a = 325,000$

$\Delta IE_C = -900,00$

Result   Year 1: $325,000 - (-780,000) - 0 = 325,000 + 780,000 - 0 = 1,105,000$

Year 2: $325,000 - (-900,000) = 325,000 + 900,000 - 0 = 1,225,000$

Year 3: $325,000 - (-900,000) = 325,000 + 900,000 - 0 = 1,225,000$

B. Change in supplier's cost

Formula (ΔIE_S)

Inserting values *Year 1:*

$(85,000 - 0) + (135,000 - 0) + (70,000 - 0) + (25,000 - 0) = 315,000$

Year 2:

$(135,000 - 0) = 135,000$

Year 3:

$(135,000 - 0) = 135,000$

In total: 585,000

C. Determining joint productivity gains

Formula $JPG = (\Delta EE_C - \Delta IE_C - (\Delta IE_S)$

where:

JPG = Joint productivity gain; $(\Delta EE_C - \Delta IE_C)$ = a change in customer's value-in-use (includes the customer's relational investment of 120,000 for the first year); ΔIE_S = change in supplier's costs

(Table II Contd.)

(Table II Contd.)

Inserting values	*Year 1:*

Inserting values *Year 1:*

$(\Delta EE_C - \Delta IEC) = (325{,}000 - (-780{,}000)) - 0) = (1{,}105{,}000 - 0)$

$\Delta IES = (315{,}000 - 0)$

Year 2:

$(\Delta EE_C - \Delta IE_C) = (1{,}225{,}000 - 0)$

$\Delta IE_S = (135{,}000 - 0)$

Year 3:

$(\Delta EE_C - \Delta IE_C) = (1{,}225{,}000 - 0)$

$\Delta IE_S = (135{,}000 - 0)$

Result   Year 1: $(1{,}105{,}000 - 0) - (315{,}000) = 790{,}000$

Year 2: $(1{,}225{,}000 - 0) - (135{,}000) = 1{,}090{,}000$

Year 3: $(1{,}225{,}000 - 0) - (135{,}000) = 1{,}090{,}000$

Total (Years 1-3): $790{,}000 + 1{,}090{,}000 + 1{,}090{,}000 = 2{,}970{,}000$

Note: [a]Zero (0) denotes the existing level of revenues when compared to a revenue increase in the proposal. In this case the start level is zero. However, in other cases it could amount to some other figure

Table III

Formula	Customer:

Formula   Customer:

$CVC = ((\Delta EE_C - \Delta IE_C) - \Delta IE_S) \times (1\text{-}P)$

Supplier:

$PVC = ((\Delta EE_C - \Delta IE_C) - \Delta IE_S) \times P$

Inserting values   Customer:

$(\Delta EE_C - \Delta IE_C) - \Delta IE_S - 2{,}970{,}000$

$(1\text{-}P) = (1 - 0.30) = 0.70$

Supplier:

$(\Delta EE_C - \Delta IEC) - \Delta IES = 2{,}970{,}000$

$(P) = (0.30)$

Result   Customer:

$CVC = 2{,}970{,}000 \times 0.70 = 2{,}079{,}000$

Supplier:

$PVC = 2{,}970{,}000 \times 0.30 = 891{,}000$

Table IV

Formula	Reciprocal return on relationship (ROR)
	$$ROR_R = \frac{((\Delta EE_C - \Delta IE_C) - \Delta IE_S)}{\Delta C_C + \Delta C_S} \times 100$$
Inserting values	$ROR_R = (2{,}970{,}000/(585{,}000 + 120{,}000)) \times 100$
Result	$ROR_R = (2{,}970{,}000/705{,}000) \times 100 = 421\%$

engagement (ROR_R). This means estimating how much better off both parties would be jointly if they went ahead with the proposal Table IV.

The second step involves determining return on relationship (ROR) for each of the parties individually. The process is shown in Table V.

Case Summary

As the case analysis illustrates, the relational business engagement would imply a healthy business opportunity for both the customer and the supplier. Throughout the

Table V

Formula	Customer:
	$$ROR_C = \frac{((\Delta EE_C - \Delta IE_C) - \Delta IE_S) \times (1-P)}{\Delta C_C} \times 100$$
	Supplier:
	$$ROR_S = \frac{((\Delta EE_C - \Delta IE_C) - \Delta IE_S) \times (P)}{\Delta C_S} \times 100$$
Inserting values	Customer:
	$ROR_C = (2{,}970{,}000 \times 0.70/120{,}000) \times 100$
	Supplier:
	$= (2{,}970{,}000 \times 0.0/585{,}000) \times 100$
Result	Customer:
	$ROR_C - (2{,}970{,}000 \times 0.70/120{,}000) \times 100$
	$= 17.3 \times 100\% = 1{,}730\%$
	Supplier:
	$ROR_S = (2{,}970{,}000 \times 0.30/585{,}000) \times 100$
	$= 1.5 \times 100\% = 150\%$

three-year contract period, both companies would indeed earn an impressive profit in excess of current margin levels. In real terms, the return on relationship for the customer (ROR_C) would amount to 1,730 percent whereas the return on relationship for the supplier (ROR_S) would be 150 percent. The reciprocal return on relationship—the return on the relationship as such (ROR_R)—is 421 percent, or in excess of four times the combined costs of the joint investment in the relationship. With both parties confident in the soundness of the opportunity, all that was needed now was to plan how to move ahead with the process and to ensure an end-to-end value realization for both the customer and the supplier. A big difference between ROR_C and ROR_S, as in this case, may of course trigger continued discussions about how the mutually created incremental value should be split, and further price negotiations.

Discussion and Implications for Research

The study demonstrates ways of moving from viewing customers as assets to understanding and measuring relationships between business parties as an asset. This is an interesting research avenue to pursue. Furthermore, the approach to relationship development and management as an investment that yields a return that can be calculated is an answer to the recently voiced call for marketing to produce and disseminate useful marketing metrics to finance and accounting (e.g. Wiesel *et al.*, 2008). Simultaneously, it also answer the call for supporting more transparency in financial reporting of intangible assets, such as customer bases, portfolios and relationships, for the benefit of investors' decision making (e.g. Whitwell *et al.*, 2007). As Kumar and Petersen (2005) notice, increasingly firms assume that marketing and finance work together. The article provides metrics that helps marketers to move closer to finance. Moreover, as normally used marketing metrics, such as customer life time value and customer equity have not created any real attention in finance circles (Gleaves *et al.*, 2008), the way of approach investments in customers and relationships as well as of calculating return on relationships presented in the present article maybe more successful in doing so. Herein ample opportunities for further research can be found.

The importance of moving away from traditional approaches to productivity assessment, where productivity is considered a one-sided construct, and treated as separate issues for the supplier and customer, towards a relationship-oriented joint productivity construct is demonstrated in the study. Only the development of joint productivity gains enables a valuation of relationship development in the form of incremental value, which can be used as a base for assessing reciprocal return on the relationship efforts. Furthermore, it is demonstrated how this incremental value can be shared between the business parties as returns on the relationship for the supplier and customer, respectively. The value sharing—the process of splitting the incremental value between the supplier and the customer—achieved through a price mechanism, based on a negotiation process between the parties, and the ROR process model introduced here is also a basis of value-based pricing. The potential of the process flow model (see Figures 3 and 4), including service perspective, practice matching, joint productivity gain calculation, incremental value assessment, value sharing, and reciprocal and party-separate ROR calculation, for developing such pricing models should be studied. When motivating a price tag on service, this model may also be helpful. Here interesting research opportunities exist.

The article has a number of additional research implications. First of all, the article develops a conceptual model and metrics for understanding and measuring return on relationships in a relational business engagement, and although the study the present article is based on includes several empirical tests of the model and the metrics, only one empirical case is presented in this context. Hence, further research is required to test the usefulness of the model and metrics.

Furthermore, how the antecedents for mutual value creation indicated in the model influence the party's willingness to engage in mutual value creation is only conceptually developed. The role and relative importance of the various antecedents, and how they have an impact on the practice matching process should be further developed and empirically studied. Also the nature of the practice matching process, and what it takes from a managerial perspective to successfully implement it need further research.

As pointed out by Jap (1999) in her research into "pie extension", interorganizational collaboration aiming at jointly creating incremental value and returns on joint investments in a relationship may be a source of competitive advantage, due to "... the inimitable nature, which is due to the specific investments and coordinated efforts of the dyad" (p. 471). Further research on the magnitude of the competitive advantage created by the mutual value creation and sharing process is warranted by our study. Also under what external conditions competitive advantage can be achieved needs to be studied.

Finally, although it has been noted throughout the article that frequently relationships in the marketplace are not dyadic only but exist in networks of relationships, the conceptual foundation and metrics have been developed for dyadic business engagements. This has been a deliberate choice. Mutual value creation in larger networks than dyads adds considerable complexity, and the metrics become more complicated. Therefore, keeping in mind the initial stage of research into the field, starting with a network context would not have been productive. At this point it was determined more fruitful to consider a business dyad. This already makes the development of considerable new insight possible. However, further research into understanding return on relationships and measuring it in network contexts is, of course, an important research task for the future.

Implications for Management

The article points out a number of important management implications. First of all, it provides a system for analyzing how a relationship can be developed with an aim to making both the supplier and the customer better off by engaging in a relational business engagement. It demonstrates the need for the parties to open up their books and in a transparent way approach the development process. If the parties are not prepared to share enough information about their operational principles, and cost and revenue drivers, a solid basis for developing a win-win relational business is not established. If this base is lacking, a win-win business engagement is difficult, if not impossible to achieve. Successful implementation of the process of practice matching aiming at aligning the business party's processes, resources and competencies is a prerequisite. However, this requires a transparent approach from the two (or several parties) involved.

Although they were not tested in this study, the model of mutual value creation pointed at a number of supplier-side and customer-side antecedents for successful practice matching. The parties must understand each other's business logic and be prepared to engage in matching practices with each other, and in the final analysis, if needed, be prepared to change their operational processes and routines. A willingness to do this, and ability to communicate one's intentions in a trustworthy manner are imperative. As Canning and Brennan (2004) observe in their discussion of interfirm adaptation, "... managers from each company are involved in exchanged episodes in order to decide how to realize the sought after change" (p. 12). To be prepared to open up one's books and engage in the practice matching process requires that a considerable amount of trust in the other party exists, or is allowed to develop during the process.

The article also demonstrates how a relationship can be seen as a mutual investment, where reciprocal return on this investment in the relationship can be assessed, and moreover, how this investment pays off as ROR for the supplier and customer, respectively. The metrics developed, and used in the study, provide the instrument to do the needed calculations.

The joint productivity approach presented in the present article opens up a new way of treating productivity management and the assessment of productivity gains. Unlike the established productivity models that see productivity management as separate processes in selling and buying firms (or several firms in a network), the joint productivity construct is based on the view that a relational business engagement is a truly two-sided endeavor. Hence, it is claimed that in order to implement relational business aiming at a win-win situation, productivity as a phenomenon and the management of productivity have to be considered a joint issue. It is not enough that the parties in the engagement attempt to become more productive separately. Instead they should aim at becoming more productive together. In fact, because effects on the other party in a relationship are considered an exogenous issue, pursuing higher productivity separately probably has a detrimental effect on the joint well-being of the parties. When the incremental value created mutually is assessed by the business parties, and the reciprocal return on the relationship is calculated, such effects have to be treated as endogenous variables (compare Jap, 1999). Hence, when adopting a relationship marketing approach, management must learn how to understand and analyze, and ultimately manage productivity jointly. In the article a conceptual understanding of joint productivity as well as measurement formulas to be used for calculating joint productivity are presented.

In the article the importance of understanding value creation as a mutual phenomenon between the two (or several) parties is emphasized, and a model of mutual value creation is presented. This is a basis for understanding how joint productivity, shared value and eventually return on relationships are calculated. In pointing out that it is not enough to offer solutions to the customer's various everyday operational and administrative processes aiming at improving operational efficiency only, but that the firm instead should offer support to the customer's business performance and business effectiveness, it has implications for sales and sales management as well, emphasizing the importance of value-based selling, and of selling solutions as service to customers.

Notes

1. The joint productivity concept and metrics for calculating joint productivity gains and value sharing were originally developed in Helle (2009), Helle (2011) and presented in a service logic in manufacturing context in Grönroos and Helle (2010).
2. This figure is a combination and further development of two figures in Grönroos and Helle (2010).
3. There are a number of antecedents of a successful mutual value creation process, both of customer value creation and supplier value creation. However, these are not tested in the present study. As indicated in Figure 2, there are both customer-side and supplier-side antecedents. For a customer to involve itself in practice matching with a supplier, the customer must be willing to match relevant practices with corresponding supplier practices, and this in turn requires that there is an understanding of the supplier's business logic. As supplier-side antecedents, an understanding of the customer's business process and of which customer practices are critical to the business outcome is instrumental. The attitudes towards the customer and the supplier's ability to communicate its willingness to engage in practice matching and mutual value creation are other supplier-side antecedents. Customer-side antecedents of supplier value creation include the customer's understanding of the supplier's business logic, and the customer's willingness to open its books and engage with the supplier in practice matching and mutual value creation. Supplier-side antecedents include the supplier's ability to support its customer's practices and business outcome. Other antecedents are the customer's trust in and commitment to a supplier as well as the customer's loyalty to a supplier.
4. It is interesting to observe that in a recently published article on how to save capitalism, Porter and Kramer (2011) suggest that firms should focus on shared value. However, in their approach to value sharing they do not include the customer. Instead they focus on other parties in the value chain as well as the community in which firms operate.
5. For the sake of an example, let us assume a joint productivity gain of 100. Given a $p = 20$, the provider obtains a 20 percent share of the joint-productivity gain of 100; i.e. 20 units of money. For the customer, in turn, this would imply a 1-P share of the joint productivity gain; that is, 1-0.2 = 0.8 (80 percent). As a consequence, the share of the productivity gain that accrues as value to the customer would be 80 units of money.
6. The case study pertains to a four-year study into mutual value creation and service business models in manufacturing firms carried out by Pekka Helle.

References

Amit, R. and Shoemaker, P.J.H. (1993), "Strategic assets and organizational rent", *Strategic Management Journal*, Vol. 14 No. 1, pp. 33-46.

Ang, L. and Buttle, F.A. (2002), "ROI on CRM: a customer-journey approach", *Conference Proceedings of the IMP (Industrial Marketing and Purchasing) Conference, Perth, Australia, December*, (also: www.crm2day.com/crm_aca demic_papers/).

Axelsson, B. and Wynstra, F. (2002), *Buying Business Services*, John Wiley & Sons, Chichester.

Berry, L.L. (1995), "Relationship marketing of services—growing interest, emerging perspectives", *Journal of the Academy of Marketing Science*, Vol. 23 No. 4.

Blattberg, R.C. and Deighton, J. (1996), "Manage marketing by the customer equity test", *Harvard Business Review*, Vol. 74, July-August, pp. 136-44.

Blattberg, R.C., Getz, G. and Thomas, J.S. (2001), *Customer Equity: Building and Managing Relationships as Valuable Assets*, Harvard Business School Press, Boston, MA.

Boddy, D., McBeth, D. and Wagner, B. (1999), "Implementing collaboration between organizations: an empirical study of supply chain partnering", *Journal of Management Studies*, Vol. 37 No. 7, pp. 1003-17.

Brennan, D.R. and Canning, L. (2002), "Adaption process in supplier-customer relationships", *Journal of Customer Behaviour*, Vol. 1 No. 2, pp. 117-44.

Brennan, D.R. and Turnbull, P.W. (1999), "Adaptive behavior in buyer-supplier relationships", *Industrial Marketing Management*, Vol. 28 No. 5, pp. 481-95.

Brennan, D.R., Turnbull, P.W. and Wilson, D.T. (2003), "Dyadic adaption in business-to-business markets", *European Journal of Marketing*, Vol. 37 Nos 11/12, pp. 1636-65.

Bursk, E.C. (1966), "View your customers as investments", *Harvard Business Review*, Vol. 44, May-June, pp. 91-4.

Canning, L. and Brennan, D.R. (2004), "Strategy as the management of adaptation", paper presented at the IMP Annual Conference, Copenhagen.

Christopher, M., Payne, A. and Ballantyne, D. (1991), *Relationship Marketing. Bringing Quality, Customer Service, and Marketing Together*, Butterworth Heinemann, Oxford.

Courbois, R. and Temple, P. (1975), "La methode des "Comptes de surplus" et ses applications macro-economiques", 160 des Collect, INSEE, Serie C (35), pp. 100.

Cravens, D.W., Greenlay, G., Piercy, N.F. and Slater, S. (1997), "Integrating contemporary strategic management perspectives", *Long Range Planning*, Vol. 30, August, pp. 493-506.

Cravens, D.W., Holland, C.W., Lamb, C.W. and Moncrieff, W.C. (1988), "Marketing's role in product and service quality", *Industrial Marketing Management*, Vol. 17, pp. 285-304.

Davis, H.S. (1955), *Productivity Accounting, Research Studies XXXVII*, University of Pennsylvania, PA.

Devinney, T.M., Stewart, D.W. and Schocker, A.D. (1985), "A note on the application of portfolio theory: a comment on Cardozo and Smith", *Journal of Marketing*, Vol. 49 No. 4, pp. 107-12.

Dhar, R. and Glazer, R. (2003), "Hedging customers", *Harvard Business Review*, Vol. 81 No. 5, pp. 86-92.

Fournier, S., Dobscha, S. and Mick, D.G. (1998), "Preventing the premature death of relationship marketing", *Harvard Business Review*, January-February, pp. 42-51.

Gleaves, R., Burton, J., Kitshoff, J., Bates, K. and Whittington, M. (2008), "Accounting is from Mars, marketing is from Venus: establishing common ground for the concept of customer profitability", *Journal of Marketing Management*, Vol. 24 Nos 7-8, pp. 825-45.

Gollop, F.M. (1979), *Accounting for Intermediate Input: The Link between Sectoral and Aggregate Measures of Productivity Growth. Measurement and Interpretation of Productivity*, National Academy of Sciences.

Grönroos, C. (1994), "Quo vadis, marketing? Toward a paradigm shift in marketing", *Journal of Marketing Management*, Vol. 10 No. 5, pp. 347-60.

Grönroos, C. (2000), *Service Management and Marketing. A Customer Relationship Management Approach*, 2nd ed., John Wiley & Sons, Chichester.

Grönroos, C. (2003), "Taking a customer focus back into the boardroom: can relationship marketing do it?", *Marketing Theory*, Vol. 3 No. 1, pp. 171-3.

Grönroos, C. (2008), "Service logic revisited: who creates value? And who co-creates?", *European Business Review*, Vol. 20 No. 4, pp. 298-314.

Grönroos, C. (2011), "A service perspective on business relationships: the value creation, interaction and marketing interface", *Industrial Marketing Management.*, Vol. 40 No. 2, pp. 240-7.

Grönroos, C. and Helle, P. (2010), "Adopting a service logic in manufacturing: conceptual foundation and metrics for mutual value creation", *Journal of Service Management*, Vol. 21 No. 5, pp. 564-90.

Gummesson, E. (1987), "The new marketing: developing long-term interactive relationships", *Long Range Planning*, Vol. 20 No. 4, pp. 10-20.

Gummesson, E. (1995), "Relationship marketing: its role in the service economy", in Glynn, W.J. and Barnes, J.G. (Eds), *Understanding Service Management*, John Wiley & Sons, New York, NY, pp. 244-68.

Gummesson, E. (2004), "Return on relationships (ROR): the value of relationship marketing and CRM in business-to-business contexts", *Journal of Business & Industrial Marketing*, Vol. 19 No. 2, pp. 136-48.

Gummesson, E. (2006), "Many-to-many marketing as grand theory: a Nordic school contribution", in Lusch, R.F. and Vargo, S.L. (Eds), *Toward a Service-dominant Logic of Marketing: Dialog, Debate, and Directions*, M.E.Sharpe, New York, NY, pp. 339-53.

Gummesson, E. (2008), *Total Relationship Marketing. Marketing Management, Relationship Strategy, CRM, and a New Dominant Logic for the Value-creating Network Economy*, 3rd ed., Butterworth Heinemann, Oxford.

Gupta, S. (2009), "Customer-based valuation", *Journal of Interactive Marketing*, Vol. 23 No. 2, pp. 169-78.

Gupta, S. and Lehman, D.R. (2003), "Customers as assets", *Journal of Interactive Marketing*, Vol. 17 No. 1, pp. 9-24.

Gupta, S. and Lehman, D.R. (2005), *Managing Customers as Investments*, Wharton School Publishing, Upper Saddle River, NJ.

Gupta, S., Hanssens, D., Hardie, B., Kahn, W., Kumar, V., Lin, N., Ravishanker, N. and Sriram, S. (2006), "Modeling customer lifetime value", *Journal of Service Research*, Vol. 9 No. 2, pp. 139-55.

Håkansson, H. (Ed.) (1985), *International Marketing and Purchasing of Industrial Goods. An Interaction Approach*, John Wiley & Sons, New York, NY.

Hallén, L., Johansson, J. and Seyed-Mohammed, N. (1991), "Interfirm adaption in business relationships", *Journal of Marketing*, Vol. 55, April, pp. 29-37.

Helle, P. (2009), *Towards Understanding Value Creation from the Point of View of Service Provision*, Conference report, EIASM Service Marketing Forum, Capri.

Helle, P. (2011), "Re-conceptualizing value-creation: from industrial business logic to service business logic", Working Paper 554, Hanken School of Economics Finland.

Jap, S.D. (1999), "Pie-expansion efforts: collaboration processes in buyer-supplier relationsips", *Journal of Market Research*, Vol. 36 No. 4, pp. 461-75.

Jap, S.D. (2001), "Pie-sharing in complex collaboration contexts", *Journal of Market Research*, Vol. 38 No. 1, pp. 86-99.

Kumar, V. and George, M. (2007), "Measuring and maximizing customer equity: a critical analysis", *Journal of the Academy of Marketing Science*, Vol. 35 No. 2, pp. 157-71.

Kumar, V. and Petersen, J.A. (2005), "Using customer-level marketing strategy to enhance firm performance: a review of theoretical and empirical evidence", *Journal of the Academy of Marketing Science*, Vol. 33 No. 4, pp. 504-19.

Kumar, V., Petersen, J.A. and Leone, R.P. (2007), "How valuable is word of mouth?", *Harvard Business Review*, Vol. 85 No. 10, pp. 139-46.

Kurosawa, K. (1975), "An aggregate index for the analysis of productivity", *Omega*, Vol. 3 No. 2, pp. 157-68.

Levitt, T. (1983), "After the sale is over …", *Harvard Business Review*, Vol. 61, September-October, pp. 87-93.

Little, E. and Marandi, E. (2003), *Relationship Marketing Management*, Thomson, London.

McGovern, G.J., Court, D., Quelch, J.A. and Crawford, B. (2004), "Bringing customers into the boardroom", *Harvard Business Review*, Vol. 82, November, pp. 70-80.

MacMillan, I.C. and McGrath, R.G. (1997), "Discovering new points of differentiation", *Harvard Business Review*, Vol. 75, July/August, pp. 133-45.

Monroe, K.B. (1990), *Pricing: Making Profitable Decisions*, McGraw-Hill, New York, NY.

Morgan, R.M. and Hunt, S.D. (1994), "The commitment-trust theory of relationship marketing", *Journal of Marketing*, Vol. 58 No. 1, pp. 20-38.

Niraj, R., Gupta, M. and Narasimhan, C. (2001), "Customer profitability in a supply chain", *Journal of Marketing*, Vol. 65, July, pp. 1-16.

Pineda, A. (1990), *A Multiple Case Study Research to Determine and respond to Management Information Need Using Total-factor Productivity Measurement (TFPM)*, Virginia Polytechnic Institute and State University, Blacksburg, VA.

Porter, M.E. (1985), *Competitive Advantage*, The Free Press, New York, NY.

Porter, M.E. and Kramer, M.R. (2011), "Creating shared value", *Harvard Business Review*, Vol. 89, January-February, pp. 62-77.

Rust, R.T., Lemon, K.N. and Zeithaml, V.A. (2004), "Return on marketing: using customer equity to focus marketing strategy", *Journal of Marketing*, Vol. 68, January, pp. 109-27.

Rust, R.T., Ambler, T., Carpenter, G.S., Kumar, V. and Srivastava, R.K. (2004), "Measuring marketing productivity: current knowledge and future directions", *Journal of Marketing*, Vol. 68, October, pp. 76-89.

Ryals, L. (2002), "Are your customers worth more than money?", *Journal of Retailing and Consumer Services*, Vol. 9 No. 5, pp. 241-51.

Ryals, L. (2005), "Making customer relationship management work: the measurement and profitable management of customer relationships", *Journal of Marketing*, Vol. 69 No. 4, pp. 252-61.

Schatzki, T.R. (2001), "Introduction: practice theory", in Schatzki, T.R., Knorr Cetina, K. and von Savigny, E. (Eds), *The Practice Turn in Contemporary Theory*, Routledge, New York, NY.

Schmidt, S-O., Tyler, K. and Brennan, D.R. (2007), "Adaptation in inter-firm relationships: classification, motivation, calculation", *Journal of Services Marketing*, Vol. 21 No. 7, pp. 530-7.

Sheth, J.N. and Parvatiyar, A. (1995), "The evolution of relationship markets", *International Business Review*, Vol. 4 No. 4, pp. 397-418.

Srivastava, R.K., Shervani, T.A. and Fahey, L. (1998), "Market-based assets and shareholder value: a framework for analysis", *Journal of Marketing*, Vol. 62, January, pp. 2-18.

Stewart, D.W. (2009), "Marketing accountability: linking marketing actions to financial results", *Journal of Business Research*, Vol. 62 No. 2, pp. 636-43.

Storbacka, K. and Lehtinen, J.R. (2001), *Customer Through Win-Win Strategies*, McGraw-Hill, Singapore.

Storbacka, K., Strandvik, T. and Grönroos, C. (1994), "Managing customer relationships for profit: the dynamics of relationship quality", *International Journal of Service Industry Management.*, Vol. 5 No. 5, pp. 21-38.

Tzokas, N. and Saren, M. (2004), "Competitive advantage, knowledge and relationship marketing: where, what and how?", *Journal of Business & Industrial Marketing*, Vol. 19 No. 2, pp. 124-35.

Van Raaij, E.M., Vernooij, M.J.A. and van Triest, S. (2003), "The implementation of customer profitability analysis: a case study", *Industrial Marketing Management*, Vol. 32 No. 7, pp. 573-83.

Vargo, S.L. and Lusch, R.F. (2008), "Service dominant logic: continuing the evolution", *Journal of the Academy of Science*, Vol. 36 No. 1, pp. 1-10.

Venkatesan, R. and Kumar, V. (2004), "A customer lifetime value framework for customer selections and resource allocation strategy", *Journal of Marketing*, Vol. 68 No. 4, pp. 106-25.

Wayland, R.E. and Cole, P.M. (1994), "Turn customer service into customer profitability", *Management Review*, Vol. 83, July, pp. 22-4.

Whitwell, G.J., Lukas, B.A. and Hill, P. (2007), "Stock analysts' assessments of the shareholder value of intangible assets", *Journal of Business Research*, Vol. 60 No. 3, pp. 217-56.

Wiesel, T., Skiera, B. and Villaneuva, J. (2008), "Customer equity: an integral part of financial reporting", *Journal of Marketing*, Vol. 72, March, pp. 1-14.

Zeithaml, V. (1988), "Consumer perception of price, quality and value: a means-ends-model and synthesis of evidence", *Journal of Marketing*, Vol. 52, July, pp. 2-22.

2

A Service Perspective on Business Relationships: The Value Creation, Interaction and Marketing Interface

Industrial Marketing Management
Vol. 40, No. 2, 2011
pp. 240–247

Christian Grönroos

Adopting a service perspective or logic on business directs suppliers' focus in business relationships towards engaging with their customers' business processes. The purpose of this article is to analyze implications for value creation and marketing of adopting a service logic in business relationships. In the article it is demonstrated that a service perspective is multi-dimensional, enabling the mutual creation of value, with service as a mediating factor in that process. It is argued that value creation, purchasing, usage and marketing are intertwined processes. Here supplier-customer interactions are in a focal position. This perspective enables marketers to better understand how to develop and extend service offerings through assistance to customers' processes relevant to their businesses. Therefore, the underpinning logic of industrial interactions is analyzed in detail, extending marketing's conventional boundaries.

1. Background and Purpose

According to the service logic of the Nordic School of marketing thought, customers use resources made available to them in usage processes, where the use of these resources renders value for them. Goods, service activities, information and other kinds of resources are used in on-going relationships by customers in their manufacturing, administrative, logistical, financial and other processes so that customer value is created for them in those processes (Grönroos, 1979). As Gummesson (1995) formulates it, all kinds of resources are used by customers as service that renders value for them. Not only service activities but also goods are distribution mechanisms for service (Vargo & Lusch, 2004). These observations have also been put forward as foundational premises in the discussion of a service-dominant logic for marketing (Vargo & Lusch, 2004, 2008). Following these thoughts, suppliers in crafting value propositions for customers, regardless of the balance between goods and other resource components, aim to deliver offerings that integrate with the customers' various practices and processes. That is, service is redefined as how offerings are put to use in ways that support the creation of value from them. In this respect all firms are service businesses (Grönroos, 1997; see also Webster, 1994; Vargo & Lusch, 2004).

In the present article the straightforward expression *service logic* (Grönroos, 2006; Normann, 2001) rather than service-dominant logic is used. Adopting service as a logic for business has implications for a number of aspects of firm-customer relationships. Such implications include, for example, how customer value is created and for the roles of suppliers and customers in value creation, how value creation and marketing, purchasing and usage are intertwined phenomena, and how marketing should be understood and managed. For example, supplier-customer interactions take on a focal position in marketing. The article focuses on on-going business relationship contexts. However, a service logic may be a way of creating a relationship-based customer engagement out of a transaction-based business. The purpose of this article is to analyze implications for value creation and marketing of adopting a service logic in business relationships and how value creation and marketing as processes are intertwined with interaction as an explaining factor.

2. Service Logic and Value for Customers in Business Relationships

In on-going business relationships a multitude of more or less interactive contacts between a supplier and a customer takes place. The success of a supplier is not only dependent on how well it manages to provide, for example, a production machine or an administrative system to a customer. Whether or not this is of value for the customer is also dependent on how well time tables are kept, the timing of deliveries, how well a solution for the customer is made operational, how it is maintained, etc. In addition, the supplier's invoicing systems, ways of handling quality problems and service failures and how other customer-influencing process are handled also have an impact on what value the customer manages to create out of the core product Value for a business customer does not emerge from one resource—the core product—only, but from the whole spectrum of supplier–customer interactions that support a successful use of this core resource.

As MacMillan and McGrath (1997) observe, to differentiate a market offering a supplier must not concentrate on the core product only, but take into account the customers' various practices and ask itself, for example, the following questions: How do customers order and purchase products (goods and service activities)? How are products delivered? What happens when they have been delivered? How are they installed?

How are they paid for? How are products stored? How are they moved around? What are customers really using products for? What do they need help with when they use the products? How are products repaired and serviced? What happens when products are disposed of or no longer used?

In its contacts with a supplier a business customer moves through a chain of everyday practices that all need support, either by the supplier or by actions taken by the customer or by a third party. The customer's practices have corresponding practices on the supplier side, and this set of corresponding practices should meet in ways that help the customer's activities flow towards a successful and profitable business outcome. In the upper part of Figure 1 typical corresponding customer and supplier practices in an industrial relationship are illustrated.

According to a traditional manufacturing approach, following what could be labeled as a goods logic, the supplier, for example producing and selling a production machine, would concentrate on how well the machine fits the customer's production process—on what can be called *operational efficiency*. A dependable machine that fits the customer's production process in a technically efficient way is in the supplier's focus. A goods logic can be described as a business logic, where resources are provided to a given usage process for the customer's use in order to support that particular process in a value-creating way (Grönroos, 2006). It remains the responsibility of the customer to make sure that it can make effective use of the resource so that value can be created out of the resource purchased.

A service business, i.e. a firm that has adopted a service logic, would take a much further-reaching responsibility for a customer's everyday practices and how they ultimately support the customer's business. According to a service business logic, the supplier supports the customer's practices with an extended offering, including goods components and a range of service activities, which enable the customer to create value out of the core process (e.g. a production process). Ultimately, this extended offering provides successful support to the customer's business process. The core customer process (e.g. a production process) is supported by the core of the supplier's market offering (e.g. a production machine), whereas the customer's business is supported by the entire extended offering, including the machine *and* support to other customer processes important to the business. In this way this supplier does not only provide resources but serves its customer's business, and therefore, this offering can be characterized as an *extended service offering*.

The connection with the business process is indicated by the lower part of Fig. 1. In order to make this connection, the supplier has to gear all its processes relevant to the customer's business towards the customer's corresponding processes. In the figure this process is labeled *practice matching* and is indicated by the arrows between corresponding supplier and customer processes.[1] Hence, a service logic means that a

---

[1] Practice matching means that the supplier and the customer develop or strive to develop the way they practice corresponding processes with an aim to be able to jointly support value creation in the customer's processes and for the customer's business. Simultaneously the supplier's creation of value from this business engagement should be supported.

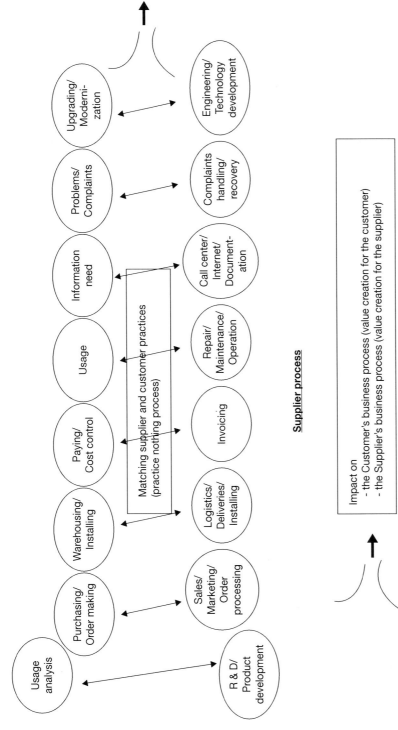

Figure 1. The Customer and Supplier Processes and Their Impact on the Business Processes

supplier does not provide resources for the customers' use only, but instead it provides support to its customers' business processes through value-supporting ways of assisting the customers' practices relevant to their business (*business effectiveness* instead of operational efficiency only).

In conclusion, service is to support customers' practices and business outcomes with a set of resources and interactive processes (Grönroos, 2008:300). In other words, in a business relationship, *an extended service offering is an interactive process consisting of several sub-processes and resources supporting corresponding customer practices in a way that helps the customer create value in all its practices (operational efficiency), and through this ultimately has a value-creating impact on the customer's business process (business effectiveness).* Order taking, deliveries, installing, product specifications and features as well as product documentation, maintenance, invoicing, complaints handling and service recovery are examples of sub-processes and resources included in such a market offering. Correspondingly, order making, storage, installing, using, maintaining, paying and cost control, having problems and mistakes corrected are examples of the customer's practices that need support. Thus the following proposition can be formulated:

1. *Implementing a service logic and providing support to the customers' business requires that the supplier extends its market offering to include activities and processes that support practices and processes that are relevant to the customers' business (i.e. that have a business effectiveness influence).*

3. What is the Value for Customers in a Business-to-Business Context?

In the literature on value creation and co-creation, value is often discussed on a philosophical level. In the most frequently used approach, value is a relationship between what one benefits and what one sacrifices (see Sánchez-Fernández & Iniesta-Bonilla, 2007). On a general level, as a working definition, value for customers can be described in the following way: *Value for customers means that they, after having been assisted by the provision of resources or interactive processes, are or feel better off than before* (Grönroos, 2008:303; slightly abbreviated; compare also Vargo, Maglio, & Akaka, 2008).

In business-to-business contexts, the support of a supplier will always have some effect on the economic result of the customer's business. The profitability of a business is dependent on how well the firm's various practices (order making, storing, producing, maintaining, paying, having mistakes corrected, etc.) function not only in terms of *operational efficiency* but also in terms of *business effectiveness*, i.e. how *effectively* various practices support either the firm's growth- and revenue-generating capacity or cost level, or both. How well such practices function and have positive effects on revenues and costs is dependent of how well they are supported by the firm's suppliers. Hence, *the roots of a firm's economic result can be traced back to how well the firm's various practices are supported by its suppliers, in terms of the revenue and cost effects created by this support.* Therefore, value for customers can be measured in monetary terms. In addition, value also has a perceptional dimension, for example, trust, commitment and attraction.

In conclusion, what value a customer can create out of the support provided by a supplier can be divided into three dimensions:

1. Effects on the customer's growth- and revenue-generating capacity
   a. Business growth opportunities (new markets, better customer or customer segment penetration)
   b. Higher margins through premium pricing
2. Effects on the customer's cost level
   c. Lower operative and/or administrative costs
   d. Higher margins through lower operating/administrative costs
3. Effects on perceptions
   e. Increased trust in the supplier
   f. Increased commitment to the supplier
   g. Increased comfort in supplier interactions
   h. Increased attraction of the supplier.

In principle the two first types of value-creating effects can be measured in monetary terms. The third effect can only be measured as perceptions and cognitive effects. From the supplier's point of view, calculating the revenue and cost effects of an extended market offering (service offering) is a way of motivating a price tag on service.

4. Value as Value-in Use—The Customer as the Value Creator

In the contemporary marketing and management literature as well as in the discussion about service logic, there is a common understanding that value is created in the users' processes as *value-in-use* (see for example, Normann & Ramirez, 1993; Holbrook, 1994, 1996; Ravald & Grönroos, 1996; Vandermerwe, 1996; Wikström, 1996; Woodruff & Gardial, 1996; Normann, 2001; Prahalad, 2004; Vargo & Lusch, 2004; Grönroos, 2006, 2008; Lush, Vargo, & O'Brien, 2007, to mention a few publications). Also in axiology, or the philosophy of value, value is considered to be created by the customers during use of goods and services (e.g., Holbrook, 1999; Lamont, 1995; Mattsson, 1991).

However, especially in publications on service as a logic for business and marketing, the expression "value creation" is used to mean more than one phenomenon. On one hand, value creation means the customer's creation of value-in-use. On the other hand, as in the expressions 'the customer is always a co-creator of value' (e.g. Vargo & Lusch, 2004, 2008) and 'the firm is not a value creator but a co-creator of value' (e.g. Lusch, Vargo, & Wessels, 2008), it is also used to mean the entire process of development, design, manufacturing and delivery as well as back-office and front-office activities *and* also including the customer's creation of value-in-use.

To avoid the confusion caused by this unspecific use of "value creation", in the present article the two above mentioned processes are conceptually kept apart. The following definitions are introduced: The term *"value creation"* and the expression *"value-creating process"* are used only for the customer's creation of value-in-use. The reason for this is that in the contemporary literature on marketing and management, as in the literature on axiology, customers are seen as the ones who create value out of resources they have obtained. Therefore, the term "value creation" is logically used for this very process of customer's creation of value and for nothing else. For the much more extensive process of developing, designing, manufacturing and delivering as well as firm's back-office and front-office activities and also including customer creation of value-in-use, the terms *"value generation"* and *"value-generating process"* are used.

Using this distinction between value creation and value generation, it is possible to create an understanding of how value for customers really emerges and to develop a terminology that can be used to explain and analyze this process. This would be one answer to the question Vargo et al. (2008) raise in a recent article: "This exploration of value co-creation raises as many questions as it answers. For example: What exactly are the processes involved in value co-creation?" (p. 451).

In the 1960s the economist and Nobel Prize winner Gary Becker (1965) described this view of value creation in a consumer context in his discussion of the household as *a utility or value producing unit.* Firms supply the household with the resources, such as goods, service activities and information, which the household needs in order to create value (or utility) for itself. Also in service marketing research this was observed very early: "A good represents potential value (or utility) for the consumer. He purchases the good and subsequently he has to initiate and implement the activities required to transform this potential value into real value for him" (Grönroos, 1979:86).

Following the value-in-use notion, it can be concluded that it is *the customer who is the value creator in a business relationship.* As an adjunct to the value-in-use notion, to say that the customer always is a co-creator of value gives the wrong impression of the pivotal role held by the customer in the creation of value-in-use. In some situations, the customer may co-create value-in-use, but the important aspect to emphasize is that the customer as the user of resources is *the* value creator. The sub-processes of the entire value-generating process including the roles of suppliers and users need to be further explored. Therefore, in a later section the roles of the supplier, and the customer, in value generation for customers will be discussed.

Since the early days of modern service marketing research, customer participation in service production processes and the customers' role as co-producers of service activities and marketing implications that follow have been recognized (Eiglier & Langeard, 1975; Grönroos, 1982). The fact that customers participate as co-producers in firms' production processes means that customers engage themselves with the firms' work or processes (see, for example, Lengnick-Hall, Claycomb, & Inks, 2000; Auh, Bell, McLeod, & Shih, 2007). Perhaps it is from this observation of customers as co-producers that the thought has emerged in the recent literature that also in the context of value creation customers are given opportunities to engage themselves with the firm's processes, but in this case as value co-creators in the firm's creation (or co-creation) of value for them. However, as it is the customers who create value, in the context of value creation this statement is misleading. Mixing co-production with value creation may have contributed to what appears to be confusing in the literature as to the roles of firms and customers in the creation of value-in-use.[2] Distinguishing between *value generation* as the entire process leading to value-in-use for a customer as the end state of that process, and *value creation* as the customer's creation of value-in-use helps overcoming this confusion. Thus the following proposition can be formulated:

2. *When adopting a value-in-use notion, the customer is the value creator.*

5.   The Roles of Value and Service in Business

Value and value creation has been found to be a foundational aspect in marketing and business (e.g., Alderson, 1957; AMA marketing redefinition attempts, 2004 and 2007; CIM the Chartered Institute of Marketing re-evaluation of the marketing definition, 2007; Drucker, 1954; Grönroos, 1997; Holbrook, 1994; Rust & Oliver, 1994; Sheth & Uslay, 2007). The objective of adopting a service logic in business is to enable value creation for both the customer and the supplier. As Gummesson (1995) observed, all kinds of resources are used by customers to *render service that create value for them.* This raises the question, what is the role of service and value, respectively in business? As Vargo & Lusch (2008; see also Lusch et al., 2008) state, service is a logic *for understanding value creation* (and marketing). This is also implied by Gummesson's (1995) observation.

Hence, what should be achieved by providing service is not service for the other party in the business engagement *per se*, but value for both parties involved in the business engagement. The ultimate goal is to support *value creation* for the customer and enable *value creation* by the supplier. Therefore, based on today's emphasis on value-in-use, the goal of business is *reciprocal value creation*, with service as a mediating factor in this process (Grönroos & Ravald, 2009).

6.   The Supplier's Role in Value Generation: Value Facilitation and Co-creation

Developing, designing, manufacturing and delivering, for which the collective term "production" is used in this article, and value creation are not the same thing. They are part of the entire process of value generation. In production processes the resources (goods, service activities and other resources) that render value for customers are produced. Production takes place in the supplier's sphere. Value creation, on the

[2] Notably, Ballantyne and Varey (2006) have suggested alterative conceptual understandings for value creation and for value production.

other hand, takes place in the customers' value-creating processes, where a range of resources are used. Their value is created out of the resources available. Value creation takes place in the customers' sphere (Vandermerwe, 1996). Hence, production and value creation are separate processes that get intertwined only under certain circumstances. They are also different constructs. Therefore, neither of them can be considered a superordinate concept.[3]

What suppliers can do in the value-generating process to support value creation is to provide their customers with resources that can be used by them, together with other available resources. In this way suppliers facilitate value creation (of value-in-use). Consequently, this task undertaken by suppliers can be labeled *value facilitation* (Grönroos, 2008:306-307; Grönroos & Ravald, 2009). However, as supplier and customer processes are in part simultaneously occurring processes, interactions between suppliers and their customers take place. During these interactions co-producing opportunities exist for customers. From a production point of view (production in this sense including both manufacturing processes and the execution of, for example, order taking, logistical, maintenance invoicing and complaints handling and problem recovery and other processes), customers may engage with the supplier's production process.

Looking at the interactions from a value creation perspective, the situation may be quite different. Value creation (of value-in-use) takes place in the user's sphere, and *therefore, it is the supplier that is invited to engage with the customer's usage processes*, in order to support the customer's value creation. This is a truly outside-in approach in accordance with the marketing concept. The supplier's involvement in its customers' usage processes during interactions with the customers opens up additional opportunities for suppliers to influence customers' value creation. During the interactions the supplier can directly work with the customers and actively influence the flow and outcome of their value-creating processes. However, according to the value-in-use notion, customers create value. As stated earlier, supplier production aims to *facilitate* customer value, but customers will always determine what is of value. Not differentiating adequately the terms *production* of resources and *facilitation* of customers' value creation by providing such resources arguably creates much confusion as to the roles of the parties in the business engagement, and the ways they can work towards the creation of value for customers.

As Storbacka and Lehtinen (2001) state, customers produce value for themselves independently, but suppliers may offer assistance. However, during part of the value-creating process, specifically during interactions with users, in addition to its role as value facilitator, *the supplier may become a co-creator of value* as well (Grönroos, 2008:307). Co-creation opportunities that suppliers have are strategic options for creating value (Payne, Storbacka, & Frow, 2008). These interactions involving co-creation of value are dialogical, where both parties influence each other's

---

[3] Value creation (or co-creation) has been suggested as a superordinate concept in relation to production (or co-production) (Vargo & Akaka, 2009).

perceptions and actions (Ballantyne, 2004; Ballantyne & Varey, 2006). Suppliers' co-creation of value-in-use for their customers takes place *together* with the customers. Because the customer creates value-in-use, without the existence of interactions the supplier has no value co-creation opportunities. Therefore, value co-creation is *a joint value creation process*, which requires the simultaneous presence of both customer and supplier. In isolation from each other, the supplier facilitates the creation of value-in-use, and the customer as sole value creator creates value-in-use. In the next sections on *interaction* and its implications for value creation and marketing the underpinning logic of suppliers' value co-creation opportunities are analyzed further.

In Figure 2 the relationships between production and value creation as well as the position of interactions in relation to the supplier's production processes and the customer's value-creating (and usage) processes are schematically illustrated. The figure shows that interactions can be viewed both from a production perspective and from a value creation perspective, respectively. From the former perspective, as illustrated in the upper left corner of the figure, interactions are joint production processes, in which the customer as *co-producer* participates with the supplier. From the latter perspective, as illustrated in the lower right corner of the figure, interactions are joint

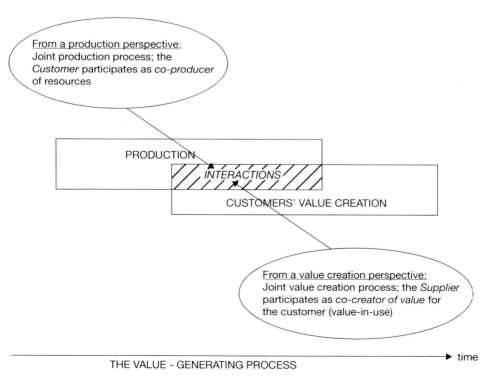

Figure 2. Value Creation and the Phases of the Value-generating Process

value creation processes, in which the supplier as *co-creator of value* participates with the customer. In this context co-creation means that two (or more) parties together influence the emergence of value-in-use.

The value-generating process is not as linear as the figure implies. The customer may also, for example, initiate the development of new resources or solutions. In that case the process of value creation may start with an interaction, where co-creation of value by the parties involved takes place. This phase may lead to another production phase, where no interactions occur. This phase may, for example, include manufacturing of a resource. After that, interactions may occur again during, for example, deliveries and installing, which enable co-creation of value for the supplier. Then the resources are used by the customer in a continuous value-creating process up until, for example, a maintenance activity again enables the supplier to get involved in the customer's value creation as co-creator of value.

Interaction and joint value creation can take place throughout the value-generating process, during development, design, manufacturing, deliveries and front-office processes. If this is the case, the customer participates as co-developer, co-designer, co-producer, etc. in the firm's processes. At the same time this enables the firm to engage itself in value co-creation within the customer's value-creating process. During non-interactive production phases the supplier is a *value facilitator* aiming at producing an output that supports or facilitates the customer's value-creating process.

Thus the following propositions can be formulated:

3. *The supplier's basic role in the value-generating process is to facilitate the customers' value creation.*
4. *During interactions with customers the supplier can engage itself with the customers' value creation and become co-creators of value with them.*

7. The Nature of Interactions and Their Implications for Joint Value Creation

No joint value creation exists and no co-creation of value can take place, unless interactions between the supplier and the customer occur. Especially within the Nordic school research tradition, the interaction concept is a key construct in relationship marketing (e.g., Grönroos, 1982; Gummesson, 2002) and in service marketing, for example in the form of buyer-seller interactions and interactive marketing (e.g., Grönroos, 1982), part-time marketers (e.g., Gummesson, 1991) and interaction quality (e.g., Lehtinen & Lehtinen, 1991). However, interaction has also been discussed to some extent within other service research traditions (e.g., Solomon, Surprenanat, & Czepiel, 1985).[4]

---

[4] For discussions of the interaction concept in other contexts, see for example Håkansson (1982), Håkansson and Snehota (1995), Dwyer, Shurr, and Oh (1987), Jap, Manolis, and Weitz (1999), Day and Montgomery (1999), Rayport and Jaworski (2005), Yadav and Varadarajan (2005), and Ramani and Kumar (2008).

In general terms *interaction is mutual or reciprocal action where two or more parties have an effect upon one another.* An inherent aspect of interaction is connectivity, i.e. the parties involved are in some contact with each other. In a business context supplier-customer interactions mean that two or more parties are in contact with each other for a business reason, and in these contacts they have opportunities to influence one another's processes.

Traditionally, in typical goods-marketing situations the supplier provides its customers with goods as input resources into their practices. The goods are more or less standardized and after delivery, unless prompted by the customer, the supplier cannot take actions to influence them. Joint R&D activities and product and service development as well as joint processes of matching corresponding supplier and customer practices (see Fig. 1) provide an interactive platform, where the customer can influence the supplier's processes and the supplier can influence the customer's value creation. By adding, for example, call center services, interactive systems for order taking, logistics or diagnosing problems a goods marketer creates interactions with its customers. In all these cases, the supplier, through the development of interactions, creates opportunities to engage itself with its customers' practices and to influence them and their outcomes.

The customer's and the supplier's practices flow partly as parallel processes. For example, order making and order taking may include interactions between people, between people and automatic systems or even between systems, or maintenance activities include interactions between people and even between automatic systems representing the supplier and the customer, respectively. The same goes for a range of supplier practices that are needed for influencing other corresponding customer practices. Such corresponding processes occur partly simultaneously and in parallel with each other. From a value creation perspective they are communicative interactive processes (Ballantyne, 2004; Ballantyne & Varey, 2006) that can *merge into one integrated process*, where both parties are active and may directly influence each other. The supplier operates as an integrated part of the customer's process, and the customer operates as an integrated part of the supplier's process.

The mere existence of an interaction does not automatically imply that direct actions that influence the other party are or even can be taken by the supplier or customer. It is important to realize that, from the supplier's point of view, the existence of interactions is only a *platform* for influencing the customers' usage processes. However, the quality of the interactions between the parties is fundamental for value co-creation (compare Fyrberg & Jüriado, 2009:422). The more actively the supplier manages to make use of the interaction platform, the more the employees and systems representing the supplier are engaged with the customers' value creation, and the more opportunities for co-creating value it has. Thus the following propositions can be formulated:

5. *Value co-creation requires that customer-supplier interactions occur.*
6. *The quality of interactions (i.e. how well the supplier can make use of them to influence the customer's value creation) has an impact on how well the supplier can make use of value co-creation opportunities.*

8.   Marketing Implications of Interactions and the Supplier's Value Co-creation Opportunities

Both in marketing practice and in academic discussions value for customers has become a key concept. In addition, as was pointed out previously, mutual value creation can be viewed as a goal of business, where service is a mediating factor. In its efforts to update its marketing definition during the 2000s, the American Marketing Association has taken a new stance and distinctly based its new view of marketing on *value creation*. In both the American Marketing Association's and The Chartered Institute of Marketing's redefinition attempts in the UK during the 2000s value has been pointed out as a pivotal issue (AMA marketing redefinition attempts, 2004 and 2007; CIM the Chartered Institute of Marketing re-evaluation of the marketing definition, 2007). Building on the AMA efforts to redefine marketing, Sheth and Uslay (2007); (see also, for example, Holbrook, 1994; Rust & Oliver, 1994; and Grönroos, 1997) have argued that focusing marketing on value creation indeed may be a contemporary marketing focus. Focusing on value creation as the ultimate goal for marketing may be an answer to the challenge posed by Alderson (1957) over half a century ago, namely that rather than finding out what utility, or value, is created by marketing, what is needed is "a marketing interpretation of the whole process of creating utility" (p. 69). It also corresponds with Drucker's (1954) conclusion that it is what customers do with firms' output and what they think is value for them that is decisive for any business.

From the underpinning logic of service, based on the notion that in order to support customers' value creation the supplier should strive to get involved in the customer's processes, such as purchasing, order making, storing goods, paying, using, maintaining, updating, having mistakes and failures corrected, getting advice, and scrap disposal, the following formulation of the goal for marketing can be derived (Grönroos, 2009:353):

> *The goal for marketing is to engage the firm with the customers' processes with an aim to support value creation in those processes, in a mutually beneficial way.*

This way of expressing marketing's goal is in line with the relationship marketing definition, which, according to Marker (Harker, 1999; Harker & Egan, 2006), best reflects the aspects of relationship marketing mentioned in the literature. According to this definition (e.g., Grönroos, 2007:275), relationship marketing is defined as the process of establishing, maintaining and enhancing, and when necessary terminating relationships with customers, for the benefit of all involved parties, through *a process of making and keeping promises*. Making promises requires that the supplier engages itself with its customers' processes in the first place (sales, marketing communication, offers, etc.). Keeping promises relates to how the supplier continuously supports the various processes relevant to its customers (order making, storing goods, paying, using, maintaining, etc.).

Keeping promises well means that the customers' processes are supported in a successful and value-creating way. Hence, the supplier's capability to support value creation through *value facilitation* (providing appropriate goods and service activities and other resources) and *value co-creation* during interactions with customers in a variety of customer practices determines its marketing success.

From a marketing point of view the value co-creation opportunities mean that, during the interactive joint value creation process with the customer, the supplier as part of the customers' processes is *part of their value creation.* This means that the supplier is not *restricted to making promises of potential value for the customers only.*[5] If that were the case, no co-production activities and especially no direct and active efforts by the supplier influencing the customer's usage and value-creating process would take place.

In summary, it can be concluded that the value co-creation opportunities for suppliers created by the adoption of a service logic on business, and the utilization of firm-customer interactions, open up new opportunities for suppliers to develop their marketing strategies in ways that previously were unique to service firms only. The analysis demonstrated how the interaction phenomenon enables a supplier adopting a service logic to break free from the goods logic restriction of being able to make promises, or offer value propositions, only. Thus the following proposition can be formulated:

7. *Suppliers adopting a service logic are not restricted to making value propositions only, but are enabled to directly engage themselves with keeping promises inherent in value propositions made.*

9. Conclusions and Implications for Management and Research

The analysis of value creation and marketing implications for business relationships, due to the adoption of a service perspective on business, reveals some new avenues for understanding business-to-business marketing. Value creation and marketing turn out to be intertwined. The opportunities for suppliers to engage themselves with their customers' value creation offer unique opportunities for suppliers to extend their marketing (and sales) activities into the customers' sphere by incorporating activities during firm-customer interactions in the marketing process. This makes new marketing strategies possible. The suppliers' active and direct involvement in the customers' value creation through value co-creation activities with them provides

---

[5] In the discussion of a service-dominant logic it is invariably claimed that service as a business perspective means that the firm can offer value propositions only (e.g. Vargo & Lusch, 2004, 2008). As a value proposition is a suggestion or promise about something that has not materialized for the customer yet, this statement must be due to a negligence or misunderstanding of the interaction concept.

interactive marketing[6] opportunities that firms adopting a conventional goods logic do not have. Hence, as has been summarized in the propositions derived from the analysis in the present article, the adoption of a service logic in business is based on the following premises:

1. Service as a phenomenon means support by one party for another party's practices and processes. In on-going business-to-business relationships the implementation of a service perspective or logic may require *practice matching* aiming at aligning corresponding supplier and customer processes and competencies.
2. In order to understand the supplier's and the customer's roles and activities, the customer's creation of value-in-use, in this article called *value creation*, and the entire process of *value generation*, starting with the development of resources and ending with the customer's creation of value-in-use out of such resources, must be kept apart conceptually.
3. Interaction is a defining characteristic of the adoption of a service logic that integrates marketing with value creation, and this has fundamental implications for both value generation and the future scope and relevance of marketing.
4. Reciprocal value creation for all parties in a business engagement is an ultimate basis of business. Service is a mediator variable in this process.
5. Suppliers cannot create value. Their role is fundamentally that of a value facilitator providing customers with value-supporting resources and interactive processes that facilitate the customers' value creation. In addition to being value facilitators, during interactions with their customers, suppliers can get opportunities to get involved in joint value creation processes and become value co-creators with them as well.
6. Value co-creation with customers offers the suppliers opportunities to extend their market offering to include activities during the customers' value-creating process. Thus, in their marketing strategies and processes firms are not restricted to making promises of potential value (or value proposition) only, but can include activities performed by people involved in interactions with customers as part-time marketers (interactive marketing) that directly and actively influence the customers' value fulfillment as well.

The implications for industrial marketing management are extensive. Marketing has mainly been a promise making process, where the responsibility for keeping promises and creating loyalty have been in the hands of other functions in a firm (see Brown, 2005:3). Now the execution of activities, such as deliveries, repair and maintenance, customer training, problem recovery, invoicing, can be incorporated in the marketing process, and when doing so, marketing becomes influential in promise keeping and loyalty creating. Long-existing concepts from service marketing research, such as interactive marketing (Grönroos, 1982), part-time marketers (Gummesson, 1991) and internal marketing (Eiglier & Langeard, 1975; Grönroos, 1982), are emphasized in business relationships.

---

[6] Interactive marketing was introduced in service marketing research as a term describing the marketing aspect of the performance of employees involved in simultaneously occurring service production and consumption processes (Grönroos, 1982).

New marketing strategies and business models can be developed, including new earnings logics based on extended market offerings integrating goods and service activities from a service business perspective. As marketing is intertwined with value and value creation, it may also be possible to develop new value-based pricing models, and find an effective way of putting a price on the service activities offered to customers.

Research opportunities follow the same paths as the above mentioned managerial implications. The adoption of service marketing concepts and models in business relationships need further research, and further refinement of such concepts to fit these contexts is required. Also research into new service logic-based business models is needed. Moreover, because a firm can create value for itself from a business relationship only if it supports its customer's value creation, the process of reciprocal value creation should be studied, and corresponding metrics for measuring such value creation developed.

References

Alderson, W. (1957). *Marketing behavior and executive action.* Homewood, IL: Richard D. Irwin.

American Marketing Association (2007, last update October). Definition of marketing. Available: http://www.marketingpower.com/AboutAMA/Pages/DefinitionofMarketing.aspx (August 25, 2009).

Auh, S., Bell, S. J., McLeod, C. S., & Shih, E. (2007). Co-production and customer loyalty in financial services. *Journal of Retailing, 83(3)*, 359–370.

Ballantyne, D. (2004). Dialogue and its role in the development of relationship specific knowledge. *Journal of Business and Industrial Marketing*, 19(2), 114–123.

Ballantyne, D., & Varey, R. J. (2006). Creating value-in-use through marketing interaction: The exchange logic of relating, communicating and knowing. *Marketing Theory*, 6(3), 335–348.

Becker, G. S. (1965, September). A theory of allocation of time. *The Economic Journal, 75* (299), 493–517.

Brown, S. W. (2005, October). When executives speak, we should listen and act differently. *Journal of Marketing, 69*, 2–4.

Day, G., & Montgomery, D. (1999). Charting new directions for marketing. *Journal of Marketing (Special Issue), 63*, 3–13.

Drucker, P. F. (1954). *The practice of management.* New York: Harper Collier Publishers.

Dwyer, F. R., Shurr, P. H., & Oh, S. (1987). Developing buyer-seller relationships. *Journal of Marketing*, 51(2), 11–27.

Eiglier, P., & Langeard, E. (1975). Principe politique de marketing pour les enterprises de service. *Working Paper.:* Institute d'Administratin des Enterprises. Université d'Aix-Marseille.

Fyrberg, A., & Jüriado, R. (2009). What about interaction? Networks and brands as integrators within a service-dominant logic. *Journal of Service Management*, 20(4), 420–432.

Grönroos, C. (1979). Service Marketing. A study of the marketing function in service firms (in Swedish with an English summary). Diss., Hanken School of Economics Finland, Marketing Technique Centre and Akademilitteratur.

Grönroos, C. (1982). An applied service marketing theory. *European Journal of Marketing*, 16(7), 30–41.

Grönroos, C. (1997). Value-driven relational marketing: From products to resources and competences. *Journal of Marketing Management*, 13(5), 407–420.

Grönroos, C. (2006). Adopting a service logic for marketing. *Marketing Theory*, 6(3), 317–333.

Grönroos, C. (2007). *Service management and marketing. Customer management in service competition.* Chichester: Wiley.

Grönroos, C. (2008). Service logic revisited: Who creates value? And who co-creates? *European Business Review*, 20(4), 298–314.

Grönroos, C. (2009). Promise management: Regaining customer management for marketing. *The Journal of Business & Industrial Marketing*, 24(5/6), 351–359.

Grönroos, C., & Ravald, A. (2009). Marketing and the logic of service: Value facilitation, value creation and co-creation, and their marketing implications. *Working paper, No. 542*, Finland: Hanken Press/Hanken School of Economics http://urn.fi/URN: ISBN:978-952-232-061-2.

Gummesson, E. (1991). Marketing revisited: The crucial role of the part-time marketer. *European Journal of Marketing*, 25(2), 60–67.

Gummesson, E. (1995). Relationship marketing: Its role in the service economy. In William J. Glynn, & James G. Barnes (Eds.), Understanding Services Management (pp. 244–268). New York: Wiley.

Gummesson, E. (2002). *Total relationship marketing*. Oxford: Butterworth Heinemann.

Harker, M. J. (1999). Relationship marketing defined? An examination of current relationship marketing definitions. Marketing *Intelligence & Planning*, 17(1), 13–20.

Harker, M. J., & Egan, John (2006). The past, present and future of relationship marketing. *Journal of Marketing Management*, 22(1–2), 215–242.

Holbrook, M. B. (1994). The nature of customer value – An axiology of services in the consumption experience. In Roland T. Rust, & Richard Oliver (Eds.), Service *Quality: New Directions in Theory and Practice*. Thousand Oaks, CA: Sage.

Holbrook, M. B. (1996). Customer value – a framework for analysis and research. In K. P. Corfman, & J. G. Lynchjr. (Eds.), *Advances in consumer research, 23*. (pp. 138–142) Provo, Utah: Association of Consumer Research.

Holbrook, M. B. (1999). Introduction to consumer value. In Morris B. Holbrook (Ed.), Customer *value. A framework for analysis and research*. London: Routledge.

Håkansson, H. (Ed.). (1982). International *marketing and purchasing of industrial goods*. New York: Wiley.

Håkansson, H., & Snehota, I. (1995). *Developing relationships in business networks*. London: Routledge.

Jap, S. D., Manolis, C., & Weitz, B. A. (1999). Relationship quality and buyer-seller interactions in channels of distributions. *Journal of Business Research*, 46(3), 303–313.

Lamont, W. D. (1995). *The value judgment.* : Edinburgh University Press.

Lehtinen, U., & Lehtinen, J. R. (1991). Two approaches to service quality dimension. *The Service Industries Journal*, 11(3), 287–303.

Lengnick-Hall, C. A., Claycomb, C., & Inks, L. W. (2000, March). From recipient to contributor: Examining customer roles and experienced outcomes. *European Journal of Marketing, 34*, 359–383.

Lush, R. F., Vargo, S. L., & O'Brien, M. (2007). Competing through service: Insights from service-dominant logic. *Journal of Retailing*, 83(1), 5–18.

Lusch, R. F., Vargo, S. L., & Wessels, G. (2008). Toward a conceptual foundation for service science: Contributions from service-dominant logic. *IBM Systems Journal*, 47(1), 5–14.

MacMillan, I. C., & McGrath, R. G. (1997, July/August). Discovering new points of differentiation. *Harvard Business* Review, 133–145.

Mattsson, J. (1991). *Better business by the ABC of values*. Lund: Studentlitteratur.

Normann, R. (2001). *Reframing business: When the map changes the landscape*. Chichester: Wiley.

Normann, R., & Ramirez, R. (1993, July-August). From value chain to value constellation: Designing interactive strategy. *Harvard Business* Review, 71, 65–77.

Prahalad, C. K. (2004). The co-creation of value – Invited commentary. *Journal of Marketing*, 68(1), 23.

Payne, A. F., Storbacka, K., & Frow, P. (2008). Managing the co-creation of value. *Journal of the Academy of Marketing Science*, 1(36), 83–96.

Ramani, G., & Kumar, V. (2008). Interaction orientation and firm performance. *Journal of Marketing*, 72(1), 27–45.

Ravald, A., & Grönroos, C. (1996). The value concept and relationship marketing. *European Journal of Marketing*, 30(2), 19–30.

Rayport, J. F., & Jaworski, B. J. (2005). *Best face forward*. Boston, MA: Harvard Business School Press.

Rust, R. T., & Oliver, R. L. (1994). Service quality: Insights and managerial implications from the frontier. In Roland T. Rust, & Richard L. Oliver (Eds.), Service *Quality: New Directions for Theory and Practice* (pp. 1–20). Thousand Oaks, CA: Sage.

Sánchez-Fernández, R., & Iniesta-Bonilla, M.Á. (2007). The concept of perceived value: A systematic review of the research. Marketing *Theory*, 7(4), 427–451.

Sheth, J. N., & Uslay, C. (2007). Implications of the revised definition of marketing: From exchange to value creation. *Journal of Public Policy & Marketing*, 26(2), 302–307.

Solomon, M. R., Surprenant, C., & Czepiel, J. A. (1985). A role theory perspective on dyadic interactions: The service encounter. *Journal of Marketing*, 49(1), 99–111.

Storbacka, K., & Lehtinen, J. R. (2001). Customer *relationship management*. Singapore: McGraw-Hill.

The Chartered Institute of Marketing (2007). Shape *the agenda. Tomorrow's world. Re-evaluating the role of marketing*.: The Chartered Institute of Marketing publications.

Vandermerwe, S. (1996). Becoming a customer "owning" company. *Long Range Planning*, 29(6), 770–782.

Vargo, S. L., & Akaka, M. A. (2009). Service-dominant logic as a foundation for service science: Clarifications. *Service Science*, 1(1), 32–41.

Vargo, S. L., & Lusch, R. F. (2004, January). Evolving to a new dominant logic for marketing. *Journal of Marketing*, 1–17.

Vargo, S. L., & Lusch, R. F. (2008). Service dominant logic: Continuing the evolution. *Journal of the Academy of Marketing Science*, 36(1), 1–10.

Vargo, S. L., Maglio, P. P., & Akaka, M. A. (2008). On value and value co-creation: A service systems and service logic perspective. *European Management Journal*, 26(3), 145–152.

Webster, F. E., Jr. (1994). Executing the new marketing concept. *Marketing Management*, 3(1), 9–18.

Wikström, S. (1996). Value creation by company-consumer interaction. *Journal of Marketing Management*, 12, 359–374.

Woodruff, R. B., & Gardial, S. (1996). *Know your customers – New approaches to understanding customer value and satisfaction*. Oxford: Blackwell.

Yadav, M. S., & Varadarajan, P. R. (2005). Understanding product migration to the electronic marketplace: A conceptual framework. *Journal of Retailing, 81*(2), 125–140.

3

Relationship Marketing as Promise Management

The SAGE Handbook of Marketing Theory
Pauline Maclaran, Michael Saren, Barbara Stern, and Mark Tadajewski (eds)
2009, pp. 397–412

Christian Grönroos

Introduction

This chapter is based on the assumption that, both from academic and practitioner perspectives, relationship marketing, as a process-oriented approach to customer management in a meaningful way, is understood as *promise management*, i.e. as a process of enabling promises to customers, making promises to them and keeping promises by meeting expectations created by promises that have been made. Consequently, the *purpose* of the present chapter is to analyse how relationship marketing can be conceptualized and managed using a promise management approach. The analysis aims at developing a marketing definition that helps academics and business practitioners alike to understand and implement a relational strategy in both business-to-business and business-to-consumer contexts. As the analysis draws to a large extent, but not entirely, on the Nordic School of thought in marketing research (see, for example, Grönroos, 2007, and Berry and Parasuraman, 1993), it is also based on the view that relationship marketing and understanding how to manage services are intertwined. Services are inherently relational, and relational marketing requires the adoption of a service logic (Grönroos, 2007).

Definitions of Relationship Marketing in the Literature

In the literature, there seems to be no agreement on how relationship marketing is best defined (see chapters in this handbook by Gadde and Håkansson, Moller et al., and Brodie et al.). In his analysis of relationship marketing definitions, Harker (1999) found that the one definition that included the most common elements of what then could be found in the scholarly literature was the following (Grönroos, 1997, slightly modified):[1]

> Relationship marketing is to identify and establish, maintain and enhance, and when necessary terminate relationships with customers (and other parties) so that the objectives regarding economic and other variables of all parties are met. This is achieved through a mutual making and fulfilment of promises.

During the time period since Harker's analysis, research does not seem to have changed the fact that this definition is the one that best covers the field (cf. Harker and Egan, 2006).

The definition includes two strengths: first, it takes a process approach to marketing, and second, it indicates by what means this process proceeds. The process moves from identifying relationships over establishing and maintaining them to enhancing and possibly dissolving them. The means of pursuing this process is making promises and keeping promises that have been made. This part of the definition draws on Calonius's (1983, 1986, 2006) suggestion of the *promise concept* as a key construct in marketing. However, as with all relationship-marketing definitions, this definition does not specify in any detail how the marketing process proceeds beyond the notion of establishing, maintaining, and enhancing relationships. In the present chapter, the progress of this process will be analysed in detail. Due to the comprehensive nature of Grönroos's definition quoted in the foregoing section, which already includes the promise concept, it seems only natural to build upon it and expand it.

Value Creation as the Goal for Marketing

Traditionally, *exchange* has been considered the fundamental construct in marketing (see, for example, Baggozzi, 1975; Hunt, 1976; Kotler, 1972; Pyle, 1931). According to this view, the goal of marketing is to create exchange of goods and services for money or the equivalent. However, concentrating on marketing as exchange draws the marketers' attention to short-term value-in-exchange and away from customers' value creation (cf. for example, Sheth and Uslay, 2007), and this conceals the importance of customers' creation of value-in-use to long-term marketing success (Grönroos, 2007, 2008). Moreover, focusing on exchange takes marketing's interest away from developing customer relationships and makes marketing focused on transactions (Grönroos, 2007). As Kotler noted, '... the core of marketing is transaction. A transaction is the exchange of values between two parties' (1972: 48). A distinction between direct and indirect exchange, as suggested by Vargo and Lusch (2008) in the discussion of service-dominant logic, does not change this in any fundamental way. On the contrary, using the term 'exchange' metaphorically weakens the exchange construct's base in economic theory and, more or less, makes its meaning and role even more elusive and difficult to use for analysis and planning.

Sheth and Uslay (2007) have suggested that, instead of focusing on exchange, marketing should take the creation of value for customers as its goal. This is not a new view voiced in the marketing literature. However, until now, it has been silenced by marketing's transaction-oriented traditions and models and marketing scholars' preoccupation with exchange. In the 1990s, Holbrook (1994) stated that the value concept is '... the fundamental basis for all marketing activity' (p. 22) and Rust and Oliver (1994) claimed that '... ultimately it is perceived value that attracts a customer or lures away a customer from a competitor' (p. 7). Directly in a relationship marketing context, Grönroos (1997) observes that 'marketing in a relational context is seen as a process that should support the creation of perceived value for customers over time' (p. 407), and Eggert et al. (2006) state that 'offering superior value to customers is essential for creating and maintaining long-term customer-supplier relationships' (p. 20). Also, American Marketing Association's (AMA's) new marketing definition, published, in 2004 and renewed in 2007, emphasizes the importance of value creation for marketing. Although the underpinning logic of AMA's attempt to define marketing has been criticized as conventional, outdated and geared towards value-in-exchange (Grönroos, 2006b), the reorientation towards value creation as such follows a general trend in business and marketing.

However, when taking value creation for customers as the goal for marketing, a focus on exchange as the foundational marketing construct is no longer supportable (Grönroos, 2007; Sheth and Uslay, 2007) but an outdated and too restrictive concept to focus on (see also Sheth and Parvatiyar, 1995; Webster, 1992). Instead, the interaction concept central to both a service and relationship marketing logic is a more productive option. As Ballantyne and Varey (2006) put it, interaction is a 'generator of service experience and value-in-use' (p. 336), and service experiences are intertwined with the development and maintenance of relationships. Furthermore, interactions help firms gain and deepen their information about customers and their preferences (Srinivasan et al., 2002).

The key advantage of customer–firm interactions for the supplier is the opportunities for the supplier to engage itself with the customers' processes that such interactions offer (Grönroos, 2008). In these interactions, the customer's processes and activities get exposed to the supplier, which enables the supplier to directly and actively take part in these processes and activities and influence the value creation that takes place in them. The supplier gets an opportunity to directly influence the customers' creation of value, something that is not possible without such interactions (Grönroos, 2008). In ongong relationships with customers, exchange still take place, of course, but focusing on exchange as a basically transaction-oriented concept does not make it possible to capture the essence of relationship development and maintenance and of value creation as value-in-use. Interaction makes this possible.

In conclusion, two concepts are of central importance for the analysis in the present chapter, viz. *value creation* and *promise management*. Hence, first of all, the marketing approach developed in this report is based on the notion that through customer-firm interactions and outcomes of these interactions, marketing aims at supporting customers' value creation. Secondly, the promise concept and promise management is a key concept for an understanding of relationship marketing. The promise concept has been developed into a promise management approach to marketing (Grönroos, 2006b).[2]

What Is Customer Value?
Who Creates It and Who Co-creates?

In management literature and in management jargon, it is claimed that value is delivered to customers. However, the phrase 'deliver value to customers' implies that value is embedded in the product (goods, service activities, ideas, information, or any type of solutions) which is delivered to customers for their use. This is a *value-in-exchange* concept, where the exchange of ready-made value embedded in the products for money is considered the central phenomenon to study. The growing importance to marketing success of interactions between customers and a set of resources of the firm is neglected.

The current research into customer value shows a clear trend away from a value-in-exchange view towards a notion of value being produced not by the supplier, but by the customer when using goods and services and when interacting with the suppliers. According to this research, there is no value for customers until they can make use of a good or a service. Value is not what goes into goods and service activities, it is what customers get out of them; i.e. value emerges in the customers' space rather than in the producer's space (Vandermerwe, 1996). Customers assess the value of goods and services based on what is received and what is sacrificed (Zeithaml, 1988). The notion that only customers can assess value to goods and services was expressed by Levitt (1983) already in the early 1980s. However, this thought was largely ignored by the academic and business communities alike. From the beginning of the 1990s onward, this *value-in-use* notion (see Woodruff and Gardial, 1996), as opposed to a value-in-exchange view, has been put forward in the marketing and management literature (see, for example, Grönroos, 2000; Gummesson, 2002; Holbrook, 1994; Jüttner and Wehrli, 1994; Monroe, 1991; Normann, 2001; Norman and Ramirez, 1993; Ravald and Grönroos, 1996; Sheth and Parvatiyar, 1995; Storbacka and Lehtinen, 2001; Vandermerwe, 1996; Wikström, 1996; Woodruff and Gardial, 1996).

Fifty years ago, Wroe Alderson (1957), whose arguments for a functionalist theory of marketing were geared towards a value-in-use concept (Dixon, 1990: 337–338 and Vargo and Lusch, 2004: 5), made the point that what marketing needs is a 'marketing interpretation of the whole process of creating value' (p. 69). He pointed out the superior role of value-in-use: 'Goods do not really have utility from the consumer viewpoint until they come into the possession of the ultimate user and form a part of his assortment' (Alderson, 1957: 70). In 1979, in a service marketing context, Grönroos concluded that 'it is ... reasonable to consider both goods and services to be bought by consumers in order to give some service or value satisfaction', and that 'a good represents potential value (or utility) for the consumer. He purchases the good and subsequently he has to initiate and implement the activities required to transform this potential value into real value for him. ... A service is in itself an activity ... with in-built ability to transform the potential value (or utility) for the consumer into real value for him' (Grönroos, 1979: 86).

Hence, value is not created in the service provider's processes of designing, delivering and pricing services, but in the customer's *value-generating processes* (Grönroos, 2000) where services and goods are consumed and used (compare Becker, 1965, who treats the household as a production unit). Value is either created by the customer in isolation or in interactions with the service provider (Grönroos, 1979, 2008; Normann and Ramirez, 1993; Prahalad and Ramaswamy, 2004; Vargo and Lusch, 2007). In the service provider's processes, *value propositions* are developed, whereas *real value* for customers is created in a customer's value-creating processes (see also Gummesson, 2007).

Co-creation demands co-production efforts of the firm and its customers. In these joint processes, if they are well handled, both customers and the firm can be expected to gain. The firm can make use of the customer's knowledge and skills to improve the quality of services as perceived by the customer and, in addition, feed the knowledge obtained in this way into its development processes (compare Schneider and Bowen, 1995). Hence, both the customer's value perception and the firm's ability to create value propositions and to support value fulfilment will benefit. In addition, the productivity of a firm's operations can benefit from co-production (Lovelock and Young, 1979) at the same time as the customers learn how to use a product and thereby both boosts productivity and their own value creation (Grönroos and Ojasalo, 2004).

A value proposition is a *suggested value* that has not been realized yet (compare Gummesson, 2007), whereas customer value is *perceived value*. At least when accepting the value-in-use notion as a better description of how customer value emerges, *delivering value to customers* is not an accurate description of reality. What marketers can do is to develop value propositions or suggested value in the form of various types of offerings and communicate them to customers and then assist customers in their value creation. 'Delivering value to customers' is based on the value-in-exchange notion and contradictory to the notion of value-in-use and the view of the customer as value creator.

Based on a value-in-use notion it is not the customer who gets engaged with the supplier's processes and becomes a value co-creator with a supplier. Rather, it is the supplier which, by developing firm–customer interactions as part of its market offerings, gets opportunities to engage itself with the customers' processes and become a co-creator of value with its customers (Grönroos, 2008). As Storbacka and Lehtinen (2001) observe, customers produce value for themselves independently, but suppliers may offer assistance. Co-creation opportunities that suppliers have are strategic options for creating value (Payne et al., 2008).

In conclusion, suppliers do not deliver value to customers; as *value facilitators* (Grönroos, 2008: 307) they support or *assist customers' value creation and possibly get involved in co-creation of value with customers*, by providing them with resources such as service processes with service employees, goods and other tangible items as well as with ideas, information, call centre advice, service recovery, payment and invoicing procedures, a whole host of various resources needed by customers (compare Grönroos, 1997).

The analysis of value for customers in a marketing context leads to the following propositions for the understanding of marketing:

> Proposition 1a: *Value is not delivered by a firm to customers but created in customer processes through assistance to those processes and through the firm's co-creation in interactions with customers.*

> Proposition 1b: *The role of marketing is, on one hand, to develop and communicate value propositions to customers, and on the other hand, to assist customers' value creation through goods, services, information, and other resources as well as through interactions where co-creation of value with the customers can take place.*

The Role of Customer Relationships in Marketing

Relationship marketing is, of course, a matter of managing customer relationships. However, as the literature on relationship marketing demonstrates, research into this field and studies of relationship marketing in practice show a variety of different views on the subject. The literature demonstrates a scale of notions of what managing customer relationships is, ranging from creating a mutual commitment and understanding of the supplier and the customer and a win-win situation (see Håkansson and Snehota, 1995; Morgan and Hunt, 1994; Sheth and Parvatiyar, 1995; Grönroos, 1999; and Gummesson, 2002) as a basis for marketing, to having customers who show a repetitive buying behaviour (see Liljander and Strandvik, 1995) to managing relationship marketing instruments such as loyalty programmes and direct mailings (Verhoef, 2003) and relationship marketing tactics (Leong and Qing, 2006) and relationships as yet another variable in the marketing mix toolbox used to manipulate customers (see the criticism of relationship marketing in practice in Fournier et al., 1998).

Moreover, as Ryals (2005) indicate, a relationship marketing approach with the goal to increase customer retention may not always be a profitable strategy, because the costs of retaining customers may be higher than the benefits to be gained from such a strategy (see also Reinartz and Kumar, 2002).

In marketing and management jargon, the term 'customer relationship' is also used in a multitude of ways. For some, it means customers with whom a behavioural and emotional connection and a mutual sense of connectedness (Lindberg-Repo and Grönroos, 2004) have been developed. Repeat purchasing behaviour *and* a larger share of customers' wallet is not enough for a relationship to have been established with a customer (a behavioural component), in addition a larger share of *their heart and mind* is also required (an emotional or attitudinal component) (Storbacka and Lehtinen, 2001). For others, every customer who has shown up at least twice or even every customer regardless of their purchasing behaviour is called a customer relationship.

Only customers can decide whether they have, or want to have, a relationship with a firm, i.e. whether a customer relationship exists or not. It seems quite obvious that all customers do not want to be in a relationship with firms whose services they are using. Customers can be in transactional modes as well as in relational modes (Grönroos, 1997; Sääksjärvi et al., 2007), and the same customer may probably shift from one mode to another depending on type of products, or supplier, or even situation. There is no research yet that would demonstrate when a customer recognizes a relationship to exist, wants a relationship to exist or shifts from a transactional to a relational mode. In fact, relationship marketing and customer relationships have mostly been studied from a management perspective based on the assumption that marketers decide whether relationships exist or not. There is not much knowledge about customers' interests in relational behaviour and about their reactions to relational approaches. The only thing we definitely seem to know is that unless the most simple and meaningless definition of customer relationships is applied, i.e. a customer that buys two or three times is a customer relationship *or* any customer is a customer relationship, all customers cannot be managed as relationships.

In addition, the research on 'Contemporary Marketing Practices' that has been published demonstrates that firms across cultures use a variety of marketing approaches, some of which can be described as relational, some of which cannot (see, for example, Coviello et al., 2002).

As a conclusion, one can note that in the literature and in management practice customer relationships and relationship marketing is considered to include a variety of levels of customer and firm commitment. To make a definition of relationship marketing useful in as wide array of situations as possible, the relational aspect should be included in a marketing definition in an implicit way only. This leads to the following propositions:

> Proposition 2a: *Customers can be in relational as well as nonrelational modes, thus they do not always appreciate being approached in a relational manner by firms, and hence, even though managing customers as relationship often may be effective, it cannot be considered a generic approach to relating a customer to the firm.*

> Proposition 2b: *In an implicit way, a marketing definition must allow both for relational and nonrelational marketing strategies and activities.*

Marketing Transcends Organizational Borders

According to conventional views, marketing is seen as one function among other organizational functions. Marketing is considered to be most efficiently and effectively planned and implemented by a separate department. In the marketing literature, the terms 'marketing', 'marketingfunction', and 'marketing department' are also most frequently used interchangeably, almost as synonyms. Inevitably, this approach to understanding marketing has been very successful for consumer goods. However, already in consumer durables where delivering, installing, and repairing equipment as well as customer advice may be important to success in the marketplace, the marketing department and a separate marketing function will find it difficult to manage or even influence all customer contacts. In services and business-to-business, often with enduring customer relationships, this is even more evident. Alone, a marketing function and marketing department cannot support the customers' value-creating processes or even develop solutions and take total responsibility for the fulfilment of value propositions (compare Brown, 2005: 3). Other processes, such as service interactions, repair and maintenance, logistics, call centres, service recovery, and complaints handling, have an often-critical responsibility for supporting customers' value creation. Few of these processes, often none of them are part of the marketing function and the responsibility of the marketing department, and the marketing department/marketing function has limited or no means of influencing how they are planned and implemented.

Both relationship marketing (e.g. Christopher et al., 1991; Grönroos, 1999; Gummesson, 2002) and service marketing (e.g. Booms and Bitner, 1982; Brown and Bitner, 2006; Grönroos, 2000; Gummesson, 1979; Zeithaml et al., 1988) as well as the IMP approach to business-to-business marketing in networks (e.g. Håkansson, 1982; Håkansson and Snehota, 1995) show that marketing cannot be separated into one function and be the responsibility of one department only. In service marketing, the links between marketing, operations, and human resources has for a long time already been recognized (Gummesson, 1979; Booms and Bitner, 1982; Eiglier and Langeard, 1975; Langeard and Eiglier, 1987; Grönroos, 2000; Lovelock, 2000). Relationship marketing and the IMP approach have come to similar conclusions (Christopher et al., 1991; Håkansson and Snehota, 1995; Grönroos, 1999; Gummesson, 2002). In addition, in his studies, Webster has pointed out the need for dispersing a marketing competence outside the marketing department and across the organization (Webster, Jr., 1992; Webster Jr. et al., 2005). Value propositions may be communicated by a separate function, but the supplier's engagement with the fulfilment of these propositions cannot. A number of other organizational functions get involved, and if those other functions do not take a customer focus, value will not emerge in the customers' processes, and marketing will probably fail.

Hence, relationship marketing cannot be viewed as a one-function process only. First of all, it can be stated that marketing as a *phenomenon* is related to the customers and to the return on the customers or segments of customers a firm serves over time. Hence, marketing requires a *customer focus*. Secondly, to get the best possible return, regardless of what they do and of which function or department they belong to, the people, systems, and processes that have an impact on the return of customers have to make sure that these customers perceive such a value in their processes that they are satisfied enough and prefer to buy again. Hence, for value to emerge in the customers' processes, everyone who is involved in both communicating value propositions and providing value support to customers' processes have to take a *customer focus* in planning and implementing what they are doing. People in the marketing department, including sales, focus on the customer is a full-time duty. For people in other departments and processes, such as operations, logistics, repair and maintenance, service recovery and complaints handling, service development, human resource management, investment, IT, and others, other duties are equally important, sometimes more important and most often perceived as more important. However, irrespective of whether, in a given situation, taking a customer focus is of substantial or marginal importance for them, it should always be part of their duties, not on a full-time scale but as Gummesson (1991) puts it as *part-time marketers*.

Hence, it can be concluded that a customer focus is part of not only what in the traditional marketing literature and vocabulary is called the marketing function, but also of many other organizational functions as well (compare Brown, 2005; Brown and Bitner, 2006; Grönroos, 1999; Gummesson, 1987; Piercy, 1985). Defining marketing as a duty for one organizational function will only work in special cases where the value support to customers' processes is embedded in standardized goods. In other situations, marketing cannot be the responsibility of one separate function only.

In conclusion, the analysis of the organizational home of relationship marketing leads to the following propositions:

> Proposition 3a: *Marketing cannot be implemented by one organizational function of marketing specialists, the full-time marketers, only.*

> Propositions 3b: *Marketing needs a customer focus throughout the organization, thus involving both full-time marketers totally or predominantly trained to take a customer focus and part-time marketers, who when performing their tasks from the outset are not at all or only partly trained to take a customer focus.*

> Proposition 3c: *To be effective marketing also requires that technologies, information systems and other systems are designed and function in a customer-focused manner.*

> Proposition 3d: *As customers participate in interactions with the firm's resources and, therefore, influence the customer orientation of these interactions, they actively participate in marketing as well. Hence, customers' role as a marketing resource, in addition to their roles as buyers and consumers and users has to be recognized in marketing.*

Elements of a Marketing Process

This chapter takes the position that marketing's goal is to assist customers' value creation. In other words, the goal for marketing is *to engage the firm with the customers' processes* with an aim to support value creation in those processes, in a mutually beneficial way (Grönroos, 2009: 353). The traditional elements of marketing mix-based definitions, for example, creating products and services, pricing, promoting, and delivering, are not enough to help marketing reach this goal. Relationship marketing, as marketing in general, is a process, and therefore, for example, promoting and pricing goods and services do not by themselves take customers from an *off* state of not having value to an *on* state of having value. There must be a process from the *off* state to the *on* state with at least some intermediate state that is facilitated by marketing. There has to be some general guidelines indicating *how* marketing activities and processes should be planned and implemented in order to achieve this move from one state to another.

Here, the promise concept provides support. The seller makes a set of promises concerning, for example, physical goods, services, financial solutions, information, interactions, and a range of future commitments. Then, if a relationship is expected to be maintained and enhanced, these promises have to be kept. Berry (1995) claims that the fulfilment of promises made to customers is the foundation for retaining customers and maintaining relationships with them. Also, in the service marketing literature, promises have been explicitly used (e.g. Bitner, 1995; Grönroos, 2000).

The *promise concept* introduced in the early 1980s in the marketing literature by Henrik Calonius is partly founded on an observation by Levitt (1981): 'When prospective customers can't experience the product in advance, they are asked to buy what are essentially promises—promises of satisfaction. Even tangible, testable, feelable, smellable products are, before they are bought, largely just promises' (p. 96). Calonius defines promises, as 'a more or less explicitly expressed conditional declaration or assurance made to another party, or to oneself, with respect to the future, stating that one will do or refrain from some specific act, or that one will give or bestow some specific thing' (1986: 518; 2006: 422).

Some of the marketing activities and processes, such as communicating and pricing, aim at making promises. Of course, customers' past experiences may also influence their perception of future promises about value propositions made to them. Promises are kept by, for example, deliveries, usage of goods and service activities, recovery of problems and mistakes, and call centre advice. As Bitner (1995) observes, promises cannot be expected to be successfully kept unless the organization is prepared to do so. Enabling promises is, therefore, an integral part of making and keeping promises. *Internal marketing*, a concept originating in service marketing research (e.g. Eiglier and Langeard, 1976; Berry, 1981; Grönroos, 1981) and later also in relationship marketing (e.g. Ballantyne, 2003; Dunne and Barnes, 2000), becomes important for marketing success. Employees involved in the fulfilment of promises, regardless of their position in the organization, have to take a customer focus. However, enabling promises also means that resources other than employees, such as goods, IT and other systems, physical resources and information, and also including as a resource external people such as the customer himself or herself and network partner employees, have to be developed in ways that support the fulfilment of promises (Grönroos, 2000).

Some marketing activities are mainly *promise making*, whereas others are mainly *promise keeping*. As research into relationship marketing and service marketing demonstrates, traditional marketing activities performed by a marketing function and full-time marketers are mainly promise making, whereas the promise-keeping activities are mainly the responsibility of other organizational functions and part-time marketers (Gummesson, 1991, 2002; see also Bitner, 1995; Grönroos, 2000). However, as Brown (2005) states in his analysis of the current state of marketing based on a discussion among management team members in large companies, '... marketing and sales often have a major role in making promises to customers and in generating new business', whereas keeping promises is the responsibility of others in an organization' (p. 3).

However, making and keeping promises is not a straightforward issue. Promises made are perceived by customers, thus creating expectations regarding what should be delivered by a firm. Such expectation may vary from person to person and even from situation to situation. As Ojasalo (2001) has pointed out in a study of professional services relationships, customers have *implicit* expectations among explicit ones, and customers easily expect that these should be fulfilled as well. In addition, there may be *fuzzy* expectations that customers have and which do not transform into explicit ones until customers experience the product. Moreover, some expectations are *unrealistic* and, if such expectations are not made realistic, customers are bound to become disappointed (Ojasalo, 2001). Hence, it is not the promises made as such that should be kept, but the individual expectations created by these promises.

In conclusion, the analysis of how value propositions lead to customers' value perceptions and to suppliers' responsibility for keeping promises lead to the following propositions:

> Proposition 4a: *Customers have explicit as well as implicit, unrealistic and fuzzy expectations and these expectations should be fulfilled by the performance of the firm.*

> Proposition 4b: *Fulfilment of promises in a customer-focused manner requires internal marketing efforts as promise enablers.*

> Proposition 4c: *Customer-focused technologies, information systems, and other systems as well as appropriate leadership are also required to support a customer-focused performance by part-time marketers.*

> Proposition 4d: *Helping customers to participate in customer–firm interactions in ways that has a favourable marketing impact on them is also required for marketing to be successful.*

> Proposition 4e: *Making promises, supported by internal activities, such as internal marketing geared towards the fulfilment of expectations created by promises made, as well as technology, systems, and leadership support, and fulfilling expectations created by promises made, form a firm's marketing process.*

Conclusion: Marketing in Relational Situations

Drawing on the discussion of recent research into customer value, relationship marketing, service marketing, and service logic as well as on the promise concept in the previous sections, the following promise management definition for marketing in relational situations can be formulated (Grönroos, 2006b: 407):

> Marketing is a customer focus that permeates organizational functions and processes, and is geared towards making promises through value proposition, enabling the fulfilment of

individual expectations created by such promises and fulfilling such expectations through assistance to customers' value-generating processes, thereby supporting value creation in the firm's a well as its customers' and other stakeholders' processes.

This definition is based on viewing value creation as the goal for marketing and interaction as a foundational construct in marketing as well as on the promise concept and is, therefore, labelled a *promise management definition* (Grönroos, 2006). The definition could also include a specification of by what means promises are made (e.g. by developing, pricing, and communicating value propositions), how promises are enabled (e.g. by internal marketing and the development of customer-focused goods and other tangible items, service processes, technologies, information systems, and other systems as well as appropriate leadership and by helping customers to use goods and service activities that have been delivered as well as to take part in the customer–firm interactions in a way that, supports a favourable marketing impact on them) and how expectations created by promises are kept by providing assistance to customers' value creation (by providing resources and processes—goods, services, information and people, systems, infrastructures, and physical resources—and interactions between the customer and these resources and processes as well as by mobilizing customers as a resource in the purchasing and consumption and usage processes). However, because these clarifications are inherent in the definition, to keep the definition as short as possible they have been omitted.

The underpinning logic of the suggested marketing definition is the following:

First of all, the definition is based on the notion that marketing's goal is to support customers' value creation. Furthermore, it builds upon the *value-in-use* concept, according to which customer value is created by the customer in customers' value-creating processes. With a set of resources, processes, and interactions, firms *provide assistance to* customers' value creation. This value-in-use approach to customer value is clearly more relevant to marketing than the value-in-exchange view, which has characterized mainstream marketing research.

Secondly, because customers probably do not always want relationships with firms and firms do not always consider creating relationships with customers as the foundation of the best possible business strategy, and the level of supplier and customer commitment sought may vary, managing, customer relationships as a phrase is not explicitly included in this definition. Moreover, research today does not provide a clear enough definition or even description of what a relationship is in a commercial context. However, this definition implicitly includes a potential for developing customer relationships. By successfully assisting customers' value creation and doing so in a way which meets individual expectations created by promises that have been made, the likelihood that customers who are in a *relational mode* will want to develop an emotional connection with the firm will increase. *In these cases, relationships will develop.* Moreover, customers who are in a nonrelational mode will probably consider doing repeat business with a firm which performs in the way outlined in the preceding section without getting relationally involved.

Thirdly, as research, for example, into relationship marketing and service marketing as well as research into business-to-business marketing according to the IMP approach demonstrate, as soon as the products provided to customers are more complicated and include more content than standardized goods, one single organizational function cannot take responsibility for total marketing. Therefore, the definition states that several organizational functions have to take a customer focus and take a responsibility for marketing. What traditionally is called the marketing function, including for example market research, advertising and other means of marketing communication, as well as sales will be to 100 percent focused on the customer, whereas other functions such as R&D, product and service development, manufacturing and service operations, logistics, procurement, repair and maintenance, call centre activities, service recovery and complaints handling wherever they are located in the organization, and human resource management and finance will have to be part-time focused on customers. Hence, marketing as a customer focus is a dimension, among others, of the planning and implementing of the tasks of these functions.

Fourthly, unlike the 4 Ps of the marketing mix, the definition does not include a list of variables that are *the* decision-making areas of marketing. Any list such as the 4 Ps endorsed by a reliable source easily becomes a law-like guideline (Kent, 1986). Hence, the promise management definition approaches what should be planned and implemented as marketing as anything that supports value formation in customers' processes by making promises, enabling these processes, and fulfilling expectations created by them. What it takes to do so efficiently and effectively will vary, sometimes less, sometimes more, from industry to industry, context to context, market to market, customer to customer, culture to culture, and even from one point in time to another.

Fifthly, enabling promises is explicitly included in the definition. If this internal support is missing or not taken care of in an adequate manner, it will be difficult to support customers' value-creating processes in a proper way, and marketing will fail.

Sixthly, the definition takes into account the role of expectations (Miller, 1977; see also Rust et al., 1994; Ojasalo, 2001) and of expectancy disconfirmation in marketing (e.g. Oliver, 1980). Communicating value propositions and making promises set expectations and the way such expectations are met by the value support provided has a decisive impact on the success of marketing. As customers' perceptions of similar promises differ, it is not the promises as such that are met but rather the customers' individual expectations created by these promises.

Finally, the definition does not explicitly include the phrases 'relationship marketing' or 'customer relationships', which makes it possible to use the definition in a variety of marketing context.

Implications for Marketing Research

The promise management definition has several advantages for marketing research (see Grönroos, 2006b). First of all, it is based on current research into customer value, according to which value for customers is created in the customer's processes, *value-in-use*, and it allows for supplier and customer co-production of solutions, and, moreover, for suppliers' value co-creation together with their customers.

Secondly, the suggested definition is geared towards the very nature of marketing as a process, and thus it shifts the interest of research into marketing from structure to process. Other definitions have always been overly preoccupied with structural elements and neglected the importance of process. The process nature has been recognized implicitly only. Of course, structural elements from traditional marketing definitions such as price and marketing communication are still important to study, but they need to be put into a process perspective.

Thirdly, the alternative definition opens up the *black box of consumption*. The consumption process becomes an integral part of marketing and the marketing process (Grönroos, 2006a). Traditionally, marketing ends with the purchase decision. Goods and services are supposed to be developed and designed so that they automatically meet the expectations of customers. According to the promise management approach, the customer's *interactions* with the resources provided by the firm become a foundational element in marketing and for marketing research. The customer may, for example, interact with service processes, a call centre, an ATM or a vending machine, an Internet web site, a telecommunication infrastructure, a delivery, installation, repair and maintenance service, a service recovery or complaints handling process, and with people, technologies, systems, information, tangible goods, and servicescapes (Bitner, 1992) involved in such interactions. Moreover, in all these interactions, the customers are present as resources, thereby being creators of value for themselves, sometimes as *sole value creators* (Grönroos, 2009: 354) using resources provided by the supplier in isolation from the supplier, sometimes together with the supplier in its capacity as co-creator of value.

Focusing on the interactions and consumption also demonstrates the need for viewing marketing as a process, including activities that go beyond a single marketing function. From a promise management perspective, marketing becomes a customer focus that should permeate organizational functions. The conventional approaches to marketing are based on a view that marketing is one function alongside other functions and, therefore, such other functions easily are perceived as nonmarketing. This view has become a straitjacket for marketing research, where at least mainstream research has not been able to cope with the changes that have taken place in the customer interfaces. Today, the content of customer interfaces has grown far beyond what a one-function marketing approach can take responsibility for.

Finally, the promise management approach recognizes the fact that everyone involved in interactions with customers are not automatically customer focused. Traditionally, marketing activities are supposed to he performed by marketing professionals only. Hence, preparing marketers for their duties has not been a central issue for marketing and for marketing research. Part-time marketers are not expected to exist and, therefore, conventional marketing approaches neither include ways of coping with them, nor trigger any interest in studying them from a marketing perspective. Enabling promises, including internal marketing, explicitly points out the need to prepare employees who are not trained as marketers and whose main task is not marketing for their marketing-related duties.

Concluding Remarks

The conventional marketing definitions with their focus on one function, exchange of pre-produced value and a structure, a set of marketing variables, rather than process, have become a hindrance for developing marketing in accordance with changes in today's business environment, at least for relationship marketing contexts. They have become equally much a straitjacket for marketing practice as for marketing research. The promise management approach helps marketing to break free from the one-function, marketing-department-based view where only full-time marketers are recognized. Its process nature helps locate the firm's true marketing resources and activities and guides planning and budgeting procedures to include all these resources and activities and not only what the marketing department (and sales) is doing. In this way, marketing becomes more relevant for the customers of a firm. If this is the case, marketing also becomes more relevant for top management and, in the final analysis, for the firm's shareholders as well.

Finally, the marketing-as-promises-management definition is derived and formulated in such a way that it fits marketing to customers who are in nonrelational modes as well. Hence, it is not restricted to relational contexts only.

Notes

1   As an example of another way of defining relationship marketing, Gummesson's definition, according to which relationship marketing is *marketing based on interactions, relationships and networks* (Gummesson, 2002), can be mentioned. This definition also takes a process-oriented view; following a set of interactions between customers and a firm and/or its network partners, relationships emerge, and this process may take place in a network.
2   The marketing definition for relationship marketing developed in this report is to a large extent based on Grönroos, Christian: On defining marketing: finding a new roadmap for marketing. *Marketing Theory*, 6(4) 2006b: 395–417, where the definition and its underpinning logic as well as the set of propositions have been previously published.

References

Alderson, W. (1957) *Marketing Behavior and Executive Action: A Functionalist Approach to Marketing Theory*. Homewood, IL: Richard D. Irwin.
Bagozzi, R.P. (1975) 'Marketing as Exchange', *Journal of Marketing*, 39(October): 32–39.
Ballantyne, D. (2003) 'A Relationship-Mediated Theory of Internal Marketing', *European Journal of Marketing*, 37(9): 1242–1260.
Becker, G.S. (1965): 'A Theory of Allocation of Time', *The Economic Journal* 75(299): 493–517.
Berry, L.L. (1981) 'The Employee as Customer', *Journal of Retailing*, 3(March): 33–40.
Berry, L.L. (1995) 'Relationship Marketing of Services—Growing. Interest, Emerging Perspectives', *Journal of the Academy of Marketing Science*, 23(4): 236–245.

Berry, L.L. and Parasuraman, A. (1993) 'Building a New Academic Field—The Case for Services Marketing', *Journal of Retailing*, 69(1): 13–60.

Bitner, M.J. (1992) 'Servicescapes: The Impact of Physical Surroundings on Customers and Employees', *Journal of Marketing*, 56(April): 57–71.

Bitner, M.J. (1995) 'Building Service Relationships: It's All About Promises', *Journal of the Academy of Marketing Science*. 23(4): 246–251.

Booms, B.H. and Bitner, M.J. (1982) 'Marketing Structures and Organization Structures for Service Firms', in J.H. Donnelly and W.R. George (eds) *Marketing of Services*, Chicago, IL: American Marketing Association, pp. 47–51.

Brown, S.W. (2005) 'When Executive's Speak, We Should Listen and Act Differently', *Journal of Marketing*, 69(October): 2–4.

Brown, S.W. and Bitner, M.J. (2006) 'Mandating a Service Revolution for Marketing', in R.F. Lusch and S.L. Vargo (eds) *The Service-Dominant Logic of Marketing: Dialog, Debate, and Directions*, Armonk, NY: M.E. Sharpe, pp. 393–405.

Calonius, H. (1983) 'On the Promise Concept', Unpublished discussion paper. Helsinki: Hanken Swedish School of Economics Finland.

Calonius, H. (1986) 'A Market Behaviour Framework', in K. Möller and M. Paltschik (eds) *Contemporary Research in Marketing*. Proceedings from the XV Annual Conference of the European Marketing Academy, pp. 515–524. Helsinki School of Economics and Hanken Swedish School of Economics Finland (republished in 2006 in *Marketing Theory*, 6(4): 419–428.

Christopher, M., Payne, A. and Ballantyne, D. (1991) *Relationship Marketing*. Oxford: Butterworth Heinemann.

Coviello, N.E., Brodie, R.J., Danaher, P.J. and Johnston, W.J. (2002) 'How Firms Relate to Their Markets: An Empirical Examination of Contemporary Marketing Practice', *Journal of Marketing*, 66(July): 33–46.

Dixon, D.F. (1990) 'Marketing as Production: The Development of a Concept', *Journal of the Academy of Marketing Science*, 18(Fall): 337–343.

Dunne, P.A. and Barnes, J.G. (2000) 'Internal Marketing: A Relationships and Value Creation View', in R. Varey and B. Lewis (eds) *Internal Marketing: Directions for Management*. London: Routledge.

Eggert, A., Ulaga, W. and Schultz, F. (2006) 'Value Creation in the Relationship Life Cycle: A Quasi-Longitudinal Analysis', *Industrial Marketing Management*, 35: 20–37.

Eiglier, P. and Langeard, E. (1975) 'Une Approche Nouvelle du Marketing des Services', *Revue Francaise de Gestion*, 2(Novembre).

Eiglier, P. and Langeard, E. (1976) *'Principe de Politique Marketing Pour les Enterprises de Service'*, Working Paper. Institute d'Administration des Enterprises, Université d'Aix-Marseille.

Fournier, S., Dobscha, S. and Mick, D.G. (1998) 'Preventing the Premature Death of Relationship Marketing', *Harvard Business Review*, 76(January–February): 42–51.

Grönroos, C. (1979): *Service Marketing. A Study of the Marketing Function in Service Firms* (in Swedish with an English summary). Diss., Stockholm and Helsinki: Akademilitteratur, Marketing Technique Centre and Hanken Swedish School of Economics, Finland.

Grönroos, C. (1981) Internal Marketing—An Integral Part of Marketing Theory', in J.H. Donnelly and W.R. George (eds) *Marketing of Services*, Chicago, IL.: American Marketing Association, pp. 238–238.

Grönroos, C. (1982) 'An Applied Service Marketing Theory', *European Journal of Marketing*, 16(7): 30–41.

Grönroos, C. (1990) 'Relationship Approach to Marketing in Service Contexts: The Marketing and Organizational Behavior Interface', *Journal of Business Research*, 20(1): 3–11.

Grönroos, C. (1997) 'Value-Driven Relational Marketing: From Products to Resources and Competencies', *Journal of Marketing Management*, 13(5): 407–419.

Grönroos, C. (1999) 'Relationship Marketing: Challenges for the Organization', *Journal of Business Research*, 46(3): 327–335.

Grönroos, C. (2000) *Service Management and Marketing. A Customer Relationship Management Approach.* Chichester: John Wiley & Sons.

Grönroos, C. (2006a) 'Adopting a Service Logic for Marketing', *Marketing Theory*, 6(3): 317–333.

Grönroos, C. (2006b): 'On Defining Marketing: Finding a New Roadmap for Marketing', *Marketing Theory*, 6(4): 395–417.

Grönroos, C. (2007) *In Search of a New Logic for Marketing. Foundation of Contemporary Theory.* Chichester: John Wiley & Co.

Grönroos, C. (2008) 'Service-Dominant Logic Revisited: Who Creates Value? And Who Co-Creates?', *European Business Review*, 20(4): forthcoming.

Grönroos, C. (2009) 'Marketing as promise management: regaining customer management for marketing', *The Journal of Business & Industrial Marketing*, 24(5/6): 351–359.

Grönroos, C. and Ojasalo, K. (2004) 'Service Productivity: Toward a Conceptualization of the Transformation of Inputs into Economic Results in Services', *Journal of Business Research*, 57(4): 414–423.

Gummesson, E. (1979) The Marketing of Professional Services—An Organizational Dilemma', *European Journal of Marketing*, 13(5): 308–318.

Gummesson, E. (1987) The New Marketing—Developing Long-Term Interactive Relationships', *Long Range Planning*, 20(4): 10–21.

Gummesson, E. (1991) 'Marketing Revisited: The Crucial Role of the Part-Time Marketer', *European Journal of Marketing*, 25(2): 60–67.

Gummesson, E. (2002) *Total Relationship Marketing.* Oxford: Butterworth Heinemann.

Gummesson, E. (2007) 'Exit *Services* Marketing—Enter *Service* Marketing', *Journal of Customer Behaviour*, 6(2): 113–141.

Håkansson, H. (ed.) (1982) *International Marketing and Purchasing of Industrial Goods.* New York: John Wiley & Co.

Håkansson, H. and Snehota, I. (1995) *Developing Relationships in Business Networks.* Routledge: London.

Harker, M.J. (1999) 'Relationship Marketing Defined? An Examination of Current Relationship Marketing Definitions', *Marketing Intelligence and Planning*, 17(1): 13–20.

Harker M.J. and Egan, J. (2006) 'The Past, Present and Future of Relationship Marketing', *Journal of Marketing Management*, 22(1–2): 215–242.

Holbrook, M.B. (1994) 'The Nature of Customer Value—An Axiology of Services in the Consumption Experience', in R.T. Rust, and O.R. Oliver (eds) *Service Quality: New Directions in Theory and Practice.* Thousand Oaks, CA: Sage Publications.

Hunt, S.D. (1976) 'The Nature and Scope of Marketing', *Journal of Marketing*, 40(July): 17–28.

Jüttner, U. and Wehrli, H.P. (1994) 'Relationship Marketing from a Value Perspective', *International Journal of Service Industry Management*, 5(5): 54–73.

Kent, R.A. (1986) 'Faith in Four Ps: an Alternative', *Journal of Marketing Management*, 2(2): 145–154.

Kotler, P. (1972) 'A Generic Concept of Marketing', *Journal of Marketing*, 36(2): 46–54.

Langeard, E. and Eiglier, P. (1987) *Servuction. Le marketing des services.* Paris: John-Wiley & Sons.

Leong Y.P. and Quing W. (2006) 'Impact of Relationship Marketing Tactics (RMTs) on Switchers and Stayers in a Competitive Service Industry', *Journal of Marketing Management*, 22(1–2): 25–59.

Levitt, T. (1981) 'Marketing Intangible Products and Product Intangibles', *Harvard Business Review*, 59(May–June): 94–102.

Levitt, T. (1983) 'After The Sale Is Over', *Harvard Business Review*, 61 (September/October): 87–93.

Levitt, T. (1986) *The Marketing Imagination.* New York: The Free Press.

Liljander, V. and Strandvik, T. (1995) 'The Nature of Customer Relationships in Services', in T.A. Swartz, D.E. Bowen and S.W. Brown (eds) *Advances in Services Marketing and Management*, Vol. 4, Greenwich, CT: JAI Press, pp. 141–167.

Lindberg-Repo, K. and Grönroos, C. (2004) 'Conceptualising Communications Strategy from a Relational Perspective', *Industrial Marketing Management*, 33: 229–239.

Lovelock, C.H. (2000) 'Functional Integration in Services. Understanding the Links Between Marketing, Operations, and Human Resources', in T.A. Swartz and D. Iacobucci (eds) *Handbook of Services Marketing & Management*, Thousand Oaks, CA: Sage, pp. 421–437.

Lovelock, C.H. and Young, R.F. (1979) 'Look to Consumers to Increase Productivity', *Harvard Business Review*, 57(May–June): 168–178.

Lusch, R.F. and Vargo, S.L. (eds) (2006) *The Service-Dominant Logic of Marketing. Dialog, Debate, and Directions*. Armonk, N.Y.: M.E. Sharpe.

Lusch, R.F., Vargo, S.L., and O'Brien, M. (2007) 'Competing Through Service: Insights from Service-Dominant Logic', *Journal of Retailing*, 83(1): 5–18.

Marketing Renaissance (2005) 'Opportunities and Imperatives for Improving Marketing Thought, Practice, and Infrastructure', *Journal of Marketing*, 69(October): 1–25.

Miller, J.A. (1977) 'Studying Satisfaction, Modifying Models, Eliciting Expectations, Posing Problems and Making Meaningful Measurements', in H.K. Junt (ed.) *Conceptualization and Measurement of Consumer Satisfaction and Dissatisfaction*, Cambridge, Mass.: Marketing Science Institute, pp. 72–91.

Monroe, K.B. (1991) *Pricing—Making Profitable Decisions*. New York: McGraw-Hill.

Morgan, R.M. and Hunt, S.D. (1994) 'The Commitment-Trust Theory of Relationship Marketing', *Journal of Marketing*, 58(January): 20–38.

Normann, R. (2001) *Reframing Business. When the Map Changes the Landscape*. Chichester, UK: John Wiley & Sons.

Normann, R. and Ramirez, R. (1993) 'From Value Chain to Value Constellation: Designing Interactive Strategy', *Harvard Business Review*, 71(July–August): 65–77.

Ojasalo, J. (2001) 'Managing Customer Expectations in Professional Services', *Managing Service Quality*, 11(3): 200–212.

Oliver, R.L. (1980) 'A Cognitive Model of the Antecedents arid Consequences of Satisfaction Decisions', *Journal of Marketing Research*, 17(November): 460–469.

Payne, A.F., Storbacka, K. and Frow, P. (2008) 'Managing the Co-Creation of Value', *Journal of the Academy of Marketing Science*, 36(1): 83–96.

Piercy, N.F. (1985) *Marketing Organization. Ana Analysis of Information Processing, Power, and Politics*. London: George Allen & Unwin.

Prahalad, C.K. and Ramaswamy, V. (2004) *The Future of Competition: Co-Creating Unique Value with Customers*. Boston, MA: Harvard Business School Press.

Pyle, J.F. (1931) *Marketing Principles*. New York: McGraw-Hill.

Ravald, A. and Grönroos, C. (1996) 'The Value Concept and Relationship Marketing', *European Journal of Marketing*, 30(2): 19–30.

Reinartz, W. and Kumar, V. (2002) 'The Mismanagement of Customer Loyalty', *Harvard Business Review*, 80(July–September): 4–12.

Rust, R.T. and Oliver, R.L (1994) Service Quality: Insights and managerial Implications from the Frontier. In R.T. Rust and R.L. Oliver (eds) *Service Quality: New Directions for Theory and Practice*, Thousand Oaks, CA: Sage, pp. 1–20.

Rust, R.T., Zahorik, A.J. and Keiningham, T.L. (1994) *Return on Quality: Measuring the Financial Impact of Your Company's Quest for Quality*. Chicago, IL: Richard D. Irwin.

Ryals, L. (2005) 'Making Customer Relationship Management Work: The Measurement and Profitable Management of Customer Relationships', *Journal of Marketing*, 69(October): 252–261.

Sääksjärvi, M., Hellén, K., Gummerus, J. and Grönroos, C. (2007) 'Love at First Sight or a Long-Term Affair? Different Relationship Levels as Predictors of Customer Commitment', *Journal of Relationship Marketing*, 6(1): 45–61.

Schneider, B. and Bowen, D.E. (1995) *Winning the Service Game*. Boston, MA: Harvard Business School Press.

Sheth, J.N. and Parvatiyar, A. (1995) 'The Evolution of Relationship Marketing', *International Business Review*, 4(4): 397–418.

Sheth, J.N. and Uslay, C. (2007) Implications of the Revised Definition of Marketing: From Exchange to Value Creation', *Journal of Public Policy and Marketing*, 26(2): 302–307.

Srinivasan, S.S., Anderson, R. and Ponnavolu, K. (2002) 'Customer Loyalty in E-Commerce: An Exploration of Its Antecedents and Consequences', *Journal of Retailing*, 78(1): 41–50.

Storbacka, K. and Lehtinen, J.R. (2001) *Customer Relationship Management.* Singapore: McGraw-Hill.

Strandvik, T. (2000) 'Relationsmarknadsföringens arbetsfält (The relationship marketing field)', in C. Grönroos and R. Järvinen (eds) *Palvelut ja Asiakassuhteet Markkinoinnin Polttopisteessä (Marketing: Services and Customer Relationships in Focus)*, Helsinki, Finland: Kauppakaari, pp. 164–77.

Vandermerwe, S. (1996) 'Becoming a Customer "Owning" Company', *Long Range Planning*, 29(6): 770–782.

Vargo, S.L. and Lusch, R.F. (2004) 'Evolving to a new dominant logic for marketing', *Journal of Marketing*, 68(January): 1–17.

Vargo, S.L. and Lusch, R.F. (2008) 'Service Dominant Logic: Continuing the Evolution', *Journal of the Academy of Marketing Science*, 36(1): 1–10.

Verhoef, P.C. (2003) 'Understanding the Effect of Customer Relationship Management Efforts on Customer Retention and Customer Share Development', *Journal of Marketing*, 67(October): 30–45.

Webster Jr., F.E. (1992) 'The Changing Role of Marketing in the Corporation', *Journal of Marketing*, 56(October): 1–17.

Webster Jr., F.E., Malter, A.J., and Ganesan, S. (2005) 'The Decline and Dispersion of Marketing Competence', *MIT Sloan Management Review*, 46(4): 35–43.

Wikström, S. (1996) 'Value Creation by Company-Consumer Interaction', *Journal of Marketing Management*, 12: 359–374.

Woodruff, R.B. and Gardial, S. (1996) *Know Your Customers—New Approaches to Understanding Customer Value and Satisfaction.* Oxford: Blackwell Publishers.

Zeithaml, V.A. (1988) 'Consumer Perception of Price, Quality and Value: A Means-End Model and a Synthesis of Evidence', *Journal of Marketing*, 52(July): 2–22.

Zeithaml, V.A., Parasuraman, A., and Berry, L.L. (1988) 'Communication and Control Processes in the Delivery of Service Quality', *Journal of Marketing*, 64(April): 35–49.

Appendix

Marketing as Promise Management—The Underpinning Logic and Definition

Propositions based on the underpinning logic of the promise management approach:

1a: *Value is not delivered by a firm to customers but created in customer processes through assistance to those processes and through the firm's co-creation in interactions with customers.*

1b: *The role of marketing is, on one hand, to develop and communicate value propositions to customers, and on the other hand, to assist customers' value creation through goods, service activities, information, and other resources as well as through interactions where co-creation of value with the customers can take place.*

2a: *Customers can be in relational as well as nonrelational modes, thus they do not always appreciate being approached in a relational manner by firms, and hence, even though managing customers as relationship often may be effective, it cannot be considered a generic approach to relating a customer to the firm,*

2b: *In an implicit way, a marketing definition must allow both for relational and non-relational marketing strategies and activities.*

3a: *Marketing cannot be implemented by one organizational function of marketing specialists, the full-time marketers, only.*

3b: *Marketing needs a customer focus throughout the organization, thus involving both full-time marketers totally or predominantly trained to take a customer focus and part-time marketers, who when performing their tasks from the outset are not at all or only partly trained to take a customer focus.*

3c: *To be effective, marketing also requires that technologies, information systems and other systems are designed and function in a customer-focused manner.*

3d: *As customers participate in interactions with the firm's resources and, therefore, influence the customer orientation of these interactions, they actively participate in marketing as well. Hence, customers' role as a marketing resource, in addition to their roles as buyers and consumers and . users has to be recognized in marketing.*

4a: *Customers have explicit as well as implicit, unrealistic and fuzzy expectations and these expectations should be fulfilled by the performance of the firm.*

4b: *Fulfilment of promises in a customer-focused manner requires internal marketing efforts as promise enablers.*

4c: *Customer-focused technologies, information systems, and other systems as well as appropriate leadership are also required to support a customer-focused performance by part-time marketers.*

4d: *Helping customers to participate in customer–firm interactions in ways that have a favourable marketing impact on them is also required for marketing to be successful.*

4e: *Making promises, supported by internal activities, such as internal marketing geared towards the fulfilment of expectations created by promises made, as well as technology, systems and leadership support, and fulfilling expectations created by promises made, form a firm's marketing process.*

Marketing as Promise Management — Definition

Marketing is a customer focus that permeates organizational functions and processes, and is geared towards making promises through value proposition, enabling the fulfilment of individual expectations created by such promises and fulfilling such expectations through assistance to customers' value-generating processes, thereby supporting value creation in the firm's as well as its customers' and other stakeholders' processes. (Grönroos, 2006b: 407)

4

Love at First Sight or a Long-Term Affair? Different Relationship Levels as Predictors of Customer Commitment

Journal of Relationship Marketing
Vol. 6, No. 1, 2007
pp. 45–61

Maria Sääksjärvi
Katarina Hellén
Johanna Gummerus
Christian Grönroos

Relationship marketing has increased in importance during the past decades. We suggest that different types of relationships exist, and propose a relationship continuum, in which the customer advances from having a relationship with a product to having one with the firm, leading to commitment towards the firm. By targeting the right type of customers, relationship strategies become enhanced, and firms can recognize the motivations customers have for engaging in a relationship with them. Maybe it is just love at first sight with a product, or a lifetime commitment towards a firm.

Relationship marketing has increased in importance during the past decade, and is today considered an important research paradigm (Grönroos 1994). The main tenet underlying this philosophy is the thought that firm success arises from developing relationships with customers, where mutual understanding of needs and wants are satisfied and based on customer retention instead of one-time purchase. The benefits of a relational approach to marketing are numerous. Suggestions involve increased revenue from long-time customers over less profitable short-time customers, saved costs by targeted advertising and positive word of mouth (Reichheld 1993; Reichheld and Sasser 1990).

During the past years, two branches within relationship marketing have evolved. One school of thought portrays relationships to be important under any circumstances, mostly due to the advantages listed above. Others, however, claim that only certain types of relationships are worth building, whereas others are not worth invested in, and should even be dissolved (Storbacka 2004). This view arises from the fact that long-term customers that firms have relationship with may not be necessarily more profitable than short-time customers (Baumgartner et al. 1995; Reinartz and Kumar 2000, 2002), and that all customers may not be interested in developing relationships with firms (Grönroos 1997).

Taking the latter view implies seeing customers as potentially being in different stages of relationships, in which customers at different relationship levels are differently receptive towards marketing messages and relational efforts. This has not been discussed more than tentatively (e.g., Grönroos 1997), although it would be valuable to know what a relationship is based on. So far, research effort has focused on estimating the financial value of customers, thereby determining which ones are worth keeping, or on examining whether there is a tendency among customers to engage in a relationship with the firm (De Wulf, Odekerken-Schröder, and Iacobucci 2001; Storbacka 1994). Merely knowing the financial value of a customer does not reveal his/her motives for engaging in a relationship, and knowing that a tendency to relationship does not reveal what the relationship is based on, as the reasons for having it could be of multiple kinds.

In this article, we focus on examining different types of relationships that customers may have with firms and on the drivers for engaging in such relationships. We separate between two different relationship levels, and propose that customers may be in any of these stages. Further, we suggest a relationship hierarchy, in which the customer gradually moves towards more intimate level of relationships with firms, starting with the initial fascination with a product to a deep, committed, relationship with a firm.

This paper is structured in the following order. First, we discuss relationship marketing. After that, we outline different relationship levels, and develop hypotheses. This is followed by method description and presentation of results. We conclude with a discussion about results and implications for academia and marketing practitioners.

Relationship Marketing

Relationship marketing emerged in the 1980s as an alternative to the prevalent marketing mix and the 4Ps' view on marketing (McCarthy 1960). Relationship marketing can be seen as a strategy for firms to satisfy the long-term value needs of its customers (Grönroos 1997). The strategy builds upon the assumption that long-term and strategically chosen customers are more profitable in the long run. Grönroos (2004, p. 101) defines relationship marketing as "a process of identifying and establishing, maintaining, enhancing, and when necessary terminating relationships with customers and other stakeholders, at a profit, so that the objectives of all parties involved are met, where this is done by a mutual giving and fulfilment of promises."

Ultimately, it is the customer who determines whether there is a relationship or not. Thus, the uppermost goal of relationship marketing is to create customer commitment (Crosby and Johnson 2001) or "an enduring desire to maintain a valued relationship" (Moorman, Zaltman, and Despandé 1992).

Recently, two streams of literature within the relationship marketing paradigm have evolved. The first school of thought recognizes the value and benefits of a relationship that they see as overriding other benefits a firm can have. Firms are recommended to recognize different relationship stages, and aim towards gaining customers at the highest phase of relationship building. Examples of these theories are the relationship ladder (Payne et al. 1998) and the relationship life cycle (Jap and Ganesan 2000; Zineldin 1996) which build on the notion of a product life cycle (e.g., Kotler and Keller 2006). These theories identify all customers as potentials for developing relationships with, and advices on how to gain customers to higher relationship levels. The other stream focuses on customer equity management, and stresses that not all customers are worth having relationships with. The idea has been approached from a portfolio strategy point of view, in which the customer base is divided based on the profit they generate (Storbacka 2004). These researchers argue that customers and the relationship they have with the firm should be seen as assets for the firm that has to be managed (Little and Marandi 2003). Although we defer from adopting a financial view on customer relationships, we find the latter stream of thought more *au par* with the notion of relationship building, as negative effects of relationships have been found, and theories in personal relationship and attachment show that not all customers may wish to have relationships in general, and thereby not with firms either. Building on the line of thought that customers may be segmented based on their relational propensity, studies have noted that customers may differ in their propensity and willingness to engage in relationships with firms and may therefore need to be treated differently by a firm's marketing efforts (De Wulf, Odekerken-Schröder, and Iacobucci 2001). Further, studies have also examined differences between transactional and relational customers (Jackson 1985), showing that they have different motivations for repeat purchase and satisfaction, and that differences in relational motivation exist among a given customer base (Garbarino and Johnson 1999).

Building further on the trans actional-relational continuum, Grönroos (1997) suggests that customers within a relational motivation may also differ. Grönroos explains his notion using the concept of relational mode, which based on Grönroos conceptualization can be defined as a consumer's relatively stable tendency to engage in a relationship with a certain company (Grönroos 1997). According to Grönroos (1997) there are two categories of relational modes, an active and a passive mode. An active relational mode is a situation when the customer actively seeks contact with a firm. A passive relational mode is a situation where the customer does not actively seek contact with the firm, but knows that if needed the firm will be there for the customer. In the regular case, a passive relational customer demands a correctly high-guided physical product and impeccable service without any hassle. This line of thought takes the separation between transactional and relational customers one step further, and recognizes that different levels of relationships exist for which firms should have different strategies. Pursuing an inappropriate strategy may hinder, rather than enhance a firm's relational efforts. For example, frequent and active contact from a firm may be regarded negatively by a passive relational customer, who wants to be left alone until she/he initiates contact with the firm. Further, resources spent on relational efforts become ill-allocated if addressed towards the wrong type of customer segment. Thus, by separating between passive and active relational customers, firms may better target their resources.

Research by De Wulf, Odekerken-Schröder and their colleagues adds another dimension to the relationship continuum. Their studies focus on relationship proneness, or the conscious predisposition that customers have towards engaging in a relationship with the firm (De Wulf, Odekerken-Schröder, and Iacobucci 2001, Odekerken-Schröder, De Wulf, and Schumacher 2003). Here, the unit of examination is the relationship between the customer and the firm, in which firms can target those customers in higher relationship proneness with their marketing efforts. Relationship proneness was suggested to lead to customer commitment and satisfaction, and is, here, seen as a continuance to relational mode.

Two Levels of Relationships

Based on the concepts of relational mode and relationship proneness, two different relational types are found: passive and active relational mode, and relationship proneness. By using these dimensions, we propose a relationship continuum, with gradually increasing intimacy within a relationship. We conceptualize relational mode to be an antecedent to relationship proneness. Relational mode is likely to be targeted towards a particular product. A passive relational mode is established when the physical product is consistently of high quality, and is often established after the initial purchase of a product. It evolves into an active relational mode, when the customer starts developing a relationship with the product. The second relationship stage occurs when customers wish to be involved with the firm, and repeatedly purchase from that firm across a range of products. This stage is the firm-level relationship, and is referred to as relationship proneness. By linking relational mode to relationship proneness, a relationship continuum emerges, in which the customer gradually builds a commitment to a firm, starting with the initial attachment to a single product. The relationship continuum can be organized as follows.

The product-level relationship (passive and active relational mode). The basis for any type of relationships is the initial attraction towards a product. A customer who finds a product attractive and has an involvement towards it, is also likely to perceive that a relationship exists between him/her and the product. The passive relational mode evolves into active when the customer's relationship becomes more intimate, and she/he develops a desire for the product.

The firm-level relationship (relationship proneness). A customer who has a relationship with a product is likely to evolve into having a relationship with the firm. Given consistently well-performing products and an emotional attachment towards them, the customer is likely to become committed to the firm as a whole.

The relationship path is one, but not the only way to reach commitment. As an alternative route to commitment, we suggest that customers can also become committed purely on the basis of product performance and functional benefits. This type of relationship is not emotionally connected, but merely functional. Both paths start with attractiveness and involvement, and end with commitment. The relational path explains the emotional connection between a customer and a product, in which a product is more than functional benefits derived from product features (cf. Fournier 1998). The functional path links to customers who are only interested in having a relationship with a firm owing to the performance of a product. Their commitment is driven by product satisfaction based on product performance, and their willingness to engage in a relationship with a firm on the notion that they expect to receive benefits such as monetary savings by having a relationship with a firm.

To test our presuppositions, we establish a framework around the concepts we propose, by placing them among commonly used antecedents and consequences to relational efforts. As antecedents, we have product attractiveness and product involvement, and as a consequence customer commitment. As previous studies also suggest satisfaction with the product to lead to relational proneness, we added satisfaction as an antecedent to it, paralleling the relationship route. Thus, our model outlines two routes: the relationship route, and the product satisfaction route to firm-level relationships. The hypothesized model is shown in Figure 1.

Product Attractiveness and Involvement

Product attractiveness. The fascination that consumers have for product starts with the initial liking or attraction towards a particular product. Visual product cues, such as design, aesthetics, or store design, may contribute to this attractiveness, alongside the product functional characteristics, such as functionality durability, or reliability. An attraction towards a product can be a "love at first sight" experience, or a more pragmatic experience (I buy this product as it helps me achieve a particular goal). In line with previous research, we propose attraction to gradually increase to an involvement with the product, in which the customer feels that the product is needed and engaging to own. Thereby, product attractiveness is a first step towards building a relationship with a product, and is predicted to lead to involvement.

H1. Perceived product attractiveness is positively related to product involvement.

Product category involvement is defined as a consumer's enduring perception of the importance of the product category (personal relevance) that results from the consumer's values, needs, and interests (Odekerken-Schröder, De Wulf, and Schumacher 2003; Zaichkowsky 1985). Higher degrees of involvement have been

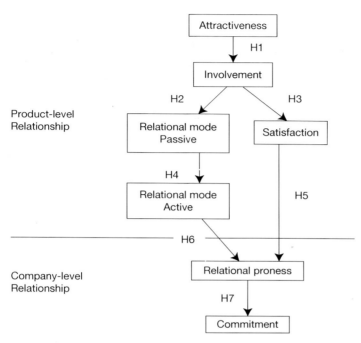

Figure 1. Hypothesized Model

shown to positively influence product evaluation, more thorough processing of advertising messages, and higher persuasion.

In the context of relationships, we predict involvement to encourage customers to engage in a relationship with a particular product. Thus, it can be viewed as the mediating step between product attraction and a relationship. In certain cases, the transition from attraction-involvement-relationship may be almost immediate. Usually, it takes time, as relationships evolve during product usage, whereas attraction often happens in a pre-purchase context. As we know, customer pre- and post-experiences may differ-products that seemed attractive during pre-purchase may evolve into post-purchase dissatisfaction (Thompson et al. 2005). Further, we know from personal relationships that not all people we fall in love with at first sight are worth having relationships with. Thus, not all products we are attracted to become involving, and not all products we become involved with are necessarily worth having relationships with. Thereby, we propose:

H2. Product involvement is likely to develop into a passive relational mode.

Relationship Levels

A passive relational mode is likely to evolve into an active one, when the customers start feeling connected to the product. In this case, the customer has become emotionally attached to the product, and wishes to develop his/her relationship with it further. The active relational mode is likely to evolve into a relationship with the whole firm. Customer-firm relationships can be depicted using relationship proneness. Customer relationship proneness is defined as a consumer's relatively stable and conscious tendency to engage in relationships with firms (De Wulf, Odekerken-Schröder, and Iacobucci 2001; Odekerken-Schröder, De Wulf, and Schumacher 2003). An active relational mode is likely to develop into relationship proneness. Customers who are connected to a product are more willing to purchase from that firm than from its competitor. By having experience with what the firm can deliver, the customer is likely to feel secure to take the relationship to the next level, that is, start exploring what other great products the firm may offer. Affect that customers have for the product is likely to spill over for the firm as a whole, thereby making customers more open and receptive towards engaging in a relationship with the firm.

> *H3.* A passive relational mode is likely to lead to an active relational mode.

> *H4.* An active relational mode contributes positively to relationship proneness.

Commitment

Relationship proneness is likely to lead to higher degrees of commitment towards a firm. According to Odekerker-Schröder and her colleagues (Odekerken-Schröder, De Wulf, and Schumacher 2003) customers who are relationally prone tend to see relational efforts through more "rose-colored glasses" and are therefore likely to appreciate the manufacturer more than other customers. Further, Garbarino and Johnson (1999) found that customers who are more relationally orientated towards a firm are driven by trust and commitment. On this basis we suggest the following hypothesis:

> *H5.* Relationship proneness has a positive influence on commitment.

An Alternative Route to Relationship Proneness and Satisfaction

Parallel to the relationships customers may have with a product, satisfaction with a firm's product may also influence their propensity to engage in a relationship with the firm. Product involvement can thus directly develop into satisfaction without the need for engaging in a relationship with the firm. This alternative route towards relationship proneness is likely to be taken by customers who are more functionally than emotionally oriented, and consider product quality to be the most important determinant for them to engage in relationships with firms. Satisfaction with a firm's products may then directly evolve into wanting to have a relationship with a firm, but often for more pragmatic reasons. For example, having a relationship with a firm is likely to benefit customers, as customers that have contacts with firms often receive special promotions and discounts that other customers may not have access to. The alternative route to firm relationship proneness builds on the following notions:

H6. Product involvement contributes positively to product satisfaction.

H7. Product satisfaction contributes positively to relationship proneness.

Method

To test the proposed model, we conducted an empirical study, using a survey methodology. The sample consisted of 100 respondents, recruited from a variety of firms (such as the high-tech, forestry, and transportation industry). The age distribution of our respondents varied from 25 to 60 years, and the sample encompassed both men and women.

Questionnaire. The questionnaire consisted of a cover letter asking consumers to participate in a study about a firm in the mobile phone industry. To conceal the purpose of the study, respondents were asked to inform us about their opinions about their mobile phone manufacturer. The questionnaire was four pages long, and covered the following scales: product attractiveness (10-item scale, Boyd and Mason 1999), involvement (8-item scale, Zaichkovsky 1985), satisfaction (3-item scale, Sharma and Patterson 2000), relationship proneness (3-item scale, De Wulf, Odenkerken-Schröder, and Iacobucci 2001), commitment (10-item scale, Bansal, Irving, and Taylor 2004), and relational mode (new scale). The relational mode scale was developed based on Raju (1980) and De Wulf, Odekerken-Schröder, and Iacobucci's (2001) ideas on relationship tactics, and adapted to the relational mode context. The new scale was pre-tested with 10 respondents. The items loaded on two factors (passive and active) and the scale was deemed suitable to use for the current study.

Method. We used PLS, partial least squares, to test our hypothesized model (Brown and Chin 2004). PLS is a structural equation modelling technique that uses a principal component-based estimation approach (Brown and Chin 2004). PLS was chosen because PLS, compared with other covariance-based analysing tools, like AMOS and LISREL, put minimal demands on measurement scales, sample size, and residual distributions (Chin, Marcolin, and Newsted 2003). PLS is suitable for exploratory research (Chin, Marcolin, and Newsted 2003) where it can suggest where relationships might or might not exist and to suggest propositions for later testing.

Sampling frame. For using PLS in data analysis, the sample size should be equal to or larger, of 10 times the largest number of structural paths directed at a particular construct in the structural model (Chin, Marcolin, and Newsted 2003). In this study, the largest number of structural paths to a construct is three (thus, $3 \times 10 = 30$, and $30 < 100$), meaning that our sample size is suitable for the model we are testing using PLS.

Measures. We ran exploratory factor analyses to confirm the reliability and unidimensionality of the scales. This step was considered necessary for estimating the discriminant validity of the scales and for testing the new scale of relational mode. Previous research indicates that the constructs may be highly correlated with each other, and may therefore not load as expected. The scales were modified as follows.

Due to low loadings or cross-loadings, two items were dropped from the product attractiveness scale, one from the product involvement scale, and three from the commitment scales. All resulting scales were deemed reliable (Cronbach's alpha > 0.70), and accounted for at least 48% of the variance in their given constructs (all Eigenvalues > 0.1, all factor loadings > 0.60). We could thus proceed to estimating the PLS model.

Results

The measurement model was examined by estimating factor item weights, the composite reliability and the average variance extracted for the constructs. The values are shown in Table 1. All exceed their recommended cutoff points, except for the AVE for involvement and commitment. However, since the values are close to the cutoff point (0.50) and the reliability of these constructs is high, we argue that their AVE values are suitable to allow for our analysis to proceed. Multi-collinearity is not a problem for the current study (not exceeding 0.7), although the correlation between attractiveness and involvement can be considered high (0.698). We propose for further research to make a stronger distinction between attractiveness and involvement, and choose to leave them as they are for our purposes, as they are not the focal constructs of our study.

Table 1
Values for the Measurement and the Structural Model

Construct	Loading	Weight	R^2	Composite Reliability	AVE	t-Values
Attraction				0.794	0.494	12.92 (H1)
Good idea	0.729	0.335				
Fun to own	0.795	0.336				
Here to stay	0.708	0.376				
Real value	0.560	0.224				
Involvement			0.487	0.884	0.462	8.59 (H2)
						4.07 (H3)
Important	0.572	0.160				
Interesting	0.785	0.172				
Exciting	0.704	0.116				
Means a lot	0.704	0.189				
Appealing	0.634	0.128				
Fascinating	0.751	0.195				

(Table 1 contd.)

(Table 1 contd.)

Construct	Loading	Weight	R^2	Composite Reliability	AVE	*t*-Values
Worthless	0.694	0.175				
Involving	0.627	0.117				
Needed	0.617	0.106				
Relation mode 1			0.349	0.800	0.504	5.64 (H4)
Personal advice	0.767	0.301				
Rely on product	0.704	0.275				
Regular interaction	−0.780	−0.324				
Old appliances	−0.569	−0.145				
Satisfaction			0.125	0.952	0.868	5.46 (H5)
Satisfied with choice	0.923	0.435				
Choose over again	0.920	0.273				
Good decision	0.951	0.365				
Relation mode 2			0.198	0.910	0.593	6.07 (H6)
Relationship desirable	0.601	0.225				
Personal comm.	0.782	0.170				
Frequent contact	0.816	0.188				
Know preferences	0.768	0.129				
Little as possible	0.764	0.171				
Appreciate attention	0.799	0.165				
Appreciate contact	0.836	0.211				
Relationship proness			0.441	0.931	0.818	11.41(H7)
Regular user	0.898	0.394				
Steady customer	0.945	0.359				
Extra mile	0.869	0.353				
Commitment			0.381	0.856	0.459	
Buy from again	0.665	0.199				
Emotional attachment	0.667	0.145				
Part of me	0.668	0.136				
Sense of belonging	0.685	0.124				
Attached	0.762	0.162				
Proud owner	0.679	0.180				
Hard to switch	0.608	0.135				

The structural model was estimated by examining R^2 values (for endogeneous constructs) and the t-values (for exogeneous constructs). As shown in Table 1, all R^2 values exceed 0.100 and are deemed significant. For estimating the significance of our paths and obtaining t-values for our constructs, we ran a bootstrapping analysis. As recommended by Brown and Chin (2004), 500 resamples were run.

Hypotheses

Our first hypotheses predicted a positive relationship between product attractiveness and involvement. This hypotheses is supported ($\beta = 0.698$, $t = 12.92$, $p < 0.001$). The second hypotheses concerned the linkage between product involvement and passive relational mode. This hypotheses is also supported ($\beta = 0.592$, $t = 8.59$, $p < 0.001$). H3 predicted a positive relationship between passive and active relational mode ($\beta = 0.354$, $t = 4.07$, $p < 0.001$), and H4 ($\beta = 0.445$, $t = 5.64$, $p < 0.001$) posited a positive linkage between an active relational mode and relationship proneness. Both of these hypotheses are supported. Our fifth hypotheses predicted that relationship proneness is liked to commitment, which is also supported ($\beta = 0.392$, $t = 5.46$, $p < 0.001$). Hypotheses 6-7 concerned an alternative route to relationship proneness through product satisfaction, in which product involvement would have a positive effect on product satisfaction, which would further lead to relationship proneness. Both of these hypotheses are supported ($\beta = 0.491$, $t = 6.07$, $p < 0.001$) for hypothesis 6 and ($\beta = 0.617$, $t = 11.41$, $p < 0.001$) for Hypothesis 7.

Conclusions and Discussion

Relationship marketing has become an integral field within marketing. Within the relationship marketing paradigm, relationships have either been viewed as predominantly positive, or as an investment strategy, in which certain relationships should be harboured, and others diversified. Previous studies identified differences between transactional and relational customers, showing that their motives for engaging in relationships differ. In this article, we examined different types of relationships customer may have towards firms. Thereby, we have extended on the relationship continuum beyond that of transactional-relational by examining different types of relationships customers may have, tapping into their motives for engaging in relationships.

In this study, we identified two relationship levels: a product-level relationship, and a firm-level relationship. Customers on the product relationship level perceive to have a relationship with a particular product, which is driven by product attractiveness and involvement. The product relationship develops from a passive into an active one, in which customers are more emotionally connected to the product than merely appreciating its features and functionality (Fournier 1998). The second relationship level is the firm-level relationship. On this relationship level, the customer perceives to have a relationship with the whole firm. This relationship level can be considered the ultimate relationship level, as it leads to customer commitment. The second relationship level may also evolve from satisfaction with products that stem from product involvement. In this case, the relationship is likely to be more cognitively than emotionally driven, and based on the functionality and the quality that the product offers.

The results of our study parallel and build on those found by previous studies. In line with Fournier (1998), we claim that a relationship often reaches beyond mere estimation of a product's functional characteristics and attributes. However, we also leave room for an alternative route for consumers who are cognitively driven and considered product satisfaction to be the driver of relationships. To the literature that separates between different types of relationships, we add by specifying the relationship levels that customers may have. We support Garbarino and Johnson's (1999) notion of relationships as the drivers of customer commitment, and establish product involvement and attractiveness as drivers of relationship engagement. Our results also parallel the relationship life cycle approach, which views relationships as dynamic, and evolving. Relationships at different levels require a different type of treatment, and should be nurtured for relational tactics to be efficient. Customers in a passive relational mode do not need to be catered to; they will contact the firm if they need something. Thereby, targeting these customers with relational tactics may backfire, as they do not wish to be pushed into a relationship, or bombarded with marketing messages. There are customers who never reach beyond this stage, and do not wish to have intimate relationships at any level. They can be compared with lifelong bachelors who never have the desire to engage deeply into something or commit to one particular product. Customers in an active relational mode already wish to have a deeper level of intimacy with the firm, and would be open towards relational tactics and marketing messages. They are happy if their preferences are known by the firm, and do not mind being connected to it. To continue buying, they demand a constantly high quality and impeccable service. Finally, the third and most intimate group of customers can be likened with firm champions, who prefer a firm's products across different brands to those of the competition. These customers want to be connected to the firm, and take pride in doing so. However, firms have to be careful in reciprocating these customers. They should be treated as assets of the firm, and cared and tendered for. If these customers do not feel that they are privileged, they may leave, or even worse, becoming an anti-firm campaigner who spreads negative word of mouth about the firm.

References

Bansal, Harvir S., Gregory P. Irving, and Shirley F. Taylor (2004), "A Three Component Model of Customer Commitment to Service Providers," *Journal of the Academy of Marketing Science*, 32(3), 234-250.

Baumgartner, Thomas, Ralf Leszinski, Roberto Paganoni, and Felix Weber (1995), "Profits in Your Backyard," *The McKinsey Quarterly*, 4, 118-127.

Boyd, Thomas C. and Charlotte H. Mason (1999), "The Link Between Attractiveness of 'Extrabrand' Attributes and the Adoption of Innovations," *Journal of the Academy of Marketing Science*, 27, 306-319.

Brown, Steven P. and Wynne W. Chin (2004), "Satisfying and Retaining Customers through Independent Service Representatives," *Decision Sciences*, 35 (3), 527-550.

Chin, Wynne W., Barbara L. Marcolin, and Peter R. Newsted (2003), "A Partial Least Squares Latent Variable Modeling Approach for Measuring Interaction Effects: Results from a Monte Carlo Simulation Study and an Electronic-Mail Emotion/Adoption Study," *Information Systems Research*, 14 (2), 189-217.

Crosby, Lawrence A. and Sheree L. Johnson (2001), "Branding and Your CRM Strategy," *Marketing Management*, 10 (2), 6-7.

De Wulf, Kristof, Gaby Odekerken-Schröder, and Dawn Iacobucci (2001), "Investments in Consumer Relationships: A Cross-Country and Cross-Industry Exploration," *Journal of Marketing*, 65, 33-50.

Fournier, Susan (1998), "Consumers and Their Brands: Developing Relationship Theory in Consumer Research," *Journal of Consumer Research*, 24 (March), 343-373.

Garbarino, Ellen and Mark S. Johnson (1999), "The Different Roles of Satisfaction, Trust, and Commitment in Customer Relationships," *Journal of Marketing*, 63 (April), 70-87.

Grönroos, Christian (1994), "From Marketing Mix to Relationship Marketing. Towards a Paradigm Shift in Marketing," *Asia/Australia Journal of Marketing*, 32 (2), 4-20.

——— (1997), "Value-Driven Relational Marketing: From Products to Resources and Competencies," *Journal of Marketing Management*, 13, 407-419.

——— (2004), "Relationship Marketing: The Nordic School Perspective," in *Hand-book of Relationship Marketing*, (Eds) Sheth, Jagdish N. and Atul Partatiyar, Thousand Oaks, CA: Sage Publications Inc., pp. 95-118.

Jackson, Barbara Bund (1985), "Build Customer Relationships That Last," *Harvard Business Review*, 63 (6), 120-129.

Jap, Sandy and Shankar Ganesan (2000), "Control Mechanisms and the Relationship Lifecycle: Implications for Safeguarding Specific Investments and Developing Commitment," *Journal of Marketing Research*, 37 (May), 227-245.

Kotler, Phillip and Kevin Lane Keller (2006), *Marketing Management*. 12th edition, Upper Saddle River, NJ: Prentice-Hall.

Little, Ebi and Ed Marandi (2003), *Relationship Marketing Management*, Thomson, GB.

McCarthy, Jerome (1960), *Basic Marketing: A Managerial Approach*. Homewood, IL: Irwin.

Moorman, Christine, Gerald Zaltman, and Rohit Despandé (1992), "Relationships Between Providers and users of Market Research: The Dynamics of Trust Within and Between Organizations," *Journal of Marketing Research*, 29 (3), 314-328.

Odekerken-Schröder, Gaby J., Kristof De Wulf, and Patrick Schumacher (2003), "Strengthening Outcomes of Retailer-Consumer Relationships: The Dual Impact of Relationship Marketing Tactics and Consumer Personality," *Journal of Business Research*, 56 (3), 177-190.

Payne, Adrian, Martin Christopher, Helen Peck, and Moira Clark (1998), *Relationship Marketing for Competitive Advantage: Winning and Keeping Customers*. Oxford: Butterworth-Heinemann Ltd.

Raju, P.S. (1980), "Optimum Stimulation Level: Its Relationship to Personality, Demographics, and Exploratory Behavior," *Journal of Consumer Research*, 7 (December), 272-282.

Reichheld, Frederick F. (1993), "Loyalty-Based Management," *Harvard Business School Review*, 2, 64-73.

——— and W. Earl Jr. Sasser (1990), "Zero Defects: Quality Comes to Services," *Harvard Business Review*, (Sept-Oct), 105-111.

Reinartz, Werner and V. Kumar (2002), "The Mismanagement of Customer Loyalty," *Harvard Business Review*, 80 (7), 86-94.

——— and ——— (2000), "On the Profitability of Long-Life Customers in a Noncontractual Setting: An Empirical Investigation and Implications for Marketing," *Journal of Marketing*, 64 (4), 17-35.

Sharma, Neeru and Paul G. Patterson (2000), "Switching Costs, Alternative Attractiveness and Experience as Moderators of Relationship Commitment in Professional, Consumer Services," *International Journal of Service Industry Management*, 11 (5), 470-90.

Storbacka, Kaj (2004), "Create Your Future by Investing in Customers," *Velocity TM*, 1st Quarter, 6(1), 19-25.

Thompson, Debora Viana, Rebecca W. Hamilton, and Roland T. Rust (2005), "Feature Fatigue: When Product Capabilities Become Too Much of a Good Thing," *Journal of Marketing Research*, 42 (4), 431-442.

Zaichkowsky, Judith Lynne (1985), "Measuring the Involvement Construct," *Journal of Consumer Research*, 12 (3), 341-52.

Zineldin, Mosad (1996), "Bank-Corporate Client 'Partnership' Relationship: Benefits and Cycle," *International Journal of Bank Marketing*, 14 (3), 14-22.

5

Taking a Customer Focus Back into the Boardroom: Can Relationship Marketing Do It?

Marketing Theory
Vol. 3, No. 1, 2003
pp. 171–173

Christian Grönroos

Marketing and marketers are becoming marginalized in a growing number of companies. The interest in shareholder value and short-term gains on the stock market has reinforced the position of managers trained in finance as the most valued persons for the top positions. However, in the final analysis the long-term economic result of a firm and value for shareholders does not come from the stock market, but from the customers of that firm.

Why is marketing about to become marginalized? There seems to be at least two different, but related, reasons for the demise of marketing. Firstly, mainstream marketing, based on the marketing mix management approach and its 4 Ps, is becoming *less relevant for customers and for the management of customers (marketing) alike.* Marketing is preoccupied with activities that only partly, if at all, are effective. In business-to-business, sales with its direct customer contacts is considered important, whereas marketing gets comparatively small budgets and plays a limited role. In services, marketing has a more dominant role with larger budgets, but it is often highly unproductive. Money is largely spent on activities that far too often have only a limited impact on customers. Only in packaged consumer goods does mainstream marketing holds on to its position, but even there changes can be seen.

Secondly, because mainstream marketing is occupied with *doing things* and *spending a budget* on marketing mix variables, marketing has become a cost issue only, instead of a balance sheet issue as well. From a shareholder perspective this is, of course, not very interesting. Hence, *marketing is not relevant for shareholders and the finance market* either. Mainstream marketing has always been defined as doing something to customers, instead of doing it for them (Dixon and Blois, 1983) and instead of *investing in customers*—a phenomenon that would be much more interesting for shareholders as well as for the business itself.

The relationship paradigm has an opportunity to make marketing relevant for shareholders, top management, customers and the management of customers again. In the age of customer relationships, where marketing is a process encompassing most of the functions, processes and departments of a firm, the support of the entire organization is imperative to success. All the resources and activities of a supplier that are imperative to the process of *supporting customers' value creation* (Grönroos, 2000; see also Ballantyne et al., this issue; Normann, 2001; Storbacka and Lehtinen, 2001; and Sheth and Parvatiyar, 1995) must be managed not from a manufacturing or an internal administrative or legal point of view only, but with a customer focus in mind as well. The definition of marketing in long-term relationship terms also makes it possible to shift the focus from marketing as a 'spending-a-budget' function, to marketing as a process of investing in customers and portfolios of customers to get a future return on that investment. When the management of customers is not viewed as a function, but as a process of acquiring customers to keep them in order to get continuous future cash flows, and as the understanding of and techniques for the calculation of customer profitability are developing (cf. Storbacka et al., 1994; Storbacka, 1994; and Gummesson, 2001), marketing can be repositioned as a balance sheet issue. Building on the relationship perspective, the following definition of marketing as investing in customers can be offered:

> Marketing is to invest in customers and customer portfolios to get wanted long-term cash flows from them. This is achieved through an exchange and fulfilment of promises which facilitates the process of acquiring customers, and maintaining and enhancing relationships with these customers, and when necessary terminating these relationships, so that the financial and non-financial goals of all parties involved in the network of suppliers, customers and other stakeholders are met.

When taking this perspective, marketing is not a function or even a separate process anymore. Marketing becomes a dimension among others of the firm's business processes. This dimension could be labelled the *customer focus dimension*. Other dimensions are, for example, technological, finance, human resource and societal dimensions.

References

Dixon, Donald F. and Blois, Keith (1983) 'Some Limitations of the 4 Ps as a Paradigm for Marketing', paper presented at the Marketing Education Group Annual Conference, Cranfield Institute of Technology, UK, July.

Grönroos, Christian (2000) *Service Management and Marketing: A Customer Relationship Management Approach.* Chichester: John Wiley & Sons.

Gummesson, Evert (2001) *Total Relationship Marketing, Rethinking Marketing Management: From 4 Ps to 30 Rs.* London: Butterworth Heinemann.

Normann, Richard (2001) *Reframing Business: When the Map Changes the Landscape.* Chichester: John Wiley & Sons.

Sheth, Jagdish N. and Parvatiyar, Atul (1995) 'The Evolution of Relationship Marketing', *International Business Review* 4(4): 397–418.

Storhacka, Kaj (1994) *The Nature of Customer Relationship Profitability—analysis of Relationships and Customer Bases in Retail Banking.* Publication of Hanken Swedish School of Economics and Business Economics, Finland, No. 55, Helsinki/Helsingfors.

Storbacka, Kaj and Lehtinen, Jarmo R. (2001) *Customer Relationship Management.* Singapore: McGraw-Hill.

Storbacka, Kaj, Strandvik, Tore and Grönroos, Christian (1994) 'Managing Customer Relationships for Profit: The Dynamics of Relationship Quality', *International Journal of Service Industry Management* 5(5); 21–38.

6

Creating a Relationship Dialogue: Communication, Interaction and Value

The Marketing Review
Vol. 1, No. 1, 2000
pp. 5–14

Christian Grönroos[1]

A relationship dialogue is a process of reasoning together in order for two or more parties to develop a common knowledge platform. Relationship marketing is facilitated provided that this knowledge platform enables a supplier to create additional value for its customers on top of the value of the goods and services which are exchanged in the relationship. For a relationship dialogue to emerge, in an on-going process the communication effects of planned communication efforts and of product and service-based interactions between a supplier and its customers have to support each other. Then the required extra value of the relationship is created and favourable word of mouth follows.

Relationship Marketing and the Need for a Dialogue

The relationship marketing perspective is based on the notion that the existence of a relationship between two parties creates additional value for the customer on top of the value of products and/or services that are exchanged (compare Ravald and Grönroos 1996). An on-going relationship may, for example, offer the customer security, and a sense of trust and minimised purchasing risks. To achieve this suppliers and service providers and their customers have to share information and keep each other informed about their requirements and intents. A relationship

---

[1] This article is based on issues discussed in Grönroos, Christian (2000): *Service Management and Marketing. A Customer Relationship Management Approach.* Chichester and New York: John Wiley and Sons.

includes at least two parties, often more in a network of relationships, and in order for the relationship to develop successfully the parties involved have to share information about needs that have to be fulfilled and solutions that can be offered. Furthermore, they have to communicate about different ways of creating and fulfilling solutions to customer needs and of handling activities such as deliveries, complaint situations, invoicing, personal interactions and a host of other interactions that may occur between two or more parties in a business situation. This goes for relationships involving individual consumers as well as for ones with business customers.

In order to manage these processes successfully the parties in a relationship will have to be able to share information and listen to each other, and not rely on persuasion and manipulation. Therefore, a true *dialogue* between the relationship partners has to emerge. Frequently, relationship marketing fails because marketers rely on relationship-like, but nevertheless manipulative, one-way communication, such as personally addressed and even personalised direct mail, to lure customers into business with the firms they represent without listening to their wishes and responding to the feedback they may give (see Fournier, Dobscha and Mick 1998).

The purpose of this article is to discuss how a dialogue between a customer and a supplier or service provider is developed and maintained in an on-going relationship and what is required for such a dialogue to emerge. It is argued that a dialogue emerges when the various kinds of planned messages sent in communication processes and interaction processes are aligned and constantly support each other. In this way the two processes of planned communication and interactions merge into a *relationship dialogue*. The approach of this article is the one of the *Nordic School* of marketing thought based on research into service management and relationship marketing.[2]

The Nature of a Dialogue

In an on-going relationship context it is not only the firm which is supposed to talk to the customer, and the customer who is supposed to listen. It is a two-way street, where both parties should communicate with each other. In the best case a dialogue develops. A dialogue can be seen as an interactive process of *reasoning together* (Ballantyne 1999/2000) so that a common knowledge platform is developing. Relationship marketing is facilitated, if this knowledge platform enables the supplier to create additional

---

[2] The school of marketing thought which internationally has been labelled *The Nordic School* emanates from Scandinavia and Northern Europe. Originally, researchers from this research tradition studied marketing in service organisations, but gradually the research interest of this school has shifted towards service management, a service perspective on management in any type of business, relationship marketing and customer relationship management. See Grönroos, Christian and Gummesson, Evert, The Nordic School of Service Marketing—An Introduction. In Grönroos, Christian and Gummesson, Evert, eds., *Service Marketing—Nordic School Perspectives*. Stockholm University, Sweden, 1985, pp. 6-11, and Berry, Leonard L. and Parasuraman, A., Building a New Academic Field—The Case of Services Marketing. *Journal of Retailing*, Vol. 69, No. 1, 1993, pp. 13-60.

value for the customer on top of the value of goods and services that are exchanged. However, this should create extra value for the supplier as well. A connection between the firm and the customer has to be made, so that they find that they can *trust* each other in this dialogue or process of reasoning together. The intent of this process is to build *shared meanings*, and get insights into what the two parties can do together and for each other through access to a *common meaning* or shared field of knowledge (see Shein 1994 and Bohm 1996). Being involved in a dialogue means that one avails oneself of existing knowledge but also is involved in *creating new knowledge* (Gummesson 1999). This sounds easy, but it may be difficult to do, because it seems as if the ability to engage in dialogue has been lost in modern societies (Senge 1990).

A dialogue requires *participation* of the parties involved (Bohm 1996). Participation takes place in interactions between the firm and its customers, but also through one-way messages, such as advertisements, brochures and direct mail. Messages through these traditional communication media should, however, contribute to the development of the shared meanings and common field of knowledge. When such messages through impersonal media and interactions between the customer and the firm support each other, the two parties are reasoning together.

There is a distinct difference between one-way messages and two-way communication through impersonal media as part of a dialogue. One-way messages have a sender and a receiver of those messages. A dialogue requires participation of the parties involved, and hence there are no senders or receivers, there are only *participants in the dialogue process*. For a dialogue to develop, the use of one-way communication also has to be adjusted to this.

For example, quite frequently marketers send out a direct marketing letter where they invite a response from the receiver. If the receiver indeed reacts with a response, this is taken as a beginning of a dialogue or perhaps even as the manifestation of a dialogue. However, creating a dialogue between a firm and a customer takes much more effort than this. A dialogue is an on-going process, where information should be exchanged between the two parties in a way that makes both the firm and the customer ready to start or continue doing business with each other. Both parties have to be *motivated to develop and maintain a dialogue*, otherwise no real dialogue will take place (Dichter 1966). This goes for individual consumers as well as for industrial customers.

The Multitude of Communication Messages in a Relationship

To maintain a dialogue not all communication contacts between the parties have to include an invitation to respond. An informative brochure and even a plain TV commercial may be part of an on-going dialogue, provided that the customer perceives that it gives information which is valuable for him or her to proceed in the relationship: for example telling the customer what piece of advice to ask for or giving him or her information needed to make the next purchase. It is also important to remember that it is not only planned communication through planned communication media (TV commercials, newspaper ads, brochures, direct mail, Internet communication, sales representatives, etc.) that maintains a dialogue. In a relationship product and service messages as well as unplanned messages, such as word-of-mouth referrals and public relations, also send messages which influence the dialogue (compare Duncan and Moriarty 1997). Products, service processes and interactions with fellow customers during the various service encounters contribute to the firm's total communication message, and thus are inputs in an on-going relationship dialogue. In this context one should also remember that *absence of communication* also sends distinct messages and therefore also contributes to the dialogue process (Calonius 1989). In Figure 1 these five sources of communication messages in on-going relationships are summarised and illustrated with examples.[3]

Planned Messages	Product Messages	Service Messages	Unplanned Messages	Absence of Communication
Mass communication (e.g. advertising) Brochures Direct Response Sales www-pages etc	Usefulness Design Appearance Raw materials Production processes etc	Interactions with service processes Deliveries Invoicing Claims Handling Product Documentation Help centre services etc	Word-of-Mouth Referrals References News Stories Gossip Internet chat groups etc	Silence following a service breakdown Lack of information about the progress of service and manufacturing processes etc

Figure 1. Sources of Communication Messages in a Relationship

In Figure 2 a *Relationship Dialogue Process* model is illustrated. The two outer circles demonstrate the two very distinct communicative processes that constantly are in progress:

- The Planned Communication Process
- The Interaction Process

[3] This figure is based on the discussion of communication messages in Duncan, Tom and Moriarty, Sandra, *Driving Brand Value. Using Integrated Marketing to Manage Profitable Stakeholder Relationships*. New York: McGraw-Hill, 1997. Duncan and Moriarty do not, however, discuss the communication impact of the fifth source of communication messages, i.e. *absence of communication*, a category of communication discussed in Calonius Henrik, 'Market Communication in Service Marketing' in Avlonitis, G.J., Papavasiliou, N.K. and Kouremenos, A.G., eds., *Marketing Thought and Practice in the 1990s*. Proceedings from the XVIIIth Annual conference of the European Marketing Academy, Athens, Geece, 1989.

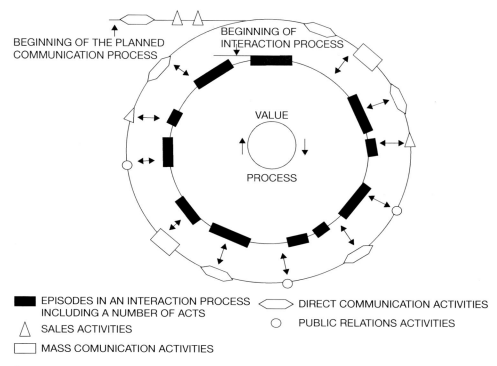

BEGINNING OF THE PLANNED COMMUNICATION PROCESS

BEGINNING OF INTERACTION PROCESS

VALUE

PROCESS

■ EPISODES IN AN INTERACTION PROCESS INCLUDING A NUMBER OF ACTS

△ SALES ACTIVITIES

▭ MASS COMUNICATION ACTIVITIES

⬡ DIRECT COMMUNICATION ACTIVITIES

○ PUBLIC RELATIONS ACTIVITIES

Figure 2. Relationship Dialogue: Integrating Interaction, Planned Communication and Value Processes

Source: Grönroos, Christian, *Service Management and Marketing. A Customer Relationship Management Approach.* Chichester and New York: John Wiley and Co, 2000, p.280.[4]

The *planned communication process* includes the communication messages which are planned and where separate and distinct communication media are used. As was said above, all types of media which are purely communication media are effective in this context (for example, TV commercials, newspaper ads, brochures, direct mail, Internet communication, sales representatives, exhibition stands, sales promotions; in the figure a limited number of examples are indicated as illustration only). For a dialogue to emerge, all planned communication messages have to be integrated into one consistent process (Schultz, Tannenbaum and Lauterborn 1992). However, this is not enough. The planned communication messages have to be consistent with the messages that are sent by the real episodes of an interaction process where customers and suppliers and service providers meet (Grönroos and Lindberg-Repo 1998).

---

[4] This figure is based on a figure in Grönroos, Christian, Relationship Marketing: The Nordic School Perspective. In Sheth, Jagdish N. and Parvatiyar, Atul, eds., *Handbook of Relationship Marketing*, Thousand Oaks, CA: Sage, 2000, pp. 95-118.

Interaction Processes as Communication

The other communicative process is a real process, where the customers' real interactions with physical products, service processes, systems and technology, e-commerce processes, administrative and financial routines, etc. occur. This is labelled the *interaction process*. All episodes in this process include an element of communication (mainly product and service messages). For example, a customer calls a help desk, because he or she has been advised to do so in a newspaper ad and gets attentive service and the pieces of information that were needed. This is a good sequence of planned communication (ad) and service messages (help desk support) which favourably supports the development of a relationship dialogue. A customer may also have answered a direct response invitation and in return received a brochure describing quick and attentive service. Following this sequence of dialogue-oriented planned communication messages with the customer's response in between the two messages, the customer decides to buy the service and gets into interactions with the service process. However, there he or she realises that the service does not fulfil the promise of quick and attentive service. What started out as a positively developing dialogue gets seriously hurt by the negative message following the customer's bad experiences with the service encounter. Messages from the planned communication process and the interaction process did not support each other and no favourable relationship dialogue developed in the long run. This, in turn, can be expected to diminish *the value of the relationship* that a given customer has perceived and appreciated. Because of the inconsistency in communication messages, the customer may feel a lack of security and the trust in the other party may be hurt. The customer does not know what to believe and what to expect in the future. The added value provided by the existence of a relationship is not developing, or if it has existed it is eroding. The *value process* in the middle of Figure 2 illustrates this effect. Of course, a good or bad relationship dialogue is not the only or even central value-creating or value-destroying element in a relationship. The existence of products and services as proper and satisfying solutions to customers' problems is of course the basic driver of value.

In conclusion, just planning and managing marketing communication through distinct communications media, even as a two-way process, is not relationship marketing and probably does not create a dialogue, although the communication efforts may look relational such as personally addressed letters inviting a customer response. The marketer and the customer are not *reasoning together* to build up a *common meaning. Only the integration of the planned communication and the interaction processes into one strategy that is systematically implemented creates relationship marketing.* Only in this way can *an on-going relationship dialogue* between the firm and its customer be maintained. This is indicated by the double-sided arrows between the two outer circles in the figure. In such a case customers' perceived value of the relationship is developing favourably, as indicated by the value process circle in the middle of Figure 2.

Learning Relationships

A successful development of a relationship requires that the two (or more) parties continuously learn from each other. The supplier or service provider gets a constantly improving understanding of the customer's needs, values and consumption or usage habits, and internal processes. The customer learns how to participate in the inter-action processes in order to get quick, smooth and accurate information, support, personal attention, well-functioning products and services, etc. This process can be characterised as a *learning relationship* (Pepper, Rogers and Dorf 1999).

An on-going dialogue supports the development of a learning relationship. On the other hand, if the co-operation between a supplier and a customer does not include elements of learning, a relationship dialogue is not developing. In fact, no real relationship where the parties involved feel a mutual way of thinking exist in that case. The customer may still continue to buy from the same supplier or service firm, at least for some time, for example because the seller offers a low price, has a technology advantage over competing firms, or is geographically located in a con-venient way. However, the co-operation is much more vulnerable to changes in the marketplace, to new competitors and to new alternative solutions that may become available.

Conclusion

In conclusion, planned marketing communication takes place in the *planned com-munication process* in Figure 2. Product and service messages are created in the *inter-action process*. Word-of-mouth referrals and other *unplanned messages* are a result of how customers and other parties perceive the two processes and how these support or counteract each other. Finally, *absence of communication* when customers expect to be kept informed and guided also sends messages about the supplier or service provider. These are also unplanned and almost invariably negative messages. As the relationship proceeds the different types of messages are developing in a continuous process and their effects are accumulating in the minds of customers. If the planned commu-nication process with its planned marketing communication activities is supporting and supported by the product and service messages (the interaction process) and not disturbed by unwanted absence of communication, favourable unplanned communi-cation *resulting in positive word-of-mouth communication* (unplanned messages) will occur (Lindberg-Repo and Grönroos 1999).

Both the firm and the customer should be expected to feel motivated to commu-nicate with each other. The customer should feel that the firm which sends a message is interested in him or her and in a convincing way argues for products, services or other elements of the total offering. He or she should also perceive that product and service messages emanating from the episodes in the interaction process in a positive way support the planned communication messages. *If this is the case, the planned communication efforts and the communication aspects of the interaction process merge into one single two-way communication process, i.e. the two processes merge into a relationship dialogue with the customer and the supplier or service provider as participants.* The nature and content of word-of-mouth referrals will probably differ depending on how long the customer has been involved in the interaction process. It can be assumed that word-of-mouth of a longstanding customer will include more holistic expressions than detailed experiences and more value-oriented than price-related expressions (Lindberg-Repo and Grönroos 1999).

If the interaction process is perceived favourably by customers and the communication messages created in the buyer-seller encounters of this process is supported by planned communication activities, the *customer perceived value* of the relationship itself is reinforced by the continuously ongoing dialogue. Thus, the development and maintenance of a *relationship dialogue* becomes an important element of successful relationship marketing. These are issues which are developed in detail in Grönroos (2000).

References

Ballantyne, David (1999/2000): Dialogue and Knowledge Generation: Two Sides of the Same Coin in Relationship Marketing. *2nd WWW Conference on Relationship Marketing*, November 1999-Februry 2000, Monash University and MCB University Press (http://www.mch.co.uk/services/conferen/nov99/rm/paper3.html).

Berry, Leonard L. and Parasuraman, A., Building a New Academic Field—The Case of Services Marketing. *Journal of Retailing*, Vol. **69**, No. 1, 1993, pp. 13-60.

Bohm, David (1996): *On Dialogue*. London: Routledge.

Calonius, Henrik (1989): Market Communication in Service Marketing, In Avlonitis, G.J., Papavasiliou, N.K. and Kouremeos, A.G., eds., *Marketing Thought and Practice in the 1990s*. Proceedings from the XVIIIth Annual Conference of the European Marketing Academy, Athens, Greece.

Dichter, Ernest A. (1966): How word-of-mouth advertising works. *Harvard Business Review*, Vol. **44**, November-December, pp. 147-166.

Duncan, Tom and Moriarty, Sandra (1997): *Driving Brand Value. Using Integrated Marketing to Manage Profitable Stakeholder Relationships*. New York: McGraw Hill.

Fournier, Susan, Dobscha, Susan and Mick, David G. (1998): Preventing the premature death of relationship marketing. *Harvard Business Review*, Vol. **76**, January-February, pp. 42-51.

Grönroos, Christian (2000): Relationship Marketing: The Nordic School Perspective. In Sheth, Jagdish N. and Parvatiyar, Atul, eds., *Handbook of Relationship Marketing*, Thousand Oaks, CA: Sage, pp. 95-118.

Grönroos, Christian (2000): *Service Management and Marketing. A Customer Relationship Management Approach*. Chichester and New York: John Wiley and Sons.

Grönroos, Christian and Lindberg-Repo, Kirsti (1998): Integrated Marketing Communications: The Communications Aspect of Relationship Marketing. *Integrated Marketing Communications Research Journal*, Vol. **4**, No. 1, pp. 3-11.

Grönroos, Christian and Gummesson, Evert, The Nordic School of Service Marketing—An Introduction. In Grönroos, Christian and Gummesson, Evert, eds., *Service Marketing—Nordic School Perspectives*. Stockholm University, Sweden, 1985, pp. 6-11.

Gummesson, Evert (1999): *Total Relationship Marketing. Rethinking Marketing Management: From 4Ps to 30Rs.* Oxford: Butterworth Heinernann.

Lindberg-Repo, Kirsti and Grönroos, Christian (1999): Word-of-Mouth Referrals in the Domain of Relationship Marketing. *The Australasian Marketing Journal*, Vol. **7**, No. 1, pp. 109-117.

Pepper, Don, Rogers, Martha and Dorf, Bob (1999): Is Your Company Ready for One-To-One Marketing? *Harvard Business Review*, Vol. **77**, January-February, pp. 151-160.

Ravald, Annika and Grönroos, Christian (1996): The Value Concept and Relationship Marketing. *European Journal of Marketing*, Vol. **30**, No. 2, pp. 19-30.

Schein, Edgar H. (1994): The Process of dialogue: creating effective communication. *The Systems Thinker*, Vol. **5**, No. 5, pp. 1-4.

Schultz, Don E., Tannenbaum, Stanley I. and Lauterborn, Robert F. (1992): *Integrated Marketing Communications.* Lincolnwood, Ill.: NTC Publishing Group.

Senge, Peter M. (1990): *The Fifth Discipline.* New York: Doubleday/Currency.

7

Relationship Marketing: The Nordic School Perspective

Handbook of Relationship Marketing
Jagdish N. Sheth, and Atul Parvatiyar (eds)
1999, pp. 95–118

Christian Grönroos

The Nordic school is a marketing school of thought that originally grew out of the research into services marketing in Scandinavia and Finland and quickly became an internationally recognized approach to services marketing research (see Berry & Parasuraman, 1993; Grönroos & Gummesson, 1985). In the 1990s it has been developing into a relationship marketing school of thought. From the beginning, the Nordic school researchers emphasized the long-term relational nature of services marketing (e.g., the buyer-seller interaction wheel in Gummesson, 1977, and the marketing and need-adaptation circle in Grönroos, 1980), but without using the term *relationship marketing*. Instead, they used terms such as *buyer-seller interactions* and *interactive marketing* (Grönroos, 1980), *customer relationship life cycle* (Grönroos, 1983), *the new marketing concept* (Gummesson, 1983), *phases of the service consumption process* (Lehtinen, 1984), *and interactive relationships* (Gummesson, 1987) to indicate the relational nature of the marketing of services.

The term *relationship marketing* was first introduced in the literature by Berry (1983) in a conference paper. Although services marketing, according to the Nordic school approach, has always been relationship oriented, this term was not used by Nordic school researchers until the end of the 1980s (e.g., Grönroos, 1989). One of the major reasons for this was the then growing interest in understanding services of the manufacturing sector, especially those of manufacturers of industrial goods. This trend was growing stronger during the latter part of that decade. Nordic school researchers realized that the introduction of services marketing concepts and models into business relationships (industrial marketing) was the beginning of a major shift in the general marketing paradigm far beyond the services marketing sphere (e.g., Blomqvist, Dahl, & Haeger, 1993; Grönroos, 1989; Gummesson, 1987, 1991;

Holmlund, 1996). According to the Nordic school of thought, this paradigm shift is predominantly but of course not solely growing out of services marketing.

Another very similar line of development also emanating from Scandinavia is the growth of the interaction and network approach to the management of business relationships (the IMP Group), which, from a start in the 1970s in Sweden in the following decade and even more so in the 1990s, has become a marketing school of thought that stresses the importance of relationships in business networks (e.g., Håkansson, 1982; Håkansson & Snehota, 1995). According to this approach, networks of companies are the dominant concept, with relationships as a subconcept that explains the development and management of networks. Mattsson (1997) discusses the similarities and differences between relationship marketing studies in the Nordic school tradition and IMP studies. In a study of business relationships, Holmlund (1996) has integrated the network approach with the Nordic school of thought in a perceived quality context, whereas Brodie, Coviello, Brookes, and Litle (1997) suggest a continuum of relational approaches.

Services in Relationship Marketing

It is not difficult to see how services marketing has become a pillar of relationship marketing. An integral part of services marketing is the fact that the consumption of a service is *process consumption* rather than *outcome consumption*, where the consumer or user perceives the service production process as part of the service consumption and not only the outcome of that process, as in traditional consumer packaged goods marketing. Thus service consumption and production have interfaces that are always critical to the consumer's perception of the service and to his or her long-term purchasing behavior. The management of these interfaces is called *interactive marketing* in the services marketing literature, and this concept has been used in the relationship marketing literature as well (see Bitner, 1995). The service provider almost always has direct contact with its customers. In these contacts relationships may easily start to develop, and if the simultaneous consumption and production processes turn out well, an enduring relationship may follow.

When manufacturers of industrial goods and equipment turn their interest from single transactions with their customers to doing business on a long-term basis, the nature of consumption changes from pure outcome consumption to ongoing process consumption or usage. In this process the customer consumes or uses the outcomes of the manufacturer's production processes (goods, equipment) that are exchanged between the parties in the relationship as well as a number of service processes that are produced and consumed or used before, during, and in between the exchanges of outcomes. The nature of this process becomes very similar to the process consumption characteristic of services.

From a marketing point of view this change of the nature of consumption or usage is emphasized even more when the outcomes (goods and equipment) constantly become more similar as competition increases. In most cases even continuous product development does not lead to a sustainable competitive advantage anymore, and hence only services—such as tailor-made design, deliveries, just-in-time logistics, installation of equipment, customer training, documentation of goods, maintenance and spare part service, customer-oriented invoicing, the handling of inquiries, service recovery and complaints management, and pricing below the market standard—are left for the marketer to use. If one does not want to use the price variable, which seldom creates a sustainable competitive advantage, only services are left for developing such an advantage.

Hence, according to the Nordic school approach, managing services is at the core of relationship building and maintenance, although relationship marketing also is supported by other factors, such as the building of networks (Håkansson & Snehota, 1995), the establishment of strategic alliances and partnership agreements (Hunt & Morgan, 1994), the development of customer databases (Vavra, 1994), and the management of relationship-oriented integrated marketing communications (Schultz, 1996; Schultz, Tannenbaum, & Lauterborn, 1992). In other approaches to relationship marketing, other elements or phenomena are seen as the primary pillars, as in the network approach or the strategic alliance and partnership approaches. It all depends on the perspective of the researcher.

There is also another characteristic of the Nordic school approach to services marketing that fits relationship building and maintenance as a marketing strategy, and that is the fact that marketing is seen more as market-oriented management than as a task for marketing specialists only, which means that marketing is viewed more as an overall process than as a separate function (Grönroos & Gummesson, 1985). Of course, transaction marketing may be justified in some cases, but as the work of Reichheld and Sasser (1990), Reichheld (1993), and Storbacka (1994) demonstrates, long-term customer relationships form a base for profitable business in a growing number of situations.

In order to implement relationship marketing, companies require a shift of focus regarding key areas of marketing. In the following sections, I discuss three such areas that are vital for the successful execution of a relationship strategy: an *interaction process* as the core of relationship marketing, a *dialogue process* supporting the development and enhancement of relationships, and a *value process* as the output of relationship marketing. First, however, I will address the service focus of relationship marketing as this is developed in the Nordic school of marketing thought.

Relationship Marketing and Service Competition

According to the Nordic school approach, marketing from a relational perspective has been defined as *the process of identifying and establishing, maintaining, enhancing, and when necessary terminating relationships with customers and other stakeholders, at a profit, so that the objectives of all parties involved are met, where this is done by a mutual giving and fulfillment of promises* (Grönroos, 1997). This definition bears clear similarities to Berry's (1983) services marketing definition from a relationship perspective and to more recently offered definitions by Hunt and Morgan (1994), Sheth and Parvatiyar (1994), and Christopher, Payne, and Ballantyne (1991). For example, marketing has been defined as the understanding, explanation, and management of the ongoing collaborative business relationship between suppliers and customers. Another well-known Nordic school definition, by Gummesson (1995), states that relationship marketing is *marketing seen as interactions, relationships, and networks.*

Both the Nordic school definitions, my own explicitly and Gummesson's implicitly, emphasize that relationship marketing is first and foremost a *process.* Most other definitions that have been offered also imply this nature of marketing. All activities that are used in marketing have to be geared toward the management of this process. Hence no marketing variables are explicitly mentioned in these definitions. According to my definition, the process moves from identifying potential customers to establishing a relationship with them, and then to maintaining the relationship that has been established and enhancing it so that more business as well as good references and favorable word of mouth are generated. Finally, if necessary, relationships that are not profitable, even in the long run, should be terminated. As Gummesson's definition implies, this process includes interactions that form relationships that may be developing in networks of suppliers, distributors, and consumers or end users.

The *focal relationship* is the one between a supplier or provider of goods or services in consumer or business markets and a buyer and consumer or user of these goods or services. Relationship marketing is first and foremost geared toward the management of this relationship. However, in order to facilitate this, other stakeholders in the process may have to be involved. Other suppliers, partners, distributors, financing institutions, and sometimes even political decision makers may have to be included in the management of the relationship if marketing is to be successful (compare Gummesson, 1995).

A shift of focus in marketing decision making from the transaction toward a process in which a relationship is built and maintained has important effects on central marketing areas (Grönroos, in press). As this process becomes as important for the customer as the outcomes, for example, in the form of goods and equipment, the nature of the product concept changes. The product as the outcome of a production process is basically a transaction-oriented construct. In a relationship perspective, physical goods and equipment (products) become a part of the process, together with other elements such as a host of services. In the best case these services enhance the value of the products, as with just-in-time deliveries, prompt service and maintenance, and customer-oriented and timely service recovery. In the worst case they damage or altogether destroy their value, as with delays in deliveries, unsuccessful maintenance, and unclear documentation about the use of equipment that has been purchased.

Customers do not look only for goods or services; they demand a much more holistic offering, including everything from information about the best and safest way to use a product to delivery, installation, updates, repairs, maintenance, and correct solutions for what they have bought. And they demand that all this, and much more, be provided in a friendly, trustworthy, and timely manner. Moreover, the core product is less often the reason for dissatisfaction than are the elements surrounding the core. As Webster (1994) has noted, "The automobile purchaser is unhappy with the car because of lousy service from the dealer; the insurance customer has problems with the agent, not with the policy" (p. 13). What Levitt (1983) concluded in the early 1980s about what should accompany the sale of the mere product—"Having been offered these extras, the customer finds them beneficial and therefore prefers to do business with the company that supplies them" (quoted in Webster, 1994, pp. 9-10)—is even more true today. By and large, customers are more sophisticated and better informed than ever and therefore more demanding, and increasing global competition offers customers more alternatives than ever before.

In a customer relationship that goes beyond a single product transaction, the outcomes themselves—including goods, services, and industrial equipment—become just one element in the *total ongoing service offering*. For a manufacturer, the physical good is a core element of this service offering, of course, because it is a prerequisite of a successful offering. However, what counts is the ability of the firm to manage the additional elements of the offering better than its competitors. The supplier has to truly *serve* its customers (Grönroos, 1996).

The product seen as a total service offering thus becomes a service including tangible elements such as physical goods and equipment and intangible elements such as a host of various types of services. In long-term relationships, firms face a competitive situation for which, in another context, I have coined the term *service competition* (Grönroos, 1996). When service competition is the key to success for practically everybody and the product has to be defined as a service, *every business is a service business* (Webster, 1994).

Shift in Focus of Central Marketing Areas

The product in a transaction-oriented approach to marketing has to be replaced with a long-term construct that fits the requirement of service competition in relationship marketing. *Interaction* is such a concept; it has been developed as one key construct in services marketing and is taken over by relationship marketing, as the Gummesson definition explicitly states. In the network approach to industrial marketing, the interaction construct has been developed as a key concept in business relationships as well (see Håkansson, 1982; Håkansson & Snehota, 1995). Thus, as the exchange of a product is the core of transaction marketing, the management of an *interaction process* is the core of relationship marketing. In this process, a supplier of goods or a service firm represented by people, technology and systems, and know-how interacts with its customer represented by everything from a single consumer to a group of buyers, users, and decision makers in a business relationship. Sometimes more parties in a network may be involved in the interactions (Grönroos, 1996; Gummesson, 1996).

In transaction marketing, marketing communication including sales is a central part of marketing. Marketing communication is predominantly mass marketing, but with a growing element of direct marketing. Sales, where appropriate, is a directly interactive element of the communication process. In the field of marketing communication, a new trend has emerged in the 1990s toward integrating communication elements such as advertising, direct marketing, sales promotion, and public relations into a two-way *integrated marketing communications* (Schultz, 1996; Schultz et al., 1992; Stewart, 1996). Also, in the Nordic school research this holistic view of marketing communication was studied to a limited extent in the mid-1980s (Grönroos & Rubinstein, 1986). This view of marketing communication was called *total communication*. Contrary to the new approach of the 1990s, it also integrated the communication effects of, for example, customer service with the effects of traditional communications media. Integrated marketing communications is clearly influenced by the relationship perspective in marketing. "As we are committed to two-way communication, we intend to get some response from those persons to whom the integrated marketing communications program has been directed.... We adapt the customer's or prospect's communication wants or needs and begin the cycle all over again. This is truly relationship marketing at its best" (Schultz et al., 1992, p. 59).

Sometimes communications researchers seem to give the impression that integrated marketing communications using various means of communications in an integrated manner is almost or totally synonymous with relationship marketing. However, in transaction marketing effective marketing communication about a bad or inappropriate product does not lead to a good result. By the same token, effective integrated marketing communications, as a purely communications program, does not develop successful and lasting relationships if the interaction process is bad. Integrated marketing communications is not the same as relationship marketing, but clearly it is an important part of a relationship marketing strategy. A two-way or dialogue marketing communication approach is needed to support the establishment, maintenance, and enhancement of the interactions process if relationship marketing is to be successful. Hence the management of a two-way communications process, or a *dialogue process*, is required in relationship marketing. It is the communications aspect of relationship marketing.

One of the most recent research streams within the Nordic school of marketing thought is related to customer perception of value created in ongoing relationships (Ravald & Grönroos, 1996). The importance of adding a relationship aspect to studies of customer value has also been demonstrated by Lapierre (1997) in Canada. In the interaction process value is transferred to and also partly created for the customer. In the dialogue communication process this creation and transfer of value should be supported before and during the interaction process of the relationship. Finally, a *value process* is needed to demonstrate how the customer indeed perceives the creation and transfer of value over time. When all three processes are in place and well understood, we have a good part of a theory of relationship marketing, or actually a theory of marketing based on a notion that the ultimate objective of marketing is to "manage the firm's market relationships" (see Grönroos, 1996, p. 11).

The Core: The Interaction Process of Relationship Marketing

As noted in the preceding section, successful marketing requires a good enough solution for the consumer or user. In transaction marketing of consumer goods, this solution is a product in the form of a physical good. In relationship marketing the solution is the relationship itself and how its functions lead to need satisfaction for the customer. As I have concluded previously, the relationship includes the exchange or transfer of physical goods or service outcomes, but also a host of service elements without which the goods or service outcomes may be of limited value or without value for the customer. For example, delayed deliveries, late service calls, badly handled complaints, lack of information, or unfriendly personnel may destroy an otherwise good solution.

The relationship, once it has been established, proceeds in an interaction process where various types of contacts between the supplier or service firm and the customer occur over time. These contacts may be very different depending on the type of marketing situation—some contacts are between people, some are between customers and machines and systems, and some are between systems of the supplier and customer, respectively. In this context, I will not be discussing the differing nature of these contacts in the interaction process depending on whether consumer goods, services, or business relationships are studied. Instead, I will examine more closely the nature of the interaction process. In the Nordic school of marketing thought this issue has been studied to some extent.

In order to understand—and, in practical marketing situations, to analyze and plan—the interaction process, one must divide it into logical parts. In the context of services, the interaction process has been studied in terms of acts, episodes, and relationships (Liljander, 1994; Liljander & Strandvik, 1995; see also Stauss & Weinlich, 1995; Storbacka, 1994; Strandvik & Storbacka, 1996). According to Liljander and Strandvik (1995), an episode is, for example, a visit to a bank office to discuss a loan, whereas an act would be the meeting with the loan officer during the visit. In the context of business relationships, IMP researchers have traditionally offered a two-level approach including short-term episodes (such as exchange of goods and services, information, and financial and social aspects) and long-term processes leading to adaptation and institutionalization of roles and responsibilities (Håkansson, 1982; Möller & Wilson, 1995). In a more generic relationship marketing context, Holmlund (1996) has recently developed the understanding of the interaction process further, in order to achieve an extended analytic depth in the analysis of relationships. In Figure 4.1, the interaction process of the ongoing relationship is divided into four levels of aggregation: the act, episode, sequence, and relationship levels.[1] Holmlund also suggests a fifth level of aggregation, a partner level, for situations in which network partners are required in a business relationship. This level is omitted here because it is specific to business-to-business relationships, whereas the four others are applicable to the analysis of relationships in general.

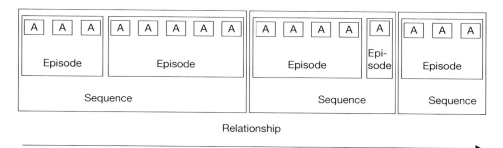

Figure 4.1. Different Interaction Levels in a Relationship

Source: Holmlund (1996, p. 49). Reprinted by permission of the author and of the Swedish School of Economics and Business Administration, Helsinki, Finland.

Acts are the smallest unit of analysis in the interaction process, such as phone calls, plant visits, service calls, and hotel registration. In the service management literature, acts are often called "moments of truth." Acts may be related to any kind of interaction elements, physical goods, services, information, financial aspects, or social contacts. "Individual act[tion]s are connected to other act[ion]s and may be analysed accordingly. Interrelated act[ion]s may therefore be grouped into interactions on a higher... level, which corresponds to episodes" (Holmlund, 1996, p. 49).

Hence interrelated acts form a minor natural entity in a relationship, an *episode* such as a negotiation, a shipment of goods, or dinner at a hotel restaurant during a stay at that hotel. Every episode includes a series of acts. For example, "a shipment may include such act[ion]s as the placement of an order by telephone, assembling and packing the products, transporting, ... unpacking, making a complaint, and sending and paying an invoice" (Holmlund, 1996, p. 49).

Interrelated episodes form the next level of analysis in the interaction process, a *sequence*. According to Holmlund (1996), a sequence can be defined in terms of a time period, an offering, a campaign or a project, or a combination of these. "This implies that the analysis of a sequence may contain all kind of interactions related to a particular year, when a particular project . . . has been carried out. Sequences may naturally overlap" (pp. 49-50). To take another type of example, in a restaurant context a sequence comprises everything that takes place during one visit to a particular restaurant.

The final and most aggregated level of analysis is the *relationship*. Several sequences form the relationship. Sequences may follow each other directly, may overlap, or may follow at longer or shorter intervals, depending, for example, on the type of business. This way of dividing the interaction process into several layers on different levels of aggregation gives the marketer, and the researcher, an instrument detailed enough to be used in the analysis of interactions between supplier or service firms and their customers. All different types of elements in the interaction process—goods and services outcomes, service processes, information, social contacts, financial activities, and so on—can be identified and put into correct perspective in the formation of a relationship over time.

The Dialogue Process of Relationship Marketing

According to the total communication concept of the 1980s, in addition to pure marketing communication activities, all contacts that a customer has with another party include a communicative element. Goods, service processes, administrative routines, invoicing, and the like communicate something about the solution and the firm offering this particular solution. However, in this context I follow the view of the integrated marketing communications concept of the 1990s regarding what is part of the communication process—that is, only communicative activities that are more or less purely marketing communication, such as traditional advertising, direct response, public relations, and also sales activities (see the definition of integrated marketing communications of the American Association of Advertising Agencies' Integrated Marketing Communications Committee, as quoted in Reitman, 1994; see also Frischman, 1994). Other than communications elements are included only if they become transparent and merge with the communications elements, as distribution and communication become the same in the case of direct-response marketing (Stewart, 1996; Stewart, Frazier, & Martin, 1996).

The characteristic aspect of marketing communication in a relationship marketing context is an attempt to create a two-way or sometimes even multiway communication process. Not all activities are directly two-way communication, but all communication efforts should lead to a response of some sort that maintains and enhances the relationship. One effort, such as a sales meeting, direct-mail letter, or information package, should be integrated into a planned ongoing process. Therefore, this communication support to relationship marketing is called a dialogue process. This process includes a variety of elements that, for example, can be divided into sales activities, mass communication activities, direct communication (other than sales efforts where a direct response is sought), and public relations (adapted from Grönroos & Rubinstein, 1986). Any other number or type of categories could of course also be used, and the suggested groups naturally include a number of subgroups. Mass communication includes traditional advertising, brochures, sales letters for which no immediate response is sought, and other similar activities, whereas direct communication includes personally addressed letters including offers, information, recognition of interactions that have taken place, and requests for data about the customer. Here a more direct response is sought in the form of feedback from previous interactions, requests for more information or an offer, data about the customer, purely social responses, and the like.

In Figure 4.2 the dialogue process is illustrated as a circle that parallels the interaction process, which includes a number of episodes consisting of individual acts. For the sake of illustration, various types of communication efforts are depicted throughout the ongoing dialogue process. As the figure shows, the dialogue process starts

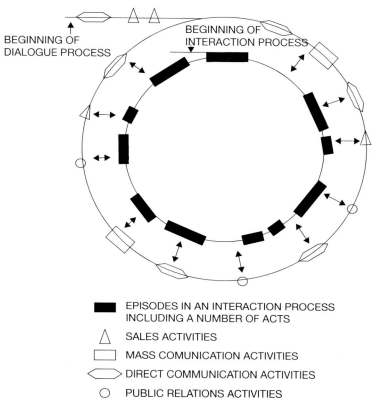

Figure 4.2. The Interaction and Dialogue Processes of Relationship Marketing

before the interaction process. This is, of course, the stage in which the relationship is established. From the point where the two processes go together, the relationship is maintained and further enhanced. At some point the relationship may be broken or terminated. The dialogue and interaction processes indeed parallel each other, which means that they should support and not counteract each other. The two-way arrows between the two circles in the figure indicate this. An activity in the dialogue process, a sales meeting or a personally addressed letter, creates an expectation, and the interaction process must follow up on this expectation. If, for example, only the dialogue process is considered part of relationship marketing, negatively perceived acts or episodes in the interactions process easily destroy the initially good impression of a communication effort, and no relationship building takes place.

    In conclusion, just planning and managing marketing communication, even as a dialogue process, is not relationship marketing, although the communication efforts may look relational, such as personally addressed letters. Only the integration of the dialogue and the interaction processes into one strategy that is systematically implemented creates relationship marketing.

The Value Process of Relationship Marketing

Clearly, relationship marketing takes more effort than transaction marketing. Therefore, a relationship marketing strategy must create more value for the customer or for some other party, such as a retailer, than the value of the mere transactions of goods or services in single episodes. The customer has to perceive and appreciate this value that is created in the ongoing relationship. Because a relationship is a process over time, value for customers is also emerging in a process over time. I refer to this as a *value process*. If relationship marketing is to be successful and accepted as meaningful by the customer, there must be such a value process paralleling the dialogue and interaction processes that is appreciated by the customer.

Traditionally, *value* has been used in the marketing and consumer behavior literature as "the value of customers for a firm." Only to some extent has "value for the customer" been discussed in the literature (e.g., Peter & Olson, 1993; Zeithaml, 1988), and then it has more or less been in a transaction marketing context. For example, Zeithaml (1988) defines customer perceived value as the consumer's overall assessment of the utility of a product based on a perception of what is received and what is given. However, as Ravald and Grönroos (1996) note:

> The relational aspect as a constituent of the offering is not taken into account. ... We suggest that the relationship itself might have a major effect on the total value perceived. In a close relationship the customer probably shifts the focus from evaluating separate offerings to evaluating the relationship as a whole.
>
> The core of the business, i.e. what the company is producing, is of course fundamental, but it may not be the ultimate reason for purchasing from a given supplier. (p. 23; see also Lapierre, 1997)

One can also imagine that even if the solution in terms of goods and services is not the best possible, the parties involved may still find an agreement if they consider the relationship valuable enough. "Value is considered to be an important constituent of relationship marketing and the ability of a company to provide superior value to its customers is regarded as one of the most successful strategies for the 1990s. This ability has become a means of differentiation and a key to the riddle of how to find a sustainable competitive advantage" (Ravald & Grönroos, 1996, p. 19; see also Heskett, Jones, Loveman, Sasser, & Schlesinger, 1994; Nilson, 1992; Treacy & Wiersema, 1993).

If transactions are the foundation for marketing, the *value* for customers is more or less totally embedded in the exchange of a product (a physical good or a service) for money in an episode. The perceived sacrifice equals the price paid for the product. However, if relationships are the base of marketing, the role of the product becomes blurred. In the case of industrial robots, to take an example from business relationships, delivery, customer training, maintenance and spare part service, information and documentation about the use of a robot, claims handling and perhaps joint development of the final robots, and a number of other activities are necessary additions to the core solution—the robot—if the customer is to be satisfied with the purchase. It is easy to see how the value of the core of the offering becomes highly questionable if the additional services are missing or not good enough. The role of the core product in the value perception of customers is indeed very much blurred in a case like this. Without the value-adding additional services, it is highly questionable whether the core product, in this case the industrial robot, has any value at all. Similar examples can easily be found in consumer and industrial services and even in consumer goods.

In a relationship context the offering includes both a *core product* and *additional services* of various kinds (as demonstrated by the example of the industrial robot). The sacrifice includes a price and also additional costs for the customer that result from the fact of being in a relationship with another party. In a relationship context such additional sacrifice can be called *relationship costs* (Grönroos, 1997). Such costs follow from the decision to go into a relationship with a supplier or service firm. Relationship costs may increase if the customer, for example, has to keep larger inventories than necessary because of the delivery policy of the supplier or suffer from higher standstill costs than expected because of delayed repair and maintenance service.

Another way of looking at value for customers is to distinguish between the core value of an offering and the added value of additional elements in the relationship. Hence *customer perceived value* in a relationship context can be described with the following two equations:

[1] $\text{Customer Perceived Value (CPV)} = \dfrac{\text{Core Solution } + \text{ Additional Services}}{\text{Price} + \text{Relationship Costs}}$

[2] $\text{Customer Perceived Value (CPV)} = \text{Core Value} \pm \text{Added Value}$

In a relationship, customer perceived value is developing and perceived over time. In Equation 1, the price has a short-term notion; in principle it is paid upon delivery of the core product. However, relationship costs occur over time as the relationship develops, the usefulness of the core solution is perceived, and the additional services are experienced in sequences of episodes and single acts. In Equation 2, a long-term notion is also present. The added-value component is experienced over time as the relationship develops. However, here it is important to observe the double signs. Often added value is treated as if something is always indeed added to a core value. This is clearly not the case, because the added value can also be negative. For example, a good core value of a machine can be decreased or even destroyed by untimely deliveries, delayed service, lack of necessary information, bad management of complaint handling, unclear or erroneous invoices, or the like. The additional services do not add a positive value; instead, they subtract from the basic core value—that is, they provide a *negative added value* or *value destruction*.

In situations with negative added value, creating added value for customers does not require the addition of new services to the offering. Instead, the firm must improve existing services in the relationship, such as deliveries, service and maintenance, and invoicing, in order to reduce or altogether eliminate the negative added value—or, rather, value destruction of these services. Probably this is a faster and more effective way of creating added value in most relationships than would be the addition of new services. When appropriate, new services can of course be included in the offering. However, firms should always remember that the value-enhancing effect of new services is counteracted and sometimes even offset by the value destruction of existing services that the customer perceives in a negative way.

The core solutions and additional services provided in the sequences of episodes in the interaction process should create a perceived value for the customer on an ongoing basis. The core value should not be counteracted by the negative added value of badly handled or untimely services. Simultaneously, the communication activities in the dialogue process should support this value process and not counteract or destroy it.

In conclusion, as is illustrated in Figure 4.3, a successful relationship marketing strategy requires that all three processes discussed above be taken into account in relationship marketing planning. The *interaction process* is the core of relationship marketing, the *dialogue process* is the communications aspect of relationship marketing, and the *value process* is the outcome of relationship marketing. If the customer value process is not carefully analyzed, wrong or inadequate actions may easily be taken in the interaction process. If the dialogue process is not integrated with the interaction process, the value process may easily take a negative turn, because customers may get conflicting signals and promises may not be fulfilled. Interaction, dialogue, and value indeed form a triplet. If any one of them is not analyzed and planned carefully, the implementation of relationship marketing may suffer.

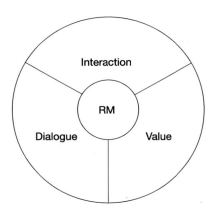

Figure 4.3. The Triplet of Relationship Marketing

Future Research Agenda

Relationship marketing is a new area in marketing research. Although relationship aspects of marketing have been studied within the Nordic school approach for about 20 years, first within the context of services marketing and later in a more general context, the area is still new, and many research opportunities present themselves. In this final section, I point out some areas for future research.

Customer interest in relationship marketing. In the literature, relationship marketing is offered as a solution for all customers in all situations where such an approach is suitable. This is probably not at all the case. Some customers may be willing to accept relational contact with a firm, whereas others may want to be in purely transactional contact. Moreover, a person may be interested in a relationship in one situation and not interested in another.

> Thus, in a given marketing situation the consumer (or user in a business-to-business relationship) is either in a *relational mode* or in a *transactional mode.* Furthermore, consumers in a relational mode can be either in an *active* or *passive* relational mode . . . . Consumers or users in an active mode seek contact, whereas consumers in a passive mode are satisfied with the understanding that if needed the firm will be there for them. (Grönroos, 1997, p. 409)

There have been some suggestions in the literature as to why customers choose to enter a relational mode and react favorably to a relationship marketing approach (e.g., Bagozzi, 1995; Sheth & Parvatiyar, 1995), but so far there has been almost no empirical research in this area. Specific research questions to be explored include the following: Why do customers choose to be in active or passive relational modes? What makes a customer move from a passive to an active mode? What types of core solutions (consumer goods or consumer services, goods and services to organizational users, and so on) tend to require a relationship marketing approach more then others? What are the exogenous conditions that trigger the choice of a passive or active relational mode? What types of activities in the interaction and dialogue processes, respectively, are suitable for various types of core solutions, markets, relational modes, and individual customers?

Internal marketing. The need for internal marketing has been recognized in the services marketing literature since the 1970s (see Grönroos, 1978). In interactions with customers, a large number of employees who do not belong to marketing departments have profound impacts on the quality perceptions and future purchasing behaviors of consumers and users. Turning these employees into true *part-time marketers* (Gummesson, 1991) is a demanding task.[2] Internal marketing is as important in relationship marketing as in services marketing. If the part-time marketers are not capable of and prepared to take their role in marketing, the interaction process will fail and the value process will be hurt. Regardless of how good the dialogue process is, marketing will be less successful, perhaps will fail altogether. However, internal marketing has been vastly neglected in academic research, partly because of its multidisciplinary nature (see Cahill, 1996; George, 1990). Gross-disciplinary research including marketing and human resource management would seem appropriate. Specific research questions would include these: What type of corporate culture nurtures a motivation among employees for relationship marketing? What types of internal activities, including training, communication, rewarding, and management guidance and support, make employees committed to relationship marketing? What is the role of top management in internal marketing? What type of external marketing communication has a positive internal effect on employees?

Organizing marketing. As the normal way of organizing marketing, traditional marketing departments may not be the best solution in relationship marketing. This area, too, has been neglected in marketing research. From the area of services marketing, one early study indicates that traditional marketing departments easily may be a hindrance to successful marketing in service firms (Grönroos, 1983; see also Piercy, 1985). The reasons for this are partly real and partly psychological. If marketing is concentrated within a marketing department only, the part-time marketers are not managed from a customer perspective. Moreover, a dominating marketing department becomes a psychological problem, because it signals to the rest of the organization that "marketing" is the same as the marketing department. Incidentally, this is also the way marketing is treated in most standard textbooks. The term *marketing department* is often used interchangeably with *marketing junction*. However, if a substantial part of the marketing impact is a result of activities outside the marketing department, new organizational innovations are needed to support successful relationship marketing. Some specific research questions include the following: What type of organizational structures support the internal processes needed to implement the interaction process successfully and integrate it with the dialogue process? What is the role of marketing and sales departments in relationship marketing? How can and should customers be integrated into the organization?

Marketing planning. Marketing planning is traditionally considered the task of the marketing department. However, if a large number of vital marketing activities take place outside this department and are the responsibility of other departments, traditional marketing planning is not enough anymore. Relationship marketing requires new planning procedures. Some specific research questions: What is the relationship between corporate planning and the planning of relationship marketing? How is a customer focus included in planning routines throughout the organization? What is the role of top management in the planning of relationship marketing?

Pricing. Traditional pricing strategies and models are based on a transaction marketing approach. Prices are set on goods and services that are exchanged in transactions. However, in an ongoing relationship price is only part of the customer's total sacrifice. The price paid in the moment of exchange can be high or low; what should count for the customer is the total sacrifice over time—that is, price and relationship costs. A lower price can be offset by higher relationship costs over time, and a higher price can be well compensated by lower relationship costs. Relationship pricing is an area where much research is needed. Specific research questions to be explored include the following: What is the relationship between price and relationship costs in various situations? How should the impact of relationship costs be calculated and included in relationship pricing? What does relationship pricing require of the accounting systems of firms?

Relationship buying. Implementing a relationship marketing strategy is difficult, but buying solutions based on a relationship approach is equally difficult. It requires a long-term cost notion, where the price as well as additional costs over the expected lifetime of the solution have to be calculated and taken into account, for example, as a net present value of lifetime use of the solution. Today there is a lack of research on relationship buying. Some suggested questions for research include these: How does one incorporate price and additional lifetime costs of a solution into one total cost measure for purchasing decisions? What changes in the purchasing routines are required in order to facilitate relationship buying? How can buyers be motivated to engage in relationship buying?

Notes

1. Holmlund (1996) uses the term *action*, but here I use the word *act*, as originally suggested by Liljander and Strandvik (1995), to describe the smallest unit of analysis in an interaction.
2. Part-time marketers are people who are not part of a marketing (or sales) department, whose main task is something other than a marketing-related one and who normally are not trained in marketing skills but who, when performing their tasks, directly or indirectly influence customer satisfaction and the future purchasing behavior of customers (Gummesson, 1991).

References

Bagozzi, R. P. (1995). Reflections on relationship marketing in consumer markets. *Journal of the Academy of Marketing Science, 23*, 272-277.

Berry, L. L. (1983). Relationship marketing. In L. L. Berry, G. L. Shostack, & G. D. Upah (Eds.), *Emerging perspectives on service marketing* (pp. 25-38). Chicago: American Marketing Association.

Berry, L. L., & Parasuraman, A. (1993). Building a new academic field: The case of services marketing. *Journal of Retailing, 69*(1), 13-60.

Bitner, M. J. (1995). Building service relationships: It's all about promises. *Journal of the Academy of Marketing Science, 23*, 246-251.

Blomqvist, R., Dahl, J., & Haeger, T. (1993). *Relationsmarknadsföring. Strategi och metod för servicekonkurrens* [Relationship marketing: Strategy and methods for service competition]. Göteborg, Sweden: IHM Förlag.

Brodie, R. J., Coviello, N. E., Brookes, R. W., & Litle, V. (1997). Towards a paradigm shift in marketing? An examination of current marketing practices. *Journal of Marketing Management, 13*, 383-406.

Cahill, D. J. (1996). *Internal marketing: Your next stage of growth.* New York: Haworth.

Christopher, M., Payne, A., & Ballantyne, D. (1991). *Relationship marketing: Bringing quality, customer service and marketing together.* Oxford: Butterworth-Heinemann.

Frischman, D. E. (1994). A voice of reality. In G. Faure & L. Klein (Eds.), *Marketing communications strategies today and tomorrow: Integration, allocation, and interactive technologies* (pp. 35-36). Cambridge, MA: Marketing Science Institute.

George, W. R. (1990). Internal marketing and organizational behavior: A partnership in developing customer-conscious employees at every level. *Journal of Business Research, 20*(1), 63-70.

Grönroos, C. (1978). A service-oriented approach to the marketing of services. *European Journal of Marketing, 12*, 588-601.

Grönroos, C. (1980, April). Designing a long range marketing strategy for services. *Long Range Planning, 13*, 36-42.

Grönroos, C. (1983). *Strategic management and marketing in the service sector.* Cambridge, MA: Marketing Science Institute.

Grönroos, C. (1989). Defining marketing: A market-oriented approach. *European Journal of Marketing, 23*, 52-60.

Grönroos, C. (1996). Relationship marketing logic. *Asia-Australia Marketing Journal, 4*(1), 1-12.

Grönroos, C. (1997). Value-driven relational marketing: From products to resources and competencies. *Journal of Marketing Management, 13*, 407-420.

Grönroos, C. (in press). Relationship marketing: Challenges for the organization. *Journal of Business Research.*

Grönroos, C., & Gummesson, E. (1985). The Nordic school of service marketing. In C. Grönroos & E. Gummesson (Eds.), *Service marketing: A Nordic school perspective* (Research rep., pp. 6-11). Stockholm: Stockholm University.

Grönroos, C., & Rubinstein, D. (1986). *Totalkommunikation. Analys och planering av företags marknadskommunikatian* [Total communication Analysis and planning of the marketing communication of firms]. Stockholm: Liber and Marketing Technique Center.

Gummesson, E. (1977). *Marknadsföring och inköp av konsulttjänster* [Marketing and purchasing of professional services]. Stockholm: Marketing Technique Center/Akademilitteratur.

Gummesson, E. (1983). *A new concept of marketing.* Paper presented at the annual European Marketing Academy Conference, Institute d'Etudes Commerciales de Grenoble, France.

Gummesson, E. (1987). The new marketing: Developing long-term interactive relationships. *Long Range Planning, 20*(4), 10-20.

Gummesson, E. (1991). Marketing-orientation revisited: The crucial role of the part-time marketer. *European Journal of Marketing, 25*(2), 60-74.

Gummesson, E. (1995). *Relationsmarknadsföring. Från 4P till 30R* [Relationship marketing: From 4P to 30R]. Malmö, Sweden: Liber-Hermods.

Gummesson, E. (1996). Relationship marketing and imaginary organizations: A synthesis. *European Journal of Marketing, 30*(2), 31-44.

Håkansson, H. (Ed.). (1982). *International marketing and purchasing of industrial goods: An interaction approach.* New York; John Wiley.

Håkansson, H., & Snehota, I. (1995). *Developing relationships in* business *networks.* London: Routledge.

Heskett, J. L., Jones, T. O., Loveman, G. W., Sasser, W. E., & Schlesinger, L. A. (1994). Putting the service-profit chain to work. *Harvard Business Review, 72*(4), 164-174.

Holmlund, M. (1996). *A theoretical framework of perceived quality in business relationships* (Research rep.). Helsinki, Finland: Swedish School of Economics and Business Administration.

Hunt, S. D., & Morgan, R. M. (1994). Relationship marketing in the era of network competition. *Marketing Management, 3*(1), 19-28.

Lapierre, J. (1997). *Development of measures to assess customer value in a business-to-business context* (Rep. No. EPM/RT 97/20). Montreal; École Polytechnique Montréal.

Lehtinen, J. R. (1964). *Asiakasohjautuva palveluyritys* [Customer-oriented service firm]. Espoo, Finland: Weilin+Göös.

Levitt, T. (1983). After the sale is over. *Harvard Business Review, 62*(1), 87-93.

Liljander, V. (1994). Introducing deserved service and equity into service quality models. In M. Kleinaltenkamp (Ed.), *Dienstleistungsmarketing—Konseptionen und Anwendungen* (pp. 1-30). Berlin: Gabler Edition Wissenschaft.

Liljander, V. & Strandvik, T. (1995). The nature of customer relationships in services. In D. Bowen, S. W. Brown, & T. A. Swartz (Eds.), *Advances in services marketing and management* (Vol. 4, pp. 141-167). Greenwich, CT: JAI.

Mattsson, L.-G. (1997). "Relationship marketing" and the "markets-as-networks approach". A comparison analysis of two evolving streams of research. *Journal of Marketing Management, 13,* 447-461.

Monroe, K. B. (1991). *Pricing: Making profitable decisions.* New York: McGraw-Hill.

Möller, K., & Wilson, D. (1995). Business relationships: An interaction perspective. In K. Möller & D. Wilson (Eds.), *Business marketing: An interaction and network perspective* (pp. 23-52). Boston: Kluwer Academic.

Nilson, T. H. (1992). *Value-added marketing: Marketing for superior results.* London: McGraw-Hill.

Peter, J. P., & Olson, J. C. (1993). *Consumer behavior and marketing strategy* (3rd ed.). Homewood, IL: Richard D. Irwin.

Piercy, N. (1985). *Marketing organisation: An analysis of information processing, power and politics.* London: George Allen & Unwin.

Ravald, A., & Grönroos, C. (1996). The value concept and relationship marketing. *European Journal of Marketing, 30*(2), 19-30.

Reichheld, F. F. (1993). Loyalty-based management. *Harvard Business Review, 71*(4), 64-73.

Reichheld, F. F., & Sasser, W. E., Jr. (1990). Zero defections: Quality comes to services. *Harvard Business Review, 69*(1), 105-111.

Reitman, J. (1994). Integrated marketing: Fantasy or the future? In C. Faure & L. Klein (Eds.), *Marketing communications strategies today and tomorrow: Integration, allocation, and interactive technologies* (Rep. No. 94-109, pp. 30-32). Cambridge, MA: Marketing Science Institute.

Schultz, D. E. (1996). The inevitability of integrated communications. *Journal of Business Research, 37*(3), 139-146.

Schultz, D. E., Tannenbaum, S. I., & Lauterborn, R. F. (1992). *Integrated marketing communications.* Lincolnwood, IL: NTC Business Books.

Sheth, J. N., & Parvatiyar, A. (Eds.). (1994). *Relationship marketing: Theory, methods and applications.* Atlanta, GA: Emory University, Center for Relationship Marketing.

Sheth, J. N., & Parvatiyar, A. (1995). Relationship marketing in consumer markets: Antecedents and consequences. *Journal of the Academy of Marketing Science, 23,* 255-271.

Stauss, B., & Weinlich, B. (1995). *Process-oriented measurement of service quality by applying the sequential prevention technique.* Presentation made at the Fifth Workshop on Quality Management in Services, EIASM, Tilburg, Netherlands.

Stewart, D. W. (1996). Market-back approach to the design of integrated communications programs: A change in paradigm and a focus on determinants of success. *Journal of Business Research, 37*(3), 147-154.

Stewart, D. W., Frazier, G., & Martin, I. (1996). Integrated channel management: Merging the communications and distributions functions of the firm. In E. Thorson & J. Moore (Eds.), *Integrated marketing and consumer psychology.* Hillsdale, NJ: Lawrence Erlbaum.

Storbacka, K. (1994). *The nature of customer relationship profitability: Analyses of relationships and customer bases in retail banking.* Helsinki, Finland: Swedish School of Economics and Business Administration.

Strandvik, T., & Storbacka, K. (1996). *Managing relationship quality.* Paper presented at the QUIS 5 Quality in Services Conference, University of Karlstad, Sweden.

Treacy, M., & Wiersema, F. (1993). Customer intimacy and other value disciplines. *Harvard Business Review, 71*(3), 84-93.

Vavra, T. G. (1994). The database marketing imperative. *Marketing Management, 3*(1), 47-57.

Webster, F. E., Jr. (1994). Executing the new marketing concept. *Marketing Management, 3*(1), 9-18.

Zeithaml, V. A. (1988). Consumer perceptions of price, quality and value: A means-end model and a synthesis of evidence. *Journal of Marketing, 52*(3), 2-22.

8

Relationship Marketing: Challenges for the Organization

Journal of Business Research
Vol. 46, No. 3, 1999
pp. 327–335

Christian Grönroos

Relationship marketing has been offered as a new marketing paradigm. However, a relationship approach to marketing challenges many fundamental cornerstones of marketing, such as the definition of marketing variables, the marketing department as a useful organizational solution, marketing planning as an effective way of planning marketing resources and activities, and others. If a firm is to take a relationship marketing approach many existing attitudes, behaviors, and structures will have to be rethought. In the present article, such behaviors and structures are challenged and eight "cornerstone" viewpoints about the implementation of relationship marketing are suggested.

The marketing mix concept was gradually developed after World War II and its 4 P model was introduced around 1960 (McCarthy, 1960). In the industrial society of the post-World War II era, marketing mix management and its transactional approach to marketing inevitably was helpful for very many industries in many markets. The rise of marketing mix management coincides with the time when the industrial society was reaching the peak of its life cycle in the Western world.

However, since that time, the market situation has changed, especially in Western economies, among other reasons because of the emergence of the postindustrial society. First, the once dominant mass markets are becoming more and more fragmented. Second, most customers no longer want to remain anonymous and want individual treatment and they are becoming more sophisticated. Third, more and more markets are maturing. Fourth, competition is increasing and becoming global. Fifth, the market offerings have become less standardized, because, in many situations, customers demand it, and new technology makes this possible in a way totally different from the past.

Relationship marketing is an emerging marketing perspective that has been discussed in the marketing literature throughout the 1990s. In marketing practice, relationship marketing is drawing more and more attention. It is suggested that a relationship approach to marketing is a new paradigm that goes back to the roots of the marketing phenomenon (Sheth and Parvatiyar, 1995). This new approach can be seen as an alternative way of looking at the marketing phenomenon as compared to the mass-marketing orientation of marketing mix management, rather than as a tool within the marketing mix.

Relationship marketing as an alternative perspective may require that basic marketing structures are reshaped. The purpose of this article is to discuss how established marketing behaviors and structures may need to be rethought. It is proposed that fundamental cornerstones of marketing need to be challenged. Eight "cornerstone" viewpoints about relationship marketing are formulated and discussed. These viewpoints are not formulated as formal propositions that can be tested. Rather, they are put forward as thought-provoking suggestions for further theoretical and empirical research. Six of the viewpoints have, however, been tested using data from quantitative and qualitative studies in New Zealand and Canada. According to preliminary results, all except the last (eighth) viewpoint are supported, and, interestingly enough, the two untested viewpoints (fourth and seventh) emerged in the qualitative studies (see Brodie, 1997).

Relationship Marketing—A Marketing Paradigm for the 1990s and Beyond

Transaction-oriented mass marketing based on the management of the 4 Ps of the marketing mix is, no doubt, still a valid marketing approach, especially for marketers of consumer packaged goods. However, from the 1970s, an alternate approach to marketing based on the establishment and management of relationships has emerged in various contexts of marketing research and practice. Elements of this new approach have been especially evident in two streams of research emanating in Scandinavia and Northern Europe and eventually spreading to other parts of the Western world. These streams of research are the Nordic School of Service (Grönroos and Gummesson, 1985; Berry and Parasuraman, 1993), which examines management and marketing from a service perspective, and the IMP Group (Håkansson, 1982; Håkansson and Snehota, 1995), which takes a network and interaction approach to understanding industrial businesses. A common denominator of these two schools of thought is that marketing is more a management issue than a function, and that managing marketing normally must be built upon relationships, not on transactions alone.

Building and managing relationship has become a philosophical cornerstone of both the Nordic School of Service and the IMP Group since the late 1970s. However, "relationship marketing" as a term was not commonly used until the latter part of the 1980s, although it was first coined in 1983 in the United States by Berry (1983). In the 1990s, the relationship marketing perspective has attracted growing attention in the United States (Kotler, 1992; Webster, 1994; Hunt and Morgan, 1994; Sheth and

Parvatiyar, 1995) as well as in Britain and Australia (Christopher, Payne, and Ballan-tyne, 1992; Brodie, Coviello, Brookes, Richard, and Little, 1997). Although the concepts used in various areas of relationship-oriented marketing differ to some extent, and the viewpoints taken are somewhat different, we can probably conclude that an understanding of services and how to manage and market services is one key to understanding the nature of relationship marketing. Another one is understanding how to manage networks (Håkansson and Snehota, 1995) and partnerships (Hunt and Morgan, 1994), and how to make use of the integrated marketing communications notion is yet another (Schultz, 1996; Stewart, 1996). However, when using a relationship approach, every firm offers services (Webster, 1994). "When *service competition* is the key to success practically for everybody and the product has to be defined as a service, *every business is a service business*" (Grönroos, 1996, p. 13).

In the literature, there is no agreement on a definition of relationship marketing. Although most definitions have common denominators, there are differences in scope. A comprehensive definition (Grönroos, 1989, 1990, 1997) states that, according to a relationship approach

> Marketing is the process of identifying and establishing, maintaining, and enhancing, and when necessary also terminating relationships with customers and other stake-holders, at a profit, so that the objectives of all parties involved are met; and this is done by a mutual exchange and fulfillment of promises. (Grönroos, 1997, p. 407)

Key aspects of such a marketing approach are not only to get customers and create transactions (identifying and establishing), but maintaining and enhancing on-going relationships are also important, and making promises is not the only responsibility of marketing, such promises must also be kept (Calonius, 1988). Profitable business relationships rely on a firm's ability to develop trust in itself and its performance with its customers and other stakeholders, and its ability to establish itself as an attractive business partner (see Halinen, 1994, who discusses the concept of *attraction* in business relationships).

Although they vary in terms of broadness and emphasis, most definitions of relationship marketing in the literature have a similar meaning (Christopher, Payne, and Ballantyne, 1992; Blomqvist, Dahl, and Haeger, 1993; Hunt and Morgan, 1994; Sheth and Parvatiyar, 1994; Gummesson, 1995). For example, Sheth and Parvatiyar (1994) state that relationship marketing is "the understanding, explanation and management of the on-going collaborative business relationship between suppliers and customers" (p. 2); whereas, Gummesson (1995, p. 16) defines relationship marketing as a marketing approach based on relationships, interactions, and networks.

In more general terms, the Grönroos definition of a relationship-oriented approach to marketing (relationship marketing) can be formulated as a generic definition: "*Marketing is to manage the firm's market relationships*" (Grönroos, 1996, p. 11; emphasis added). This definition includes the fundamental notion of marketing as a phenomenon related to the relationships between a firm and its environment. It points out that marketing includes all necessary efforts required to prepare the organization for activities and to implement those activities needed to manage the interfaces with its environment. Markets are, of course, of several kinds: customers, distributors, suppliers, networks of cooperating partners.

Relationship marketing is not a new phenomenon (Sheth and Parvatiyar, 1995). Rather, it is a return to what can be called the "roots of trade and commerce," before scientific management principles were intensively used, and before the emergence of the middleman, which broke up the relationship between suppliers and users. Marketing was based on management of relationships. The orientation toward mass production, mass distribution, and mass consumption, which at a period in the history of economic development in the Western world, well served the creation of wealth, made it difficult to maintain this basic nature of marketing. As noted previously in this article, today we have already entered a postindustrial society with a new business environment and new marketing challenges. New management principles are needed. This makes it necessary for marketing to return to its roots.

In none of the definitions of relationship marketing is the concept of *exchange* (Baggozzi, 1975), which for about two decades has been considered a foundation of marketing, explicitly mentioned. Focusing on exchange is considered too narrow a view. A relationship is also a *mindset*; hence, a relationship includes much more than exchanges. If a trusting relationship between two or several parties in the marketplace exists, exchanges should inevitably occur. However, there is so much more to an ongoing relationship that also has to be taken care of, if exchanges of offerings for money are to take place. The relationship is a more fundamental unit of study than the exchanges that occur within it. Hence, *the basic concept of marketing is the relationship itself rather than singular exchanges* that occur in the relationship. A relationship can be analyzed on several levels; for example, on relationship, sequence, episode, action, and step levels, as suggested by Holmlund (1996) and further developed by Wrange (1997).

Cornerstones of Marketing Challenged by the Relationship Marketing Perspective

Marketing mix management that continues to dominate mainstream marketing textbooks and large parts of research into marketing includes the following "cornerstones:" the marketing mix itself; the product concept; the marketing department; marketing planning; market segmentation; and market research and market share statistics. None of these, as they are treated in mainstream marketing, can be taken for granted when a relationship marketing approach is taken. They were developed in situations where a transaction-orientation approach served marketing well, and the task of getting customers dominated marketing. When marketing is based on relationships, and keeping customers is considered at least equally important as getting customers, new structures for analyzing, planning, implementing, and monitoring marketing and its effects may be needed. In fact, we argue that major changes in existing structures and behaviors are required. In the sections that follow, these six cornerstones of marketing are analyzed in view of the transition to a relationship marketing philosophy, and relationship-oriented structures are proposed.

Marketing Variables and Resources

The *marketing mix and its 4P model* define the variables that are considered part of marketing. Although the Ps are not obsolete as marketing variables today, often the philosophical foundation of the marketing mix and its Ps do not fit well in the competitive situation that has been emerging in many industries in the Western world. Mass-marketing and transaction orientation, as well as the adversarial approach to customers, do not allow the firm to adjust its market performance to the demands of more and more customers today; for example, enhanced value around the core product, reliable service to accompany the product, a trusting relationship with customers, suppliers, and distributors. As Dixon and Blois (1983) state, ". . . indeed, it would not be unfair to suggest that far from being concerned with a customer's interests (i.e., somebody *for whom* something is done), the view implicit in the 4P approach is that the customer is somebody *to whom* something is done!" (p. 4, emphasis added). Today, with more sophisticated customers, maturing markets, and intensifying global competition, this approach to customers will not serve marketers as well as it did. Cooperation, in a competitive environment, rather than an adversarial approach is a better foundation for marketing in today's market climate.

The marketing mix clearly includes such variables as advertising and other means of marketing communications, selling, and pricing that are needed in a relationship-oriented marketing approach. However, the basic tenet that the marketing mix consists of a number of predetermined groups of decision-making areas that together are what should be planned as marketing is challenged. It fits a situation where the customer is anonymous, and the market offering is a fairly simple product, such as many consumer packaged goods. When the firm can identify its customers (or distributors or suppliers), when interactions between these parties and their staff occur, and when it is important to make current customers interested in buying again (Reichheld and Sasser, 1990), marketing impact is created by a large number of people, the *part-time marketers* (Gummesson, 1987), and by other resources in the organization, in addition to the efforts of the full-time marketers in marketing departments. Hence, marketing variables can neither be predetermined, because they vary from case to case, nor separated from activities that, for example, belong to production and operations, deliveries, customer service, or a host of other business processes. We can offer the first viewpoint about how to understand the nature of marketing variables in relationship marketing:

Viewpoint 1:   In relationship marketing, the firm cannot predetermine a set of marketing variables. Instead, depending upon the stage and nature of the relationship with any given existing or potential customer, it must use all resources and activities that make a desired marketing impact by creating value and enhancing satisfaction, regardless of where in the organization they are located.

The Marketed Object

In the marketing literature, the *product concept* has a firm position. The product—a good or a service—is the core around which the rest of marketing revolves. To use the 4P model, the product has to be developed and packaged so that it can be priced, promoted, and distributed. Although the product may be complicated, including not only the technical core but also packaging and such augmenting services as warranties, it is considered more or less prefabricated before the marketing process begins. This view of the phenomenon, which is offered as a solution to customer problems, is transaction oriented. The product must exist, if a transaction is to take place at a given moment. As long as transactions or exchanges are the focus of marketing, a prefabricated product is required. However, when the focus is shifted from singular exchanges to relationships, quite another view of how solutions to customer problems develop emerges.

The technical solution embedded in a product (a physical good or a service) is only the prerequisite for a good solution to a problem. In addition, customers expect, for example, well-handled deliveries, service and maintenance, information, customer-oriented complaints-handling routines, as well as skillful and service-minded employees who demonstrate an interest in the needs and desires of customers and show service-oriented attitudes and behaviors when performing their tasks. Moreover, customers do not want to spend too much time getting their problems resolved.

When solutions to customers' problems are viewed in a relationship perspective, the traditional product becomes transparent. In fact, normally several competitors offer a similar "product." What is important is a firm's ability to create a total system of caring for its customers on an on-going basis so the customers are served better by a given supplier or service firm than by its competitors (Levitt, 1969). The customers must be truly *served*. Hence, a total *service offering* that, indeed, serves the customer must be designed. The technical solution, or the "product," becomes only one resource among many. When the solution to a customer's problem is viewed in this way, two things follow. First, the product does not exist as a prefabricated phenomenon. Second, the solution is developing over time when the firm manages its resources so that an acceptable total offering gradually emerges.

What is needed is a governing system that matches the various resources with the needs and desires of the customer over time. Of course, to some degree a prefabricated technical solution, a "product," is always needed, but it is only one technology among many used to create the offering over time. The resources that must be managed through a customer-oriented governing system can, for example, be grouped into the following categories: *people, technology, know-how,* and *time* (Grönroos, 1997). Time, of course, refers to how efficiently and effectively the firm manages *the customer's time.* People includes *both personnel and customers.* The customer also becomes a resource, because in an on-going relationship, much of what is emerging is based on customer-driven information, initiatives, and actions. Hence, we can formulate the second viewpoint about the total offering, which in a relationship marketing, context replaces the product concept.

> *Viewpoint 2:*   In relationship marketing, the firm cannot rely on a prefabricated product. It must develop such resources as personnel, technology, know-how, the customer's time, and the customer itself as a resource, as well as create a governing system that manages these resources during the on-going relationship in such a manner that a satisfactory total service offering emerges over time.

The Organizational Solution

The *marketing department*, including specialists on various sub-areas of marketing, is the traditional organization solution for managing, planning, and implementing marketing activities. This functionalistic organizational solution is inherent in the marketing mix management approach and follows the general principles of scientific management (Taylor, 1947). Specialists should perform their specialties. However (except for such cases as many consumer packaged goods), marketing is no longer the sole task of marketing specialists. Marketing is spread throughout the organization, and this is true for a growing number of businesses, in service industries, and in the manufacturing sector (Gummesson, 1987; Grönroos, 1990, 1995).

Marketing and marketers have become isolated in organizations over time. As we have observed in another context, "both from an organizational point of view and from a psychological standpoint *the marketing department is off side*" (Grönroos, 1994, p. 356; emphasis added). The marketing department cannot influence the people in the rest of the organization outside the marketing department to play their roles as *part-time marketers,* to use a term coined by Gummesson (1987). Part-time marketers are those people outside the marketing department (i.e., not marketing specialists), who are specialist in, say, maintenance, deliveries of goods, claims handling, operating telephone exchanges, or just about any type of job, where their attitudes and way of doing their job have an impact on the customer's perception of the firm and of the quality of its market offerings. Hence, they have *dual responsibilities*, both for doing their job well and in so doing, making a good marketing impression.

Gummesson observes that in industrial markets and in service businesses, the part-time marketers typically outnumber by several times the full-time marketers; that is, the specialists of the marketing and sales departments. Furthermore, he concludes that "marketing and sales departments [the full-time marketers] are not able to handle more than a limited portion of the marketing *as its staff cannot be at the right place at the right time with the right customer contacts*" (Gummesson, 1990, p. 13). Hence, the part-time marketers not only outnumber the full-time marketers, the specialists; often they are the only marketers available at crucial moments (Normann, 1983), when the marketing impact is made and a basis for customer satisfaction is laid. Moreover, the marketing department cannot plan the job of the part-time marketers or in any way take responsibility for their attitude and performance. In the final analysis, the traditional marketing department stands in the way of spreading market orientation and an interest in the customer throughout the organization (Piercy, 1985; Grönroos, 1982, 1990).

Furthermore, the specialists in a marketing department may become alienated from the customers. Managing the marketing mix means relying on mass marketing. Customers become numbers for marketing specialists, whose actions, therefore, typically are based on surface information obtained from market research reports and market-share statistics. Frequently, such "full-time" marketers may act without ever having encountered an actual customer. As we observed as early as 1982 in a study of service firms, traditional marketing departments may make a firm less customer oriented and make it more difficult to create interest in marketing among employees who do not belong to such departments (Grönroos, 1982).

Because marketing resources (i.e., part-time marketers) can be found throughout an organization, total marketing cannot be organized in the form of a traditional marketing department. Marketing responsibility must be spread organization-wide. Moreover, normally it is probably impossible for the head of a marketing department to be responsible for the marketing impact of part-time marketers and to have a decisive influence on investments in equipment and operational and administrative systems that also have a marketing impact on the customers. Only top management or the head of, for example, a regional organization or a division can take that responsibility.

Marketing specialists are, of course, still needed to perform such basic full-time marketing activities as market research, some advertising programs, and direct marketing. In addition, as specialists on their customers, they can assist top management as internal marketing facilitators; that is, as internal consultants. As Berry (1986) observes, "service marketing directors not only must persuade customers to buy (for the first time), they must also persuade—and help—employees to perform" (p. 47). Marketing specialists can help making part-time marketers understand and accept their marketing responsibility through educating employees on managerial and nonmanagerial levels about the nature, purpose, and applications of part-time marketing, they can strive to support investments in tools and systems that make it easier for part-time marketers to perform, and they can be visible supporters of good quality in the organization (Berry and Parasuraman, 1991). *Internal marketing* becomes a critical issue in relationship marketing if the organization is to be well prepared for its new marketing tasks (Grönroos, 1990). In an article about relationship marketing, Bitner (1995) emphasizes the need for a firm to manage, not only the tasks of making and keeping promises, but also the task of enabling the fulfillment of promises, if marketing is to be successful.

If the group of marketing specialists in a firm becomes too big and becomes dominant, problems with market orientation and customer consciousness may follow. The part-time marketers may not understand or accept their responsibilities as marketers. Hence, we can formulate the third viewpoint about how to organize marketing and the fourth viewpoint about preparing the part-time marketers for their marketing duties.

Viewpoint 3: In relationship marketing, marketing cannot be organized as a separate organizational unit, rather a marketing consciousness must be developed organization-wide. However, marketing specialists are needed for some traditional marketing activities and as internal consultants to top management in order to help instill such a marketing consciousness.

Viewpoint 4: Because the implementation of relationship marketing relies upon the support of a host of part-time marketers, the firm must create an internal marketing process to ensure that part-time marketers understand and accept their marketing duties and learn the skills needed to perform in a customer-oriented manner.

Planning Marketing

Marketing planning is the process of planning and developing the activities of the marketing department and budgets for those activities. As long as almost all marketing activities are in the hands of the marketing department, traditional marketing planning is acceptable. However, in a situation where much or even most of the marketing impact is the result of activities that are not the responsibility of the marketing department, it does not make sense to plan the activities of that department separately and call this "the marketing plan." Such a plan includes, of course, part of what is needed to implement relationship marketing, but today so much more that is planned as parts of other plans should also be planned from the same customer perspective as the activities of the traditional marketing plan. Just preparing a "marketing plan" within a marketing department does not mean that the firm's total marketing activities as perceived by its customers are planned. It can easily become a plan that counteracts what may be planned as part of human resource management, production and operations, for example, or is counteracted by those plans. *The result is not well-planned marketing.* What is called "the marketing plan" may only cover those external marketing activities by which the firm *gives promises* to potential and existing customers. Interactive marketing activities and the performance, attitude, and behavior of the part-time marketers are not planned with a customer perspective in mind. Hence, how *promises are fulfilled* is not well planned from a marketing point of view. If top management, the marketers, and people from other departments internally believe in such a "marketing plan," which they often seem to do, the marketing concept, that is, the notion that the interest of the customer should be kept in mind in the firm's planning processes, is unfulfilled.

Because marketing resources can be found throughout the organization, not only in the marketing department, marketing cannot be planned in the form of a traditional, separate marketing plan. Instead, the marketing impact of resources and activities that are planned elsewhere, such as in production and operations, human resources, or investment in systems and equipment, must be recognized. All resources and activities that have such an impact must be integrated, regardless of in what department they may be. This can only be done in an overall corporate plan based, not only on establishing relationships, but also on a notion of relationship building and maintenance. As we concluded in an earlier study more than 15 years ago (Grönroos, 1982), a market orientation must be instilled in all plans through a market-oriented corporate plan. This plan would then serve as a governing *relationship plan.* Hence, we can formulate the fifth viewpoint about how to plan marketing from a relationship perspective.

> *Viewpoint 5:*   Relationship marketing cannot be localized in the traditional marketing plans. Instead, a market orientation must be instilled in all plans and integrated through a market-oriented corporate plan as a governing relationship plan.

Individualizing the Customer Base

Market segmentation (Smith, 1956) is the process of identifying and evaluating subgroups of customers that are internally more homogeneous than the total market. As long as markets could be viewed as masses of anonymous customers, market segmentation served marketing well. However, when customers no longer want to be treated as numbers, but as individuals, the traditional notion of market segmentation becomes less helpful. Identifying groups of numbers that somehow look alike is, in many cases, still a valid approach to segmentation, but, it is often more important for the firm to identify its existing and potential customers as individuals representing households or organizations. *Individualizing* the market becomes more important for marketing than merely segmenting it. From a profitability point of view, getting a larger share of the purchases of such individuals may be better than getting a larger number of customers in a given market segment (Storbacka, 1997).

Because relationship marketing is based on the notion of relationships with identifiable customers who should not be treated as unknown persons but as individuals representing households or organizations, traditional segmentation is less appropriate. Instead of getting some of the business of a large segment, the firm should strive to get as much as possible of every individual customer's business (Peppers and Rogers, 1993). The basic idea behind market segmentation still holds true, of course, However, the nature of segmentation changes dramatically. It is no longer enough to distinguish between homogeneous groups of anonymous customers based on average measures. Much more detailed and individualized information in the form of, for example, customer information files (Vavra, 1994), or other types of databases must be compiled. Firms serving mass markets cannot, of course, develop as many individual and informative files as firms that have a limited number of customers. However, the basic principle should be the same in both situations. Hence, the sixth viewpoint about how to manage the customer base can be formulated.

Viewpoint 6:   In relationship marketing, marketing decisions and activities cannot be based on traditional market segmentation techniques. Choice of customers to serve and decisions about how to serve them must be based on individual customer information files and other types of databases.

Researching Customers and Monitoring Success

Market research and *market share statistics* are a way of finding out needs and expectations of customers, monitoring the level of satisfaction among the firm's customers, and evaluating the relative sales result of a firm as compared to that of the competition. When marketing is based on a notion of masses of anonymous customers, this is a practical way to monitor how well, on the average, the firm is doing. Far too often, however, market share alone is treated as a way of evaluating the success of the firm in satisfying the needs and expectations of its customers. The better the market share is maintained or increased, the healthier the customer base. Of course, this is not the case, but because frequently no other than at best ad hoc information about customer satisfaction or customer loyalty is available, good sales performance is easily taken as a measure of satisfied customers. This may, however, turn out to be a dangerous misunderstanding. Moreover, the closer natural contacts the firm has with its customers, the less justifiable it is to mix up market-share statistics with satisfaction and the health of the customer base.

Market research is often based on surveys, and because such data-gathering methods normally do not allow for obtaining in-depth information about the thoughts and intents of customers, only surface data are gathered. Such data may be useful, too, but, for example, information about customer satisfaction and about customer needs, desires, and expectations that employees who interact with customers are accumulating is neglected. The firm knows very little about the specific needs, desires, and expectations of individual customers, although the information technology available today makes it possible to develop customized databases (Vavra, 1994).

Measuring market share is an important way to monitor relative sales of a product when the product is marketed to a mass market of unknown customers. It is relatively easy to compile sales statistics. Studies of customer perceived quality and customer satisfaction measurements normally cannot be done on an equally regular basis. As a consequence, market-share statistics are sometimes regarded as a proxy for customer satisfaction. Market share can be maintained, at least for some time, even when customer satisfaction deteriorates. When a firm has direct contacts with its customers, information about the needs, desires, expectations, and future intentions of customers as well as about their quality and value perceptions and about satisfaction can be obtained directly in these contacts. This, however, requires an intelligent system for registering the bits of information many employees throughout the organization receive on a daily basis. This is vastly neglected today. However, only such direct management of the customer base gives management current and accurate information, not only about sales, but also about the needs, expectations, intentions, and level of satisfaction of its customers. Hence, we can formulate a seventh viewpoint about the need to manage the firm's customer base directly and not through market-share statistics and ad hoc customer studies alone.

Viewpoint 7: In relationship marketing, the firm should manage its customer base directly through information obtained from the continuous interfaces between customers and employees, and only support this with market-share statistics and ad hoc studies of customers.

The Rebirth of Marketing: The Relationship Approach

The marketing mix management paradigm was developed to suit the requirements of marketing during the peak of the industrial society. Today it is helpful only in some types of businesses, such as many consumer goods industries, and even there it is being questioned (Rapp and Collins, 1990; McKenna, 1991). Relationship marketing, by going back to the roots of the marketing phenomenon, offers a new approach to managing market relationships. However, it is important to understand the paradigmatic nature of this perspective. It is foremost a philosophy that guides the planning and management of activities in the relationships between a firm and its customers, distributors, and other partners. The relationship philosophy relies on co-operation and a trusting relationship with customers (and other stakeholders and network partners) instead of an adversarial approach to customers, on collaboration within the company instead of specialization of functions and the division of labor, and on the notion of marketing as more of a market-oriented management approach with part-time marketers spread throughout the organisation than as a separate function for specialists only (Grönroos, 1996).

Common mistakes when discussing relationship marketing follow from a failure to understand this philosophical shift. We must realize that it is *a new paradigm, not just a new model*, that is emerging. Sometimes relationship marketing is used more or less as a synonym for direct marketing, database marketing, or for establishing customer clubs, and it becomes just another instrument in the marketing mix toolbox to be used to create transactions. In other situations, relationship marketing is used as a synonym for developing partnerships, alliances, and networks, or as part of marketing communications only. However, it is much more than all of these. It requires a totally new approach to some of the fundamental thoughts in marketing, as is implied by the seven propositions suggested in the previous section. The transition from transaction-oriented marketing mix-based practice of marketing to a relationship-oriented one is not an uncomplicated process. The old paradigm has deep roots in the minds of academics, as well as of marketers and nonmarketers in a company. Moreover, it still has a much easier-to-use toolbox of marketing instruments available than the emerging new paradigm can presently offer.

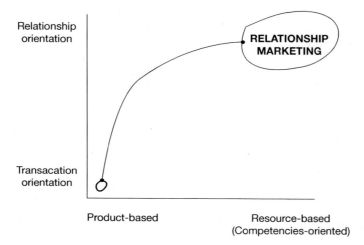

Figure 1. Relationship Marketing: The Transition Curve

Source: Strandvik and Storbacka, 1996.

Hence, as illustrated in Figure 1, the transition toward a relationship-oriented marketing approach can be understood as a learning curve or a *transition curve* (Strandvik and Storbacka, 1996). In the beginning, firms that want to implement a relational approach to marketing remain very focused on products. Hence, only easily developed relational activities are introduced. Typical examples are customized sales letters and information bulletins, customer clubs, and so forth. Such activities can easily backfire, especially if the customer is mistreated in other respects; for example, when using a service, in a recovery or complaints situation, or in just about any other interaction with the firm. Firms in this stage do not yet fully understand the philosophical nature of relationship marketing. Here, singular exchanges are still the basic focus of marketing. Today, most firms applying a relationship marketing approach are probably somewhere in this stage of the transition process. A true transition toward a relationship marketing strategy requires a focus on resources and competencies in the relationship. It is interesting that this changing demand from the market has had an impact on the strategy field that parallels the development of the relationship approach in marketing. Resources and core competencies are emphasised in the current strategy literature (Hamel and Prahalad, 1994).

In principle, the product is but one resource among others, although it is, of course, the necessary prerequisite for a successful relationship. The relationship itself becomes the focus of marketing.

However, as noted earlier, the roots of the old paradigm are very deep in the minds of most people, regardless of whether they are in managerial positions, or they are full-time marketers, or should consider themselves to be part-time marketers. Therefore, it may be difficult to instill a new philosophical approach in which marketing is practically every employee's business as part-time marketers or managers of part-time marketers. Getting the commitment of everyone to the new marketing philosophy and its consequences for marketing in practice may be difficult or even impossible. As we observed in another context (Grönroos, 1994), "the use of the marketing mix paradigm and the 4 Ps has made it difficult for the marketing function to earn credibility" (p. 356). Far too many people feel uncomfortable with the thought of being involved in marketing. Some firms have solved this problem not only by downscaling or terminating their marketing departments altogether but also by *banning the use of the term marketing* (Grönroos, 1982, 1994). Such terms as "customer contacts" and "customer satisfaction" have been used instead of "marketing" to describe the same phenomenon; i.e., the management of the firm's market relationships. Sometimes we need this kind of semantic nicety. It is not too far-fetched to assume that in the future this will occur in a growing number of cases. Therefore, an eighth, and final, viewpoint about relationship marketing as the rebirth of marketing is offered.

Viewpoint 8:   To create an understanding of relationship marketing in an organization and to implement a culture of relationship marketing, it may be necessary to replace the term "marketing" with a psychologically more readily accepted term to describe the task of managing the firm's customer relationships (see Appendix).

References

Berry, Leonard L.: Relationship Marketing, in *Emerging Perspectives of Services Marketing*, Leonard L. Berry, G. Lynn Shostack, and G. D. Upah, eds., American Marketing Association, Chicago, IL. 1983, pp. 25–28.

Berry, Leonard L.: Big Ideas in Services Marketing. *Journal of Consumer Marketing* 3 (Spring 1986).

Berry, Leonard L, and Parasuraman, A.: Building a New Academic Field—The Case of Services Marketing. *Journal of Retailing* 69 (1993): 13–60.

Bitner, Mary Jo: Building Service Relationships: It's All About Promises. *Journal of the Academy of Marketing Science* 23 (1995): 246–251.

Blomqvist, Ralf, Dahl, Johan, and Haeger, Tomas: *Relationsmarknads-foring. Strategi och metod fö servicekonkurens* (Relationship Marketing. Strategy and Methods for Service Competition). IHM Förlag, Göteborg, Sweden. 1993.

Brodie, Roderick J.: From Transaction to Relationship Marketing: Propositions for Change, in New *and Evolving Paradigms: The Emerging Future of Marketing*, Tony Meenaghan, ed., The American Marketing Association Special Conferences, University College, Dublin, Ireland. 1997, pp. 615–616.

Brodie, Roderick J., Coviello, Nicole E., Brookes, Richard W., and Little, Victoria: Toward a Paradigm Shift in Marketing? An Examination of Current Marketing Practices. *Journal of Marketing Management* 13 (1997), pp. 383–406.

Calonius, Henrik: A Buying Process Model, in *Innovative Marketing—A European Perspective*, Proceedings of the XVIIth Annual Conference of the European Marketing Academy, Blois, Keith, and Parkinson, S., eds., University of Bradford, England, 1988.

Christopher, Martin, Payne, Adrian, and Ballantyne, David: *Relationship Marketing. Bringing Quality, Customer Service, and Marketing Together*, Butterworth, London. 1992.

Dixon, Donald F., and Blois, Keith: *Some Limitations of the 4 Ps as a Paradigm for Marketing*, Marketing Education Group Annual Conference, Cranfield Institute of Technology, UK, July 1983.

Grönroos, Christian: *Strategic Management and Marketing in the Service Sector*. Swedish School of Economics and Business Administration, Helsingfors, Finland, 1982 (published in 1983 in the United States by Marketing Science Institute and in the UK by Studentlitteratur/Chartwell-Bratt).

Grönroos, Christian: Defining Marketing: A Market-Oriented Approach. *European Journal of Marketing* 23 (1989): 52–60.

Grönroos, Christian: Relationship Approach to the Marketing Function in Service Contexts: The Marketing and Organizational Behavior Interface. *Journal of Business Research* 20 (1990): 3–12.

Grönroos, Christian: Quo Vadis, Marketing? Toward a Relationship Marketing Paradigm. *Journal of Marketing Management* 10 (1994): 347–360.

Grönroos, Christian: Relationship Marketing: The Strategy Continuum. *Journal of the Academy of Marketing Science* 23 (1995): 252–254.

Grönroos, Christian: The Relationship Marketing Logic. *Asia–Australia Marketing Journal* 4 (1996): 7–18.

Grönroos, Christian: Value-Driven Relational Marketing: From Products to Resources and Competencies. *Journal of Marketing Management* 13 (1997): 407–419.

Grönroos, Christian, and Gummesson, Evert: The Nordic School of Service Marketing, in *Service Marketing—Nordic School Perspectives*, Christian Grönroos, and Evert Gummesson, eds., Stockholm University, Stockholm, Sweden. 1985, pp. 6–11.

Gummesson, Evert: The New Marketing—Developing Long-Term Interactive Relationships. *Long-Range Planning* 20 (1987): 10–20.

Gummesson, Evert: *Relationsmarknadsföring. Fran 4P till 30R* (Relationship marketing. From 4P to 30R). Liber-Hermods, Malmö, Sweden. 1995.

Håkansson, Håkan, ed.: *International Marketing and Purchasing of Industrial Goods*, Wiley, New York. 1982.

Håkansson, Håkan, and Snehota, Ivan: *Developing Relationships in Business Networks*, Routledge, London. 1995.

Hamel, Gary, and Prahalad, C. K.: *Competing For the Future. Breakthrough strategies for seizing control of your industry and creating the markets of tomorrow*, Harvard Business School Press, Boston, MA. 1994.

Holmlund, Maria: *A Theoretical Framework of Perceived Quality in Business Relationships*. Research report 36, CERS, Center for Relationship Marketing and Service Management, Swedish School of Economics and Business Administration, Helsinki, Finland. 1996.

Hunt, Shelby D., and Morgan, Robert M.: Relationship Marketing in the Era of Network Competition. *Marketing Management* 3 (1994): 19–30.

Kotler, Philip? It's Time for Total Marketing. Business *Week* ADVANCE *Executive Brief* 2 (1992).

Levitt, Theodore: *The Marketing Mode*, McGraw-Hill, New York. 1969.

McCarthy, E. Jerome: *Basic Marketing*, Irwin, Homewood, IL. 1960.

McKenna, Regis: *Relationship Marketing. Successful Strategies for the Age of the Customer*. Addison-Wesley, Reading, MA. 1991.

Normann, Richard: *Service Management*, Wiley, New York. 1993.

Peppers, D., and Rogers, Mary: *One-to-One Future: Building Relationships One Customer at a Time*. Currency/Doubleday, New York. 1993.

Piercy, Nigel: *Marketing Organisation. An Analysis of Information Processing, Power, and Politics,* George, Allen & Unwin, London. 1985.

Rapp, Stan, and Collins, Tom: *The Great Marketing Turnaround*, Prentice-Hall, Engelwood Cliffs, NJ. 1990.

Sheth, Jagdish N., and Parvatiyar, Atul, eds.: *Relationship Marketing: Theory, Methods, and Applications,* 1994. Research Conference Proceedings, Center for Relationship Marketing, Emory University, Atlanta, GA. June 1994.

Sheth, Jagdish N., and Parvatiyar, Atul: Relationship Marketing in Consumer Markets: Antecedents and Consequences. *Journal of the Academy of Marketing Science* 23 (1995): 255–271.

Schultz, Don E.: The Inevitability of Integrated Communications. *Journal of Business Research* 37 (1996): 139–146.

Smith, W. R.: Product Differentiation and Market Segmentation as Alternative Marketing Strategies. *Journal of Marketing* 21 (July 1956): 3–8.

Storbacka, Kaj: Segmentation Based on Customer Profitability—Retrospective Analysis of Retail Bank Customer Bases. *Journal of Marketing Management* 13 (1997): 479–492.

Strandvik, Tore, and Storbacka, Kaj: Managing Relationship Quality. Proceedings of The QUIS 5 Quality in Services Conference, University of Karlstad, Sweden. 1996.

Steward, D. W.: Market-Back Approach to the Design of Integrated Communications Programs: A Change in Paradigm and a Focus on Determinants of Success. *Journal of Business Research* 37 (1996): 147–154.

Taylor, Frederick W.: *Scientific Management*, Harper & Row, London. 1947. (a volume of two papers originally published in 1903 and 1911 and written testimony for a Special House Committee in the United States in 1912).

Vavra, Terry G.: The Database Marketing Imperative. *Marketing Management* 1 (1994): 47–57.

Webster, Frederick E., Jr.: Executing the New Marketing Concept. *Marketing Management* 3 (1994): 9–18.

Wrange, Kim: *Customer Relationship Termination*. Research report, CERS, Center for Relationship Marketing and Service Management, Swedish School of Economics and Business Administration, Helsinki, Finland. 1997.

Appendix. Eight Viewpoints about Relationship Marketing

Viewpoint 1: In relationship marketing, the firm cannot predetermine a set of marketing variables. Instead, depending upon the stage and nature of the relationship with any given existing or potential customer, it must use all resources and activities that make a desired marketing impact by creating value and enhancing satisfaction, regardless of where in the organization they are located.

Viewpoint 2: In relationship marketing, the firm cannot rely on a prefabricated product. It must develop such resources as personnel, technology, know-how, the customer's time, and the customer itself as a resource, as well as create a governing system that manages these resources during the on-going relationship in such a manner that a satisfactory total service offering emerges over time.

Viewpoint 3: In relationship marketing, marketing cannot be organized as a separate organizational unit, rather a marketing consciousness must be developed organization-wide. However, marketing specialists are needed for some traditional marketing activities and as internal consultants to top management in order to help instill such a marketing consciousness.

Viewpoint 4: Because the implementation of relationship marketing relies upon the support of a host of part-time marketers, the firm must create an internal marketing process to ensure that part-time marketers understand and accept their marketing duties and learn the skills needed to perform in a customer-oriented manner.

Viewpoint 5: Relationship marketing cannot be localized in the traditional marketing plans. Instead, a market orientation must be instilled in all plans and integrated through a market-oriented corporate plan as a governing relationship plan.

Viewpoint 6: In relationship marketing, marketing decisions and activities cannot be based on traditional market segmentation techniques. Choice of customers to serve and decisions about how to serve them must be based on individual customer information files and other types of databases.

Viewpoint 7: In relationship marketing, the firm should manage its customer base directly through information obtained from the continuous interfaces between customers and employees, and only support this with market-share statistics and ad hoc studies of customers.

Viewpoint 8: To create an understanding of relationship marketing in an organization and to implement a culture of relationship marketing, it may be necessary to replace the term "marketing" with a psychologically more readily accepted term to describe the task of managing the firm's customer relationships.

9

Value-Driven Relational Marketing: From Products to Resources and Competencies

Journal of Marketing Management
Vol. 13, No. 5, 1997
pp. 407–419

Christian Grönroos

Marketing from a relational perspective, or relationship marketing, requires that a firm offers more resources and activities than a core product (goods or services) in order to satisfy the long-term value needs of its customers. In the present article a value-driven approach to how such long-term needs are fulfilled is discussed. The analysis goes beyond the product concept and develops a resources-and-competencies approach to the market offer. However, a relational approach to marketing can be expected to be successful only if the firm adopts a true relational intent and the customer is in a relational mode. Therefore, the concepts of relational and transactional intent and relational and transactional mode, respectively, are also introduced and discussed.

Introduction

Marketing from a relational perspective has been defined as the process of identifying and establishing, maintaining, enhancing, and when necessary terminating relationships with customers and other stakeholders, at a profit, so that the objectives of all parties involved are met, where this is done by a mutual giving and fulfilment of promises (cf. Grönroos 1996),[1] or as a marketing

---

[1] Recently Shelby Hunt has offered a definition with the same meaning. See Hunt and Morgan (1994, p 23). In a similar way, Sheth and Parvatiyar (1994) define relationship marketing as "the understanding, explanation and management of the ongoing collaborative business relationship between suppliers and customers". See also Christopher *et al.* (1992) and Blomqvist *et al.* (1993). Also compare Berry (1983).

approach involving interactions, relationships and networks (Gummesson 1995).[2] In this article we focus on how to understand the product concept in such a marketing context. The basic perspective is that of the Nordic School of service research, which has been identified as one of the major research traditions in the discipline (cf. Berry and Parasuraman 1993), and its extension into relationship marketing. Marketing in a relational context is seen as a process that should support the creation of perceived value for customers over time.

Only the relationship between a firm and a customer is taken into account in this context. Moreover, a dyadic situation is focused upon. It should, however, be possible to extend the analysis to other relationships in networks using the same argument. Such an extension is outside the scope of the present article.

First, the nature of a relational approach to marketing is discussed and the concepts of relational intent and relational mode are introduced. Then the meaning of value and customer perceived value in a relational context is analysed, and finally the product concept is discussed in a value-driven relational context as compared to a transactional context. It is argued that the traditional product concept is too simplistic, and that one has to understand the management of resource structures and competencies of a firm beyond the product construct to be able to create value-driven solutions for customers in relational contexts.

Relational Intent versus Transactional Intent

In the on-going discussion about relationship marketing it is frequently argued that relationships between, for example, a firm (supplier of goods or service firm) and its customers do not necessarily always *exist*, and that either part may not *want to have* a relationship with the other part. However, it would be more fruitful to look at the situation in *a* different way. We argue that *latent relationships* do always exist, and that either the firm or the customer, or both, may choose to activate that latent relationship, depending on their strategies, needs, wishes and/or expectations or choose not to do it.

Thus, the firm may choose either a relational strategy or a transactional strategy. On the other hand a customer may want either to have a transactional contact with a firm or become engaged with the firm in a more relational manner. The main thing is, therefore, not whether a relational strategy is possible or not, but whether a firm finds it profitable and in other respects suitable to develop a relational strategy or a transactional strategy. For example, a marketer of canned juice may choose to activate the

---

[2] This new marketing paradigm has been called *relationship marketing*. It would be more accurate to use the term *relational marketing*, because it indicates an alternative way of looking at the marketing phenomenon, whereas the term relationship marketing easily is interpreted as just a subset of something else, or in the worst case as yet another tool in the marketing mix. However, because relationship marketing already has become a widely used term, it is used in this article as well interchangeably with the expression relational marketing to mean an approach to marketing that is based on a relational perspective.

latent relationships with consumers who could be open for a relational engagement with the firm by adding a note on the cans encouraging consumers to give feedback. In addition the marketer develops a system for actively answering consumers' phone calls, faxes or e-mail messages to make a continuing dialogue with the consumers possible. This is a relational marketing strategy that may well suit this type of goods and market situation. Some consumers may want to activate the latent relationship and indeed get in contact with the marketer. Others may recognise the invitation to give feedback and feel pleased with the fact that they have been given an opportunity that they for some reason do not choose to use. Still, in their minds the value of this particular brand has increased. In the latter case the consumers mentally and passively engage in a relationship, whereas in the first case they actively do so. Finally, some consumers may not evaluate this relational invitation at all. They are not relationally interested consumers in this market. For them a strategy based on transactional intent works well.

On the other hand, a marketer of the same packaged goods may choose not to invite this type of feedback or to do it without really developing a system for showing consumers who indeed contact the firm that it really cares. In this latter case the marketing strategy is transactional. If there is an invitation for consumers to give feedback but no intention to follow up on such feedback in a customer-orientated way, the activity that may look relational is based on transactional thinking. Rather the activity is used as what could be called a transactional tool. For transaction-oriented consumers this may work well, for others is may become a source of discontent if the consumer chooses to give feedback and gets no response.

Similar examples of a relational approach as the consumer packaged goods one (canned juice) can easily be found from the fields of business-to-business marketing and services marketing. However, because marketing situations differ, the nature and contents of relationships vary even to a large degree. For example, a relationship would probably be much more extensive and multi-faceted in an average business-to-business marketing situation (cf. Holmlund and Törnroos 1996). Thus, depending on the situation, a relational strategy will probably require very different types of activities, to both their nature and scope.

Customers, individual consumers and organisational users can be seen as interested in either a relational or transactional contact with a firm. Regarding different types of goods and services or industrial solutions the same individual or organisation can probably take a different interest. Thus, in a given marketing situation the consumer (or user in a business-to-business relationship) is either in a *relational mode* or in a *transactional mode*. Furthermore, consumers in a relational mode can be either in an *active* or a *passive* relational mode, as the example with canned juice illustrated. Consumers or users in an active mode seek contact, whereas consumers in a passive mode are satisfied with the understanding that if needed the firm will be there for them.

Why people enter a relational mode and choose to react favourably to a relationship marketing approach by a firm is a topic that has not been studied very much so far. Sheth and Parvatiyar (1995) argue that the primary reason is to reduce choices.

Baggozzi (1995), on the other hand, says that this is probably not a pervasive motive. As antecedents to reduction in choices he offers the possibility that customers may enter relationships in order to be able to fulfil goals to which they have earlier committed or tentatively committed. Goals may, of course, be of very different nature, such as profitability, cost reduction, comfort, health and self esteem. As another antecedent he offers the possibility that some customers may sometimes feel that being involved in a relationship is an end in itself.

Strategic Conclusions for Marketing

For marketing strategy the important thing here is not whether relationship marketing is possible in a given situation or not, rather it is a question of whether the company finds it profitable and suitable to base its strategy on a *relational intent* or not. In principle, a relational strategy is always possible, because there are always latent relationships. However, it is not always the best choice to activate these latent relationships by developing a marketing strategy based on a relational intent. In some situations, if the customers are not in a relational mode or if a relational strategy cannot be justified from an economic standpoint, it may be more profitable and suitable to adopt a *transactional intent* and create a marketing strategy that is transactional in nature. It all depends on the nature of the product, the market situation, the needs and wishes of the customers, the competitive situation, etc. We do, however, believe that a relationship intent is required in more and more situations, because of the general development of the environment surrounding the marketers.

As illustrated by Figure 1, three modes of consumers and users (active and passive relational and non-relational or transactional, respectively) and two types of marketing efforts (based on a relational intent or based on a non-relational or transactional intent, respectively) can be combined into a *relationship configuration matrix*. By analysing where in this configuration matrix the current or potential customer falls, the firm can see what type of marketing strategy seems to be most appropriate.

		FIRM Efforts based on	
		Relational intent	**Non**-relational intent
	Active relational mode	1	2
CUSTOMER or USER	**Passive** relational mode	3	4
	Non-relational mode	5	6

Figure 1. Relational Configuration Matrix

In a *non-relational intent/non-relational mode* configuration (cell 6) a transactional strategy leading to the exchange of a product for money (moving to cell 6) makes sense, because this creates the value the customers are looking for. Anything else would not produce additional value.

In a *relational intent/non-relational mode* configuration (cell 5) a transactional approach leading to the exchange of a product for money (moving to cell 6) makes sense as well. In fact, anything else would be a waste of efforts, because the consumers or users are not in a relational mode.

In all other configurations (cells 1, 2, 3 and 4) the customers are looking for something in addition to the product to satisfy their or an organisation's *value needs*. By value needs we mean the total value created by the core offering and other resources and activities in the relationship that a customer is requiring in order to feel satisfied. Value creation goes beyond the product. In these cases a marketing strategy based on a relational intent (moving to cells 1 and 3) obviously makes sense.

A relational intent is a philosophical way of thinking about a given market situation that probably leads to the development of a relational marketing strategy. If the firm adopts a relational intent in a given situation, it believes that in this particular business, for this given product or types of products, for this particular customer or group of customers, or for the existing competitive situation activating the latent relationships may be a better way of serving the customers than relying on a transactional strategy. The actions taken will be quite different. This has a decisive impact on the *value perception* of customers. By value perception we mean the way and to what extent the value created by a firm is perceived by customer.

The relational intent, contrary to the transactional intent, implies a long-term notion. This does not, however, mean that the firm and the customer always would engage in on-going interaction or dialogue with each other. Sometimes the customer perceives and appreciates the relational intent knowing that the firm will be there for him or her if and when needed. Hence, the long-term notion is there, because of the actions of the firm based on a relational intent, even if no on-going relationship is visible. Of course, customers who are not looking for such a relational intent will not be impressed by such a strategy. If the relationship manifests itself in dialogue and interactions, these may be continuous or discrete, depending on the situation at hand.

Customer Perceived Value in a Relational Context

A focus on value for customers has emerged as an important marketing concept especially during the 1990s.

"Value is considered to be an important constituent of relationship marketing and the ability of a company to provide superior value to its customers is regarded as one of the most successful strategies for the 1990s. This ability has become a means of differentiation and a key to the riddle of how to find a sustainable competitive advantage" (Ravald and Grönroos 1996. p. 19; cf. Heskett *et al.* 1994, Nilson 1992; Treacy and Wiersema 1993).

If transactions are the foundation for marketing, the *value* for customers is more or less totally embedded in the exchange of a product (a physical good or a service) for money. However, if relationships are the base of marketing, the role of the core product becomes blurred. In the case of canned juice, the possibility to give feedback, the feeling that the marketer and the producer care about the opinion of the consumer, add to the value perception of consumers who are interested in this. In the case of industrial robots, to take an example that is very different from a packaged consumer goods, delivery, customer training, maintenance and spare part service, information and documentation about the use of the robot, claims handling and perhaps joint development of the final robots, and a number of other activities, are necessary additions to the core solution—the robot—if the customer is to be satisfied with what has been bought. The firm needs to understand when and how much such efforts are required in a relationship and how they should be delivered to create an added value that meets the value needs of the customer.[3] It is easy to see how the value of the core of the offering becomes highly questionable if the additional services are missing or not good enough. The role of the core product to the value perception of customers is indeed very much blurred in a case like this. Without the value-adding additional services it is highly questionable whether the core product, in this case the industrial robot, has any value at all.

Traditionally, the marketing and consumer behaviour literature mainly includes models of the value of a customer. The value concept from a value-to-customer perspective exists only to a limited extent in the marketing literature (Ravald and Grönroos 1996). There is, however, a growing interest in value from this point of view (cf. Monroe 1991; Peter and Olsen 1993; Zeithaml 1988). There seems to be an agreement that value is a function of what a customer gets, the solution provided by an offering, and the sacrifice of the customer to get this solution. As Zeithaml (1988) puts it "...perceived value is the consumer's overall assessment of the utility of a product based on a perception of what is received and what is given." In a relational context the offering includes both a core product and additional services of various kinds (for instance, as demonstrated by the examples of canned juice and industrial robots). The sacrifice includes a price and also additional costs for the customer that occur from the fact that one is in a relationship with another party. In a relationship context such additional sacrifice can be called *relationship costs* (Grönroos 1992). They can be divided into at least three categories: direct costs, indirect costs, and psychological costs.

Direct relationship costs are costs that follow from a decision to go into a relationship with another party. The customer may have to invest in office space or have a given number of man years available to be able to use, for example, a computer system for administrative purpose. This is a direct cost of engaging in a relationship with a

---

[3] Lele (1994; quoted in Peters 1994) divide the purchasing and consumption or usage processes into three stages—in purchase, product in use, in disposal—and demonstrates how service elements in a relationship correctly used add value over time to the total offering. In business-to-business relationships it would be meaningful to add a pre-purchase stage to the three stages suggested by Lele.

supplier of such a system. *Indirect relationship costs* are costs that occur because the offering does not function as promised: e.g. costs caused by problems to make the computer system function in the intended way, costs of unexpected service needs, costs of delayed deliveries, etc. These costs resemble what in the quality literature is called quality costs, i.e., costs that are caused by quality problems. Finally, the *psychological costs* are caused by the fact that the customer fears or knows that problems in the relationship will occur, which in rum leads to a situation where he or she cannot fully concentrate on other tasks and duties. Direct and indirect relationship costs can be calculated, whereas psychological costs normally can only be perceived.

Another way of looking at value for customers is to distinguish between a core value of an offering and an added value or value added. Hence, *Customer Perceived Value* can be described with the following two equations:

$$\text{Customer Perceived Value (CPV)} = \frac{\text{Core Solution} + \text{Additional Services}}{\text{Price} + \text{Relationship Cost}} \quad [1]$$

$$\text{Customer Perceived Value (CPV)} = \text{Core Value} \pm \text{Added Value} \quad [2]$$

As a relational view is taken. Customer Perceived Value is developing and perceived over time. In Equation [1] the price has a short-term notion, in principle it is paid upon delivery of the core product. However, relationship costs occur over time as the relationship develops, the usefulness of the core solution is perceived and the additional services are experienced. In Equation [2] a long-term notion is also present. The Added Value component is experienced over time as the relationship develops. However, here it is important to observe the double signs. Often added value is treated as if something is always indeed added to a core value. This is clearly not the case, because the added value can also be negative. For example, a good core value of a machine can be decreased or even destroyed by untimely deliveries, delayed service, etc. The additional services do not add a positive value, instead they subtract from the basic core value, i.e. they provide a *negative added value.*

The objective of a successful relational marketing strategy should be to provide a customer with additional services supporting the core of the offering that minimises the indirect and psychological relationship costs. The total offering should be designed so that it does not create unnecessary direct relationship costs.

The Product in a Transactional Context

In a transactional situation the core product is exchanged for money, and not much more in terms of additional services or additional sacrifice is supposed to influence the perceived customer value of the transaction. In the marketing literature the product concept has a key position, for example, as one of the four decision making variables in the transaction-oriented 4 P model of the marketing mix management paradigm.

The core product may be packaged in order to create more interest, but it remains a transactional concept. The *augmented product* notion (cf. Levitt 1969) that has been introduced in the literature includes auxiliary services such as warranties in addition to packaging. Levitt (1969) concluded almost three decades ago that:

> "the *new competition* is not between what companies produce in their factories, but between what they add to their factory output in the form of packaging, services, advertising, customer advice, financing, delivery arrangements, warehousing, and other things that people value" (p.2).

This model has a relational notion, but unfortunately it has been incorporated in translational contexts.

In a relational context value for the customer is not embedded in a transactional exchange of a product for money. Instead customer perceived value is created and perceived over time as the relationship develops. Hence, because the product basically is a transaction-related concept, it becomes less valuable as a means of describing how customer perceived value is created in a relational context.

A product is a result of how various resources, such as people, technologies, raw materials, knowledge and information have been managed so that a number of features that customers in target markets are looking for are incorporated into it. Thus, a product as a more or less pre-fabricated package of resources and features that is ready to be exchanged has evolved. The task of marketing (including sales) is to find out which product features the customers are interested in and to give promises to a segment of potential customers through external marketing activities such as sales and advertising campaigns. If the product includes the features that the customers want, it will almost by itself fulfil the promises that have been given to the customers. This marketing situation is illustrated in the *transactional marketing triangle*[4] in Figure 2.

In Figure 2 the three key parties of marketing in a transactional context are shown. These are the firms represented by a marketing and/or sales department, the market and the product. Normally, marketing (including sales) is the responsibility of a department (or departments) of specialists or the full-time marketers (and salespeople) (cf. Gummesson 1995). Customers are viewed in terms of markets of more or less anonymous individuals. The offering very much revolves around the product, goods or services, as the dominating element. Along the sides of the triangle three key functions of marketing are displayed, namely, to give promises, to fulfil promises, and to enable promises (cf. Calonius 1988; Bitner 1995).[5] Promises are normally given through mass marketing and in business-to-business contexts also through sales.

---

[4] This way of illustrating the field of marketing is adapted from Philip Kotler (1991), who uses it to illustrate the holistic concept of marketing of the Nordic School approach to services marketing and management.

[5] Henrik Calonius (1988) has suggested that the promise concept, and the notion of marketing's role in giving and fulfilment of promises, should be given a central position in marketing. Recently, Mary Jo Bitner (1995) added the expression "enabling promises" in me context of internal marketing.

Figure 2. The Product-Oriented Marketing Perspective: The Transactional Marketing Triangle
Source: Grönroas (1996).

Promises are fulfilled through a number of product features and enabled through the process of continuous product development based on market research performed by full-time marketers and on technological capabilities of the firm. The value customers are looking for is guaranteed by appropriate product features. "The idea of marketing as a sequence of activities giving and fulfilling promises is not expressed explicitly in the transactional marketing literature, probably because it is taken for granted that the products are developed with such features that any promises which external marketing and sales have given are kept" (Grönroos 1996, p. 9).

Beyond Products—Resources and Competencies in a Relational Context

In a relational context resources that are used over time in the relationship have to be managed throughout the relationship. The notion of a product with features that customers are looking for is too simplistic. In many cases it is not known in the beginning of a relationship or at any point of time during an on-going relationship what resources should be used and to what extent and in what configuration they should be used. For example, the service requirements of a machine that has been delivered to a customer may vary, the need to provide training of the customer's personnel and the need to handle claims may vary, and the firm has to adjust its resources and its way of using its resources accordingly.

In Figure 3, the *relational marketing triangle*, marketing in a relational context is illustrated in the same way as transaction marketing was in Figure 2. The relational context of Figure 3 represents marketing as it is developing in a constantly growing number of businesses. As can be seen most elements in the figure are different. The firm may still have a centralised marketing and sales staff, called here the full-time marketers, but they do not represent all the marketers and salespeople of the firm. Markets as masses of more or less anonymous individuals are considered less suitable.

Figure 3. The Resources and Competency Perspective: The Relational Marketing Triangle
Source: Grönroos (1996).

Customers, individual consumers and households and organisational customers alike, like to be treated on a much more individual basis. In principle, no customer must remain anonymous to the firm if this can be justified from an economic or practical standpoint (cf. Peppers and Rogers 1993) or if the customer does not want it.

Furthermore, the product becomes transparent. Instead resources that when they are used create value for the customer are in the forefront. Of course, the product is still there, but it has conceptually been divided into its basic elements, i.e. the various resources, technology, knowledge, etc., that form the product. Depending on type of offering, products as prefabricated packages of resources do exist. However, often there are so many other resources required in the relationship that cannot be prepackaged so that the notion of a product as a prefabricated package of resources becomes less meaningful. And in the case of services that are processes and not things it becomes quite unclear if a product can exist in the first place. Even if service firms try to create products they do not come up with more than to a larger or lesser degree standardised ways of using existing resources in the simultaneous service creation and delivery and service consumption processes.

> "They (service firms) only have a set of resources and, in the best case scenario, a well-planned way of using these resources as soon as the customer enters the arena" (Grönroos 1996, p. 10).

Customer-perceived value follows from a successful and customer-oriented management of resources relative to the customer sacrifice.

For marketers of other types of offerings than services a similar type of situation occurs when the marketing situation is seen from a relational perspective. Actually this follows naturally from the notion that any firm that adopts a relational strategy becomes a service business (cf. Grönroos 1996 and Webster 1994). "A growing number of (manufacturing) industries face a competitive situation for which we ... have coined the term "*service competition*", and have to understand the nature of service management" (Grönroos 1996, p. 13; emphasis added). For a manufacturer the physical good, standardised or complicated, is a core element in the offering, because it is a prerequisite for a successful perceived customer value. Today the core is, however, very seldom enough to create successful results, competitive customer perceived value and a lasting position on the marketplace. What counts is the ability of the firm to manage its resources to create a holistic offering over time that evolves into an acceptable perceived customer value. Too many competitors can offer a similar core of the total offering, and sometimes to a lower price.

In Figure 3 the resources of a firm are divided into five groups: personnel; technology; knowledge and information; customer's time and the customer. Many of the people representing the firm are creating value for customers in manufacturing, deliveries, customer training, claims handling, service and maintenance, etc., and some of them are directly engaged in resales and cross-sales activities. Thus, they are involved in marketing as *part-time marketers* to use an expression coined by Gummesson (1991). Also, other types of resources influence the value perception of the customer, and hence are important from a marketing perspective as well. Technologies, the knowledge that employees have and that is embedded in technical solutions, and the way of managing the customer's time are such resources. Moreover, the customer himself or herself as individual consumer or representing organisations often become a value-generating resource. The impact of customers on the final development or design of a technical solution, or on the timeliness of a service activity may be critical to the value perception of the customer. In the services marketing literature the marketing effect of the performance of such resources is termed *interactive marketing* (cf. Grönroos 1982).

In summary, in a relational approach to marketing the transactional product concept becomes more complicated. The product as a pre-fabricated package of resources has to be broken down into its parts, a *set of resources* needed to create a good customer perceived value. In addition, the firm has to have *competencies* to acquire and/or develop the resources needed. Thus, a *governing system* is needed, whereby the resources are managed and used in such a way that an intended customer perceived value indeed is created for each customer.

Promises given by sales and external marketing are fulfilled through a process of managing the various types of resources. In order to prepare an appropriate set of resources continuous product development in its traditional form is not enough. Instead internal marketing and a continuous development of the competencies and resource structure of the firm are needed.

Conclusion

If marketing is to be developed based on a relational intent and geared to the creation of good customer perceived value, the simplistic concept of a product as a prefabricated package of resources is not sufficient. Instead, one has to go beyond the product concept to understand the value-creating benefits of an offering. In a relational context a core benefit—the technical solution achieved by a physical good or a service—is accompanied by additional services. The number of such services may be very limited, as in the case of canned juice, or large, as in the case of industrial robots. A well-developed and managed set of core benefits and additional services will help the customer to keep the various types of relationship costs down and thus creates a positive added value to the core value of the technical solution. On the other hand, a badly managed set of core benefits and additional services may lead to increased relationship costs and a diminishing positive added value or even a negative added value.

To be able to manage the value creation in a relational context the firm has to focus on the resources—personnel, technologies, knowledge and information, customer's time and the customer itself—as well as on the competencies of the firm to acquire and manage these resources. In this article we have focused on the relationship between a firm and its customers only. The same arguments apply also when discussing the relationship between a firm and, for example, a distributor. In the larger context, when studying the network of vertically and horizontally related partners, the situation gets more complicated. In principle, the same resource-and-competency approach to understanding the "product" in a relational context seems applicable.

References

Bagozzi, R.P. (1995) "Reflections on Relationship Marketing in Consumer Markets", *Journal of the Academy of Marketing Science*, **23**, No. 1, pp. 272–277.

Berry, L.L. (1983), Relationship Marketing, In *Emerging Perspectives of Services Marketing.* (Eds) Berry, L.L. Shostack, G.L. and Upah, G.D., Chicago, Ill.: American Marketing Association, pp. 25–28.

Berry, L.L. and Parasuraman, A. (1993). "Building a New Academic Field—The Case of Services Marketing", *Journal of Retailing*, 69, No. 1, pp. 13–60.

Bitner, M.J. (1995), "Building Service Relationships: It's All About Promises", *Journal of the Academy of Marketing Science*, **23**, No. 4, pp. 246–251.

Blomqvist, R., Dahl, J. and Haeger, T. (1993), *Relationsmarknadsföring. Strategi och metod för servicekonkurrens* (Relationship Marketing. Strategy and Methods for Service Competition). Göteborg, Sweden: IHM Förlag.

Calonius, H. (1988), "A Buying Process Model. In *Innovative marketing—A European Perspective.*" (Eds) Blois, K. and Parkinson, S. Proceedings from the XVIIth Annual Conference of the European Marketing Academy, University of Bradford, England.

Christopher, M., Payne, A. and Ballantyne, D. (1992), *Relationship Marketing. Bringing Quality, Customer Service and Marketing Together.* London: Butterworth.

Grönroos, C. (1982), *Strategic Management and Marketing in the Service Sector* Helsingfors, Finland: Swedish School of Economics and Business Administration (published in 1983 in the U.S. by Marketing Science Institute and in the UK by Studentlitteratur/Chartwell-Bratt).

Grönroos, C. (1992), "Facing the Challenge of Service Competition: The Economies of Service", In *Quality Management in Services* (Eds), Kunst, P. & Lemminck, J. Van Gorcum, Assen, Maastricht, pp. 129–140.

Grönroos, C. (1996), "Relationship Marketing Logic" *Asia-Australia Marketing Journal*, **4**, No. 1, pp. 7–18.

Gummesson, E. (1991), "Marketing Revisited: The Crucial Role of the Part-Time Marketers" *European Journal of Marketing*, **25**, No. 2, pp. 60–67.

Gummesson, E. (1995), *Relationsmarknadsföring. Från 4P till 30R* (Relationship marketing. From 4P to 30R). Malmö, Sweden: Liber-Hermods.

Heskett, J.L., Jones, T.O., Loveman, G.W., Sasser, W.E. and Schelsinger, L.A. (1994), "Putting the Service-Profit Chain to Work" *Harvard Business Review*, March-April, pp. 164–174.

Holmlund, M. and Törnroos, J.-Å. (1996), "What are Relationships in Business Networks. Abstract". In *Interactions, Relationships and Networks.* Gemünden, H.G., Ritter, T. and Walter, A., (Eds). Proceedings of the 12th International Conference on Industrial Marketing and Purchasing, Vol. 2, University of Karlsruhe, Germany, September, pp. 855–856.

Hunt, S.D. and Morgan, R.M. (1994), "Relationship Marketing in the Era of Network Competition. Marketing *Management*, **3**, No. 1, pp. 19–30.

Kotler, P. (1991), *Marketing Management. Analysis, Planning, and Control* (7th Edn.), Englewood Cliffs, NJ.: Prentice-Hall.

Lele, M.M. (1994), "Managing Customer Satisfaction". Seminars in Marketing Management, University of Chicago. Cited in Peters, G., *Benchmarking Customer Service.* New York: Pitman Publishing, pp. 12–15.

Levitt, T. (1969), *The Marketing Mode.* New York: McGraw-Hill.

Monroe, K.B. (1991), *Pricing—Making Profitable Decisions.* New York: McGraw-Hill.

Nilson, T.H. (1992), *Value-Added Marketing: Marketing for Superior Results.* London: McGraw-Hill.

Peter, J.P. and Olson, J.C. (1993), *Consumer Behavior and Marketing Strategy* (3rd Edn). Homewood, IL.: Irwin.

Peppers, D. and Rogers, M. (1993), *One-to-One Future: Building Relatitmships One Customer at a Time.* New York; Currency/Doubleday, 1993.

Ravald, A. and Grönroos, C. (19%). "The Value Concept and Relationship Marketing", *European Journal of Marketing*, **30**, No. 2, pp. 19–30.

Sheth, J.N. and Parvatiyar, A. (Eds) (1994), *Relationship Marketing: Theory, Methods, and Applications*, 1994 Research Conference Proceedings, Center for Relationship Marketing, Emory University, Atlanta, GA, June.

Sheth, J.N. and Parvatiyar, A. (1995), Relationship Marketing in Consumer Markets: Antecedents and Consequences. *"Journal of the Academy of Marketing Science"* **23**, No. 4, pp. 255–271.

Treacy, M. and Wiersema, F. (1993), "Customer intimacy and other value disciplines". *Harvard Business Review*, January–February, pp. 84–93.

Webster, F.E. Jr. (1994), "Executing the New Marketing Concept", *Marketing Management* **3**, No. 1, pp. 9–18.

Zeithaml, V. A. (1988), "Consumer Perceptions of Price, Quality and Value: A Means-End Model and Synthesis of Evidence". *Journal of Marketing*, **52**, July, pp. 2–22.

10

Relationship Marketing: Strategic and Tactical Implications

Management Decision
Vol. 34, No. 3, 1996
pp. 5–14

Christian Grönroos

Discusses the logic of the re-emerging relationship approach to marketing and presents key strategic as well as tactical implications for a firm attempting to apply a relationship marketing strategy. Notes that major changes in the business philosophy may be required if relationship marketing is truly to be adopted. Otherwise the firm may just be paying lip-service to the new philosophy. Using direct marketing techniques and developing partnerships alone are not sufficient. Relationship marketing requires much more than that.

The "New" Relationship Marketing Perspective: Once Upon a Time ...

In a village in ancient China there was a young rice merchant, Ming Hua[1]. He was one of six rice merchants in that village. He was sitting in his store waiting for customers, but the business was not good.

One day Ming Hua realized that he had to think more about the villagers and their needs and desires, and not only distribute rice to those who came into his store. He understood that he had to provide the villagers with more value and not only with the same as the other merchants offered them. He decided to develop a record of his customers' eating habits and ordering periods and to start to deliver rice to them.

To begin with Ming Hua started to walk around the village and knock on the doors of his customers' houses asking how many members were there in the household, how many bowls of rice they cooked on any given day and how big the rice jar of the household was. Then he offered every customer free home delivery and to replenish the rice jar of the household automatically at regular intervals.

For example, in one household of four persons, on average every person would consume two bowls of rice a day, and therefore the household would need eight bowls of rice every day for their meals. From his records Ming Hua could see that the rice jar of that particular household contained rice for 60 bowls or approximately one bag of rice, and that a full jar would last for 15 days. Consequently, he offered to deliver a bag of rice every 15 days to this house.

By establishing these records and developing these new services, Ming Hua managed to create more and deeper relationships with the villagers, first with his old customers, then with other villagers. Eventually he got more business to take care of and, therefore, had to employ more people: one person to keep records of customers, one to take care of bookkeeping, one to sell over the counter in the store, and two to take care of deliveries. Ming Hua spent his time visiting villagers and handling the contacts with his suppliers, a limited number of rice farmers whom he knew well. Meanwhile his business prospered.

This old story from China demonstrates how Ming Hua, the rice merchant, through what today would be called a relationship marketing strategy, changes his role from a transaction-oriented channel member to a value-enhancing relationship manager. Thus, he creates a competitive advantage over his competitors who continue to pursue a traditional strategy. His strategy includes three typical tactical elements of a relationship strategy:

1   seek direct contacts with customers and other stakeholders (such as rice farmers);
2   build a database covering necessary information about customers and others;
3   develop a customer-oriented service system.

We can also distinguish three important strategic issues of a typical relationship marketing approach:

1   to redefine the business as a service business and the key competitive element as service competition (competing with a total service offering instead of with rice alone);
2   to look at the organization from a process management perspective and not from a functionalistic perspective (to manage the process of creating value for the villagers);
3   to establish partnerships and a network to be able to handle the whole service process (close contacts with well-known rice farmers).

The story of Ming Hua tells us first of all that relationship marketing is not something new that has emerged in the 1980s or 1990s. A story of this kind illustrates not only an isolated phenomenon, but a common way of thinking at least in some context at some period of time. In modern western economic history, at least the industrial revolution and the evolution of scientific management[2,3], which helped society to achieve other important goals, in spite of some examples of the contrary, turned relationship thinking into a secondary issue[4]. Mass orientation and the occurrence of the middleman in distribution channels, as well as specialization and the division of labour, became top priorities. The dominance of the mass marketing-oriented and highly management-oriented marketing mix approach to marketing from the 1960s onwards has not allowed for a relationship perspective either [5].

Second, the story of Ming Hua illustrates six key aspects of a successfully implemented relationship marketing strategy, three strategic issues (service business orientation, process management perspective, partnership and network formation) and three tactical issues (direct customer contacts, customer databases, customer-oriented service system). In the rest of this article, relationship marketing as a philosophy will first be touched on, and then the strategic and tactical issues of such a strategy will be examined to some extent.

A Transition from a Product-oriented Approach to a Resource-Oriented Approach

Since the 1960s the marketing mix management approach, with its 4P model, has dominated the marketing literature and marketing research and practice. Academics and practitioners alike have been so preoccupied with this approach that it long ago achieved a paradigmatic position (compare [6,7]). Sometimes the marketing mix is called a model of marketing only. However, it has had, and in many situations still has, such a profound influence on the marketing thought of academics and practitioners as well as on the directions of marketing research and on the organization and implementation of marketing in practice that it is better described as a paradigm, and moreover as the dominating marketing paradigm of the last decades.

Although the Ps are not at all useless as marketing variables, the philosophical foundation of the marketing mix and its Ps are not very well fitted to the competitive situation that has been emerging in most industries in the western world for some time already The mass marketing and transaction orientation, as well as the adversarial approach to customers and the functionalistic organizational solution inherent in the marketing mix approach, do not allow the firm to adjust its market performance to the demands of more and more customers today, i.e. enhanced value around the core product, reliable service to accompany the product, a trustworthy relationship with customers, suppliers, distributors, etc.

It is interesting that these changing demands from the market have had an impact on the strategy field that parallels the development of relationship marketing. The strategic orientation towards core competences am resources as the basis for successful and profitable market relationships stresses the issue of what firms can do *for* customers in the form of a total service offering, rather than what it can do *to* customers with existing products or technologies based on a trans actional marketing mix management approach[8,9].

Figures 1 and 2[10,11] illustrate the shift towards a resource-based relational approach to marketing from a product-based transactional approach. In Figure 1, the three key parties of marketing in a transactional approach are shown. These are the firm represented by a marketing and/or sales department, the market and the product. Marketing (including sales) is the responsibility of a department of specialists. The customers are viewed in terms of markets of more or less anonymous individuals or

Figure 1. The Product-Oriented Marketing Perspective: A Transaction Marketing Approach

Figure 2. The Resource-Oriented Marketing Perspective: A Relationship Marketing Approach

organizations. The offering very much revolves around products. goods or services, as the dominating elements. Along the sides of the triangle, three other key aspects of marketing are depicted: giving promises through external marketing (normally mass marketing) and sales, keeping promises through product features, and preparing for the fulfilment of promises through continuous product development. The idea of marketing as a sequence of activities giving and fulfilling promises is not expressed explicitly in the transactional marketing literature, probably because it is taken for granted that the products are developed with such features that any promises which external marketing and sales have given are kept.

In Figure 2, which represents today's market situation for a constantly growing number of businesses, most of the elements are different. The firm may still have a centralized marketing and sales staff, called here the full-time marketers, but they do not represent all the marketers and salespeople of the firm. Markets as masses of more or less anonymous individuals or organizations no longer exist. Customers, individual customers and households and organizational customers alike, like to be treated on a much more individual basis. In principle, no customer must remain anonymous to the firm.

Finally, the product has disappeared. This is a fundamental element, especially in the Nordic School approach to services. Service companies do not have products in the traditional, well-defined and packaged sense of the marketing mix; however, even though they try to create such products, they only have a set of resources and, in the best case scenario, a well-planned way of using these resources as soon as the customer enters the arena. For manufacturers doing business with organizational buyers and users, a development in the same direction is currently taking place. Hence, regardless of what type of business the firm is operating in, it has to be able to manage key resources so that a successful total offering is developed. This offering, of course, also includes a core product of some sort, which for manufacturers is a physical good, but as this product can be offered by many other competitors in the marketplace it often becomes rather transparent from the customer's point of view. Other elements of the offering which, together with the core product, fulfil the customer's needs, wants, desires and expectations, often in a prolonged time perspective, become imperative to successful fulfilment of promises given by external marketing and sales.

Basically, at least four types of resources to be used to create customer care, including the core product, can be identified: personnel, technology, knowledge and time. Many of the people involved have an effect on the total quality perception and satisfaction of customers, and some may also perform resales and cross-sales activities. Thus, they are involved in marketing. Also, the other types of resources influence satisfaction and the perception of total quality, and hence are important from a marketing perspective as well. This type of marketing is called interactive marketing in the services marketing literature[12]. The issues of what promises are indeed given and how are they to be fulfilled becomes something which has to be explicitly addressed in marketing. Finally, continuous product development is not sufficient any more as a foundation for successful marketing. Continuous development of all types of resources, including internal marketing, becomes important from a marketing point of view.

As the figures demonstrate, the marketing context has changed dramatically. This calls for a new marketing philosophy.

The Relationship Marketing Philosophy

From the 1970s an alternative approach to marketing based on the establishment and management of relationships has emerged within two streams of research emanating from Scandinavia and northern Europe, and eventually spreading to growing parts of the Western world. These streams of research are the Nordic School of Service[13], which looks at management and marketing from a service perspective, and the IMP Group[14], which takes a network and interaction approach to understanding industrial businesses. A common denominator of these two schools of thought is that marketing is more a management issue than a function, and that managing marketing, or market-oriented management as marketing is frequently called, normally has to be built on relationships rather than transactions. Building and managing relationships has become a philosophical cornerstone of the Nordic School of Service and the IMP Group since the late 1970s. However, "relationship marketing" as a term was not used until the latter part of the 1980s. It was first coined in the USA in 1983[15-17], and the relationship marketing approach is spreading there[18-22] and also in an Anglo-Australian context[23].

In the literature there is no agreement on a definition of relationship marketing, even if most definitions have many common denominators. There are, however, differences in scope. A rather comprehensive definition states that: "Relationship marketing is to identify and establish, maintain, and enhance relationships with customers and other stakeholders, at a profit, so that the objectives of all parties involved are met"; and "that this is done by a mutual exchange and fulfilment of promises"[12] (see also [22-29]).

This definition is supplemented by a statement that such a marketing approach should lead to a trusting relationship between the parties involved. Key aspects of such an approach to marketing are that not only getting customers and creating transactions (identifying and establishing) are important, but also maintaining and enhancing ongoing relationships; that not only giving promises is the responsibility of marketing, but also the task of fulfilling promises; and that profitable business relationships rely on the capability of a firm to develop trust in itself and its performance among its customers and other stakeholders. Internal marketing becomes a critical issue in relationship marketing if the organization is to be well prepared for its new marketing tasks[5,24]. In a recent article about relationship marketing, Bitner[30] emphasizes the need for a firm to manage not only the task of giving and fulfilling promises but also the task of enabling the fulfilment of promises if marketing is to be successful.

Another relationship marketing definition by Gummesson[31] points out three key aspects of relationship marketing. He defines relationship marketing as a marketing approach that "is based on relationships, interactions and networks".

In more general terms the Grönroos definition of relationship marketing can be formulated as a generic marketing definition: "Marketing is to manage the firm's market relationships." This definition includes the fundamental notion of marketing as a phenomenon basically related to the relationships between a firm and its environment. It points out that marketing includes all necessary efforts required to prepare the organization for, and implement activities needed to manage, the interfaces with its environment. Markets are, of course, of several kinds: customers, distributors, suppliers, networks of co-operating partners, etc. Transaction-oriented activities heavily relying on the 4Ps are but a special case with uncomplicated and mostly non-personal relationships. This definition makes it possible to develop marketing strategies according to a relational approach or a transactional approach depending on what suits any given market situation best[32].

In none of these definitions is the concept of exchange[33], which for about two decades has been considered a foundation of marketing, included. Focusing on exchange is considered too narrow a view. A relationship includes much more than exchanges, and if a trusting relationship between two or several business partners exists, exchanges should inevitably occur from time to time. However, there is so much more to an ongoing relationship which also has to be taken care of, if exchanges of offerings for money are to take place. Moreover, what actually is exchanged is not very straightforward when products are replaced by management of resources such as personnel, technology, knowledge and time so that the firm can take care of the needs, wants, desires and expectations of its customers and other partners. Hence, the basic concept of marketing is the relationship itself rather than singular exchanges which occur in the relationship. Thus, the concept exchange relationship which is frequently used is a contradiction[34]. Exchange is a concept with a short-term notion where something is given to someone else, whereas relationship has a long-term notion implying an association of two parties. The combination of the two does not make sense.

In order to execute relationship marketing the Ps of the marketing mix, such as advertising, pricing and selling, can and should be applied, but in addition a host of other resources and activities are needed. Most of these additional resources and activities, relating, for example, to delivering, installing, updating, repairing, servicing and maintaining goods or equipment, or to billing, complaints handling, customer education and other activities, are not considered part of the marketing function. Most of the people involved in such activities are not part of a marketing and/or sales department. Nevertheless, their attitudes towards customers and their behaviours and ways of executing their tasks are imperative to successful maintenance and enhancement of customer relationships and other types of market relationships. In many situations their impact is more important to long-term success in the marketplace than that of the full-time marketers. As Evert Gummesson has pointed out, marketing departments (the full-time marketers) "are not able to handle more than a limited portion of the marketing *as its staff cannot be at the right place at the right time with the right customer contacts*"[35]. He has coined the term "part-time marketer"[36] for the people outside marketing departments whose attitudes and behaviours have a decisive marketing impact on customer satisfaction and the quality perception of customers and on their future buying and word-of-mouth behaviour.

This view of marketing is based on a totally different philosophy from the marketing mix management approach. The relationship philosophy relies on co-operation and a trusting relationship with customers (and other stakeholders and network partners) instead of an adversarial approach to customers, on collaboration within the company instead of specialization of functions and the division of labour, and on the notion of marketing as more of a market-oriented management approach with part-time marketers spread throughout the organization than as a separate function for specialists only.

Strategic Issues in Relationship Marketing

The three strategic issues in relationship marketing were identified as:

1   defining the firm as a service business;
2   managing the firm from a process management perspective;
3   developing partnerships and networks.

All three issues will be briefly discussed in this section.

Defining the Firm as a Service Business

A key requirement in a relationship marketing strategy is that a manufacturer, whole-saler, retailer, a service firm or any supplier knows the long-term needs and desires of customers better and offers added value on top of the technical solution embedded in consumer goods, industrial equipment or services. Customers do not only look for goods or services, they demand a much more holistic service offering including every-thing from information about how best and most safely to use a product, to deliver-ing, installing, updating, repairing, maintaining and correcting solutions they have bought. And they demand all this, and much more, in a friendly, trustworthy and timely manner. Levitt's[36] conclusion in an article about what should accompany the sale of the mere product, "having been offered these extras, the customer finds them beneficial and therefore prefers to do business with the company that supplies them", is even more true in today's business environment.

In a customer relationship that goes beyond a single transaction of a product, the product itself as a technical solution involving goods, services or industrial equipment becomes just one element in the total, ongoing service offering. For a manufacturer, the physical good is a core element of the service offering, of course, because it is a prerequisite for a successful offering. In today's competitive situation this core is very seldom enough to produce successful results and a lasting position on the mar-ketplace. What counts is the ability of the firm, regardless of its position in the distribution channel, to manage the additional elements of the total offering better than the competitors. Moreover, the core product is less often the reason for dissat-isfaction than the elements surrounding the core. As Webster[21, p. 13] exemplifies, "the automobile purchaser is unhappy with the car because of lousy service from the dealer; the insurance customer has problems with the agent, not with the policy". In other words, competing with the core of the offering is not enough, compet-ing with the total offering, where the core product becomes only one element, or rather one service, of the total service offering is what counts. The transition from the product as the dominating element of the offering to management of human resources, technology, knowledge and time for the firm to create successful market offerings is evident.

In Figure 3 the black arrow from the factory towards the customer demonstrates the traditional product-oriented approach, where the factory and the management of what takes place in the factory are considered the key to success in the marketplace. Services are considered add-ons to the factory output. The so-called scientific manage-ment philosophy or "Taylorism"[3] with its roots in the turn of the century is based on this factory focus. However, although this approach to management has been highly successful in the past, it does not reflect the current competitive situation any more. As we are approaching the turn of the millennium, a new management perspective is needed. As is indicated by the second arrow in the figure, from the customer towards the factory, the various service elements of the firm are the first elements of the output of the firm that the customer sees and perceives. The various service elements create

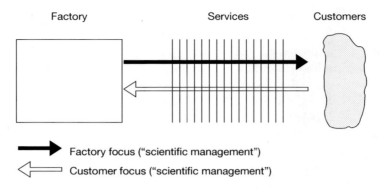

Figure 3. A Customer Focus: The Firm as a Service Business

added value for the customer, whereas the factory output is only a necessary prerequisite for value.

A growing number of industries, manufacturers and service firms alike, face a competitive situation for which we, in another context, have coined the term "service competition", and have to understand the nature of service management as a new management approach geared to the demands of the new competitive situation[4]. The product seen as a total service offering thus becomes a service. Today the firm which does not understand that but continues to compete as if the core product was the most important, or in the worst case the only important, element in the offering, will undoubtedly suffer hardships and eventually fail. When service competition is the key to success for practically everybody and the product has to be defined as a service, every business is a service business[21].

A Process Management Perspective

An ongoing relationship with customers, where customers look for value in the total service offering, requires internal collaboration among functions and departments which are responsible for different elements of the offering, such as the core product itself, advertising the product, delivering the product, taking care of complaints and recovering mistakes and quality faults, maintaining the product, billing routines, product documentation, etc. The whole chain of activities has to be co-ordinated and managed as one total process. Moreover, from profitability and productivity perspectives only activities which produce value for customers should be tolerated. Other resources and activities need to be excluded from the process. In a traditional, functionalistic, organizational setting this can hardly be achieved. Therefore, relationship marketing for the same reasons as modern lean management principles requires a process management approach.

A process management perspective is very different from the functionalistic management approach based on scientific management. Functions and a functionalistic

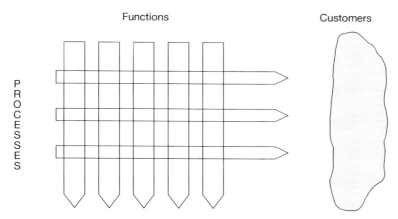

Functions   Customers

Figure 4. A Process Focus: The Firm as a Value-generating Operation

organization allow for suboptimization, because each function and corresponding department is more oriented towards specialization within its function than collaboration between functions. As is indicated in Figure 4, the various functions are not necessarily directing their efforts towards the demands and expectations of the customers. This easily creates subvalues but not total value. Customers are not looking for a combination of sub-optimized output which does not support a total value for them. For example, an outstanding technical solution and a cost-effective transportation system may be optimal from the supplier's point of view, but for the customer it is often equivalent to an unreliable supplier, i.e. low value.

Project and taskforce organizations are first attempts to break free from the straitjacket of a functionalistic organization, so that the various functions are geared towards working according to the horizontal arrows in Figure 4. However, in order to be able to produce maximum total value in a co-ordinated relationship with customers, the firm has to go much further. A process management approach to the whole operation of the firm has to be taken. Traditional departmental boundaries are torn down and the workflow, including traditional sales and marketing activities, productive, administrative and distributive activities with a host of part-time marketing activities involved, are organized and managed as value-creating processes which enable and strengthen relationship building and management.

Partnerships and Networks

As relationship marketing is based on cooperation rather than an adversarial situation, firms will not view one another from a win-lose perspective, but will rather benefit from a win-win situation, where the parties involved will be best off as partners. Furthermore, manufacturers and service firms will frequently find that they cannot supply customers with the total offering needed on their own, and that it would be too expensive to acquire the necessary additional knowledge and resources to produce the required elements of the offering themselves. Hence, it may be more effective and profitable to find a partner to supply the complementary elements of the offering needed to develop a successful relationship with a customer[37]. Partnerships and networks of firms are formed horizontally and vertically in the distribution channel and in the supply chain. As Hunt and Morgan[22, p. 25] put it, "the paradox of relationship marketing is that being an effective competitor in the era of network competition also means being an effective co-operator". This, of course, demands the existence of one of the key ingredients of relationship marketing, trust between the parties in a network; otherwise they will not feel committed to the mutual cause.

Tactical Issues in Relationship Marketing

Three tactical elements of a relationship marketing strategy were identified in the beginning of the article:

1   seeking direct contacts with customers;
2   building a database;
3   developing a customer-oriented service system.

In this section we shall discuss each of them separately.

Seeking Direct Contacts with Customers

Relationship marketing is based on a notion of trusting co-operation with known customers. Hence, firms have to get to know their customers much better than is the case today In the extreme case, which is quite possible in many consumer service markets such as household insurance and industrial markets (e.g. merchant banking and the paper and pulp industry), the firm can develop segments of one customer[38]. In the other extreme (consumer goods to mass markets), customers cannot be identified in the same way. However, manufacturers or retailers should develop systems which provide them with as much information about their customers as possible so that, for example, advertising campaigns, sales contacts and complaints situations can be made as relationship-oriented as possible. Modern information technology provides the firm with ample opportunities to develop ways of showing a customer that he or she is known. Also, traditional advertising campaigns become too expensive and ineffective if they cannot be better directed towards at least more or less well-known customers so that a dialogue can be initiated. Pure one-way market communication costs too much and produces too little[39,40].

Quite regardless of how close to the ideal situation of segments of one customer a firm can get, one should always use available face-to-face contacts with customers, or means provided by information technology, to get as close as possible to the customers.

Developing a Database

Traditionally, marketing operates with little and incomplete information about customers. In order to pursue a relationship marketing strategy, the firm cannot let such ignorance last. A database consisting of customer information files has to be established[41,42]. If such a database does not exist, customer contacts will be handled only partially in a relationship-oriented manner. If the person involved in a particular interaction with a customer has first-hand information about the customer and knows the persons he or she is in contact with, the interaction may go well. However, in many situations, people who, for example, answer customers' phone calls, meet a customer at a reception desk or make maintenance calls, etc. will not be personally familiar with the customer. A well-prepared, updated, easily retrievable and easy-to-read customer information file is needed in such cases to make it possible for the employee to pursue a relationship-oriented customer contact. In addition, a good database will be an effective support for cross-sales and new product offerings.

In addition to the primary use of databases to maintain customer relationships, databases can be used for a variety of marketing activities, such as segmenting the customer base, tailoring marketing activities, generating profiles of customer types, supporting service activities and identifying high-likelihood purchasers[41].

A customer information file for relationship marketing purposes should also include profitability information, so that one knows the long-term profitability of the customers in the database, a measure for which Storbacka has coined the term "customer relationship profitability"[43]. If such long-term profitability information is lacking, the firm may easily include segments of unprofitable customers in its customer base.

Creating a Customer-oriented Service System

Because successfully executed relationship marketing demands that the firm defines its business as a service business and understands how to create and manage a total service offering, i.e. manage service competition, the value-generating processes of the organization have to be designed to make it possible to serve customers and produce and deliver a total service offering. In other words, the firm has to know service management[12,44]. The philosophy and principles of service management are in many respects decisively different from those of scientific management[45]. Four types of resources are central to the development of a successful service system; employees, technology, customers and time.

Customers take a much more active role than they normally are given. The perceived quality of the service offering depends partly on the impact of the customer and indeed, fellow customers. The service system is, to a growing extent, built on technology. Computerized systems and information technology used in design, production, administration, service and maintenance have *to* be designed from a customer-service perspective, and not only or mainly from internal production and productivity-oriented viewpoints. The success of relationship marketing is, to a large extent, dependent on the attitudes, commitment and performance of the employees. If they are not committed to their role as part-time marketers and are not motivated to perform in a customer-oriented fashion, the strategy fails. Hence, success on the external market-place requires initial success internally in motivating employees and getting their commitment to the pursuit of a relationship marketing strategy Relationship marketing is, therefore, highly dependent on a well-organized and continuous internal marketing process[12, chs 10,11; 46]. Time is also a critical resource to manage (see Figure 2). Customers have to feel that the time they spend in the relationship with a supplier or service firm is not wasted. Badly managed time creates extra costs for all parties in a relationship.

Towards a Relational Strategy: The Transition Curve

If a firm is truly to implement a relationship marketing strategy, it has to understand the philosophical nature of such a strategy. Although traditional means of competition, such as the 4Ps of the marketing mix, are still applicable, relationship marketing is based on a totally different philosophy of how to approach customers and other stakeholders. Common mistakes when discussing relationship marketing follow from a failure to understand this philosophical shift. We have to realize that it is a new paradigm, not just a new model that is emerging. Sometimes relationship marketing is used more or less as a synonym for direct marketing or database marketing, or for establishing customer clubs, and it becomes just another instrument in the marketing mix toolbox to be used in accordance with the marketing mix management philoso-phy In other situations, relationship marketing is used as a synonym for developing partnerships, alliances and networks. However, it is much more than that and, as has been demonstrated in this article, forming partnerships and networks is only one strategic aspect of developing and implementing a relationship marketing strategy.

In Figure 5 the nature of the transition from a product-based transaction marketing approach to a resource-based and competences-related relationship marketing strategy is schematically illustrated as a transition curve[47]. In the beginning, firms which wish to implement a relationship marketing approach are normally still very focused on their products. Hence, only easily developed relational activities are introduced. Typical examples are customized sales letters and information bulletins, and customer clubs, etc. Such activities easily backfire, especially if the customer is mistreated in other respects, for example when using a service, in a recovery or complaints situation or in almost any interaction with the firm. Firms in this stage do not yet fully understand the philosophical nature of relationship marketing. Singular exchanges are still the basic focus of marketing. Today, most firms which apply a relationship marketing approach are probably somewhere in this stage of the transition process. A true transition towards a relationship marketing strategy requires a focus on competences and resources (see Figure 2) in the relationship. The relationship itself becomes the focus of marketing. It is understood that the products themselves are transparent from

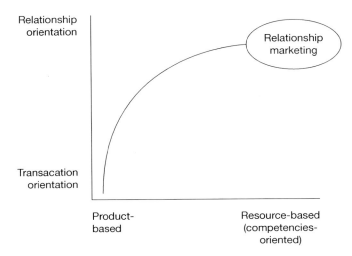

Figure 5. Changes in the Marketing Paradigm: The Transition Curve

Source: Adapted from [47].

the customer's point of view. Gradually a firm may approach a position on the transition curve where relationship marketing both as a philosophy and a way of behaviour is genuinely appreciated.

Every firm, regardless of its business, can benefit from a relationship marketing approach. In some situations, such as business-to-business situations and for service industries, this approach is easier to implement; in others (for many consumer goods industries), it is more difficult. However, in the business environment and marketing situation that is emerging in more and more industries and on an ever-growing number of markets, a relationship marketing strategy is becoming a necessity for survival. Relationship marketing is the biggest paradigmatic shift marketing theory and practice has seen during the last 50 years. It is taking marketing thought back to its roots[48].

Notes and References

1   I was told the story of Ming Hua, the Chinese rice merchant, by students attending a course on service management which I am teaching in an executive programme at Thammasat University in Bangkok.

2   Smith, A., *The Wealth of Nations. An Inquiry into the Nature and Cause of the Wealth of Nations*, Methuen, London, 1950 (the original published 1776).

3   Taylor, F.W., *Scientific Management*, Harper & Row, 1947 (a volume of two papers originally published in 1903 and 1911 and a written testimony for a Special House Committee in the USA in 1912).

4   Grönroos, C., "From scientific management to service management. A management perspective for the age of service competition", *International Journal of Service Industry Management*, Vol. 5 No. 1, 1994, pp. 5-20.

5   Grönroos, C., "Quo vadis, marketing? Toward a relationship marketing paradigm", *Journal of Marketing Management*, Vol. 10, 1994, pp. 347-60.

6   Kuhn, T.S., *The Copernican Revolution*, Harvard University Press, Cambridge, MA, 1957.

7   Kuhn, T.S., *The Structure of Scientific Revolutions*, The University of Chicago Press, Chicago, IL, 1962.

8   Hamel, G. and Prahalad, C.K., *Competing for the Future. Breakthrough Strategies for Seizing Control of your Industry and Creating the Markets for Tomorrow*, Harvard Business School Press, Boston, MA, 1994.

9   Dixon, D.F. and Blois, K.J., *Some Limitations of the 4Ps as a Paradigm for Marketing*, Marketing Education Group Annual Conference, Cranfield Institute of Technology, July 1983. (The authors claim that the 4Ps of the marketing men are more oriented towards doing something *to* the customer rather than *for* the customer).

10 This way of illustrating the field of marketing is adapted from Philip Kotler[11], who uses it to illustrate the holistic concept of marketing of the Nordic School approach to services marketing and management.

11 Kotler, P., *Marketing Management. Analysis, Planning, and Control*, (7th ed.), Prentice-Hall, Englewood Cliffs, NJ, 1991.

12 Grönroos, C., *Service Management and Marketing. Managing the Moments of Truth in Service Competition*, Free Press/Lexington Books, Lexington, MA, 1990.

13 Berry, L.L. and Parasuraman, A., "Building a new academic field—the case of services marketing", *Journal of Retailing*, Vol. 69 No. 1, 1993, pp. 13-60.

14 Håkansson, H. (Ed.), *International Marketing and Purchasing of Industrial Goods*, Wiley, New York, NY, 1982.

15 Berry, L.L., "Relationship marketing", in Berry, L.L., Shostack, G.L. and Upah, G.D. (Eds), *Emerging Perspectives of Service Markeing*, American Marketing Association, Chicago, IL, 1983, pp. 25-8.

16 Berry, L.L., "Relationship marketing of services—growing interest, emerging perspectives", *Journal of the Academy of Marketing Science*, Vol. 23 No. 4, 1995, pp. 236-45.

17 Sheth, J.N. and Parvatiyar, A., "Relationship marketing in consumer markets—antecedent and consequences", *Journal of the Academy of Marketing Science*, Vol. 23 No. 4, 1995, pp. 255-71.

18 *Marketing Science Institute Review*, "Philip Kotler explores the new marketing paradigm", *Marketing Science Institute Review*, Spring 1991.

19 Kotler, P., "It's time for total marketing", *Business Week ADVANCE Executive Brief*, Vol. 2, 1992, pp. 1, 4-5.

20 Webster, F.E. Jr, "The changing role of marketing in the corporation", *Journal of Marketing*, Vol. 56, October 1992, pp. 1-7.

21 Webster, F.E. Jr, "Executing the new marketing concept", *Marketing Management*, Vol. 3 No. 1, 1994, pp. 9-18.

22 Hunt, S.D. and Morgan, R.M., "Relationship marketing in the era of network competition", *Marketing Management*, Vol. 3 No. 1, 1994, pp. 19-30.

23 Christopher, M., Payne, A. and Ballantyne, D., *Relationship Marketing. Bringing Quality, Customer Service and Marketing Together*, Butterworth, London, 1992.

24 Grönroos, C., "Relationship approach to the marketing function in service contexts: the marketing and organizational behavior interface", *Journal of Business Research*, Vol. 20 No 1, 1990, pp. 3-12.

25 Recently Shelby Hunt has offered a definition with the same meaning, see [22, p. 23].

26 In a similar way, Sheth and Parvatiyar[27] define relationship marketing as "the understanding, explanation and management of the ongoing collaborative business relationship between suppliers and customer".

27 Sheth, J.N. and Parvatiyar, A. (Eds), *Relationship Marketing: Theory, Methods, and Applications, 1994 Research Conference Proceedings*, Center for Relationship Marketing, Emory University, Atlanta, GA, June 1994, p. 2.

28 Blomqvist, R., Dahl, J. and Haeger, T., *Relation smarknads-föring. Strategi och metod för servicekonkurren (Relationship Marketing. Strategy and Methods for Service Competition)*, IHM Förlag, Göteborg, 1993.

29   Sheth, J.N. and Parvatiyar, A., "The evolution of relationship marketing", *International Business Review*, Vol. 4 No. 4,1995, pp. 397-418.

30   Bitner, M.J., "Building service relationships: it's all about promises", *Journal of the Academy of Marketing Science*, Vol. 23 No. 4,1995, pp. 246-51.

31   Gummesson, E., *Relationsmarknadsföring. Från 4P till 30R (Relationship Marketing. From 4P to 30R)*, Liber-Hermods, Malmö, 1995.

32   Grönroos, C., "Relationship marketing: the strategy continuum", *Journal of the Academy of Marketing Science*, Vol. 23 No. 4, 1995, pp. 252-4.

33   Baggozzi, R.P., "Marketing as exchange", *Journal of Marketing*, Vol. 39, October 1975, pp. 32-9.

34   Craig-Lees, M. and Caldwell, M., *Relationship Marketing: An Opportunity to Develop a Viable Marketing Framework, 1994 Research Conference Proceedings,* Center for Relationship Marketing, Emory University, Atlanta, GA, June 1994.

35   Gummesson, C., *The Part-time Marketer*, Centre for Service Research, Karlstad, 1990.

36   Gummesson, E., *The Part-time Marketer*, Centre for Service Research, Karlstad, 1990

37   Ring, P.S. and Van de Ven, A.H., "Structuring cooperative relationships between organizations", *Strategic Management Journal*, Vol. 13, 1992, pp. 483-98.

38   Peppers, D. and Rogers, M., *One-to-One Future: Building Relationships One Customer at a Time*, Currency/Doubleday, New York, NY, 1993.

39   Rapp, S. and Collins, T., *The Great Marketing Turnaround*, Prentice-Hall, Englewood Cliffs, NJ, 1990.

40   McKenna, R., *Relationship Marketing. Successful Strategies for the Age of the Customer*, Addison-Wesley, Reading, MA, 1991.

41   Vavra, T.G., "The database marketing imperative", *Marketing Management*, Vol. 2 No. 1, 1994, pp. 47-57.

42   The author of[41] describes how and by whom such a customer information file should be developed and what it should consist of.

43   Storbacka, K., *The Nature of Customer Relationship Profitability. Analyses of Relations and Customer Bases in Retail Banking*, Swedish School of Economics and Business Administration, Helsingfors, 1994.

44   The term "service management" was originally introduced in Normann, R., *Service Management*, Wiley, New York, NY, 1984 (published in Swedish in 1982).

45   See the special issue on service management of the *International Journal of Service Industry Management*, Vol. 5 No. 1, 1994.

46   George, W.R. and Grönroos, C., "Developing consumer-conscious employees at every level", in Congram, C. A. and Friedman, M.L. (Eds), *Handbook of Marketing for the Service Industry*, AMACON, New York, NY, 1991, pp. 85-100.

47   Strandvik, T., *Visionär kvalitet (Visionary Quality)*, Research report, Swedish School of Economics and Business Administration, Helsingfors, 1995 (forthcoming).

48   Grönroos, C., *The Rebirth of Modern Marketing—Six Propositions about Relationship Marketing*, Working paper, Swedish School of Economics and Business Administration, Helsingfors, 1995.

Application Questions

1   Write a shout description of your organization without reference to products, i.e. as a "set of resources ... and a well-planned way of using these resources as soon as the customer enters the arena".

2   What are your key marketing promises? What are your assurance strategies to keep them?

3   Is relationship marketing the conceptual and practical way we will approach marketing in the future?

11

Relationship Marketing: The Strategy Continuum

Journal of the Academy of Marketing Science
Vol. 23, No. 4, 1995
pp. 252–254

Christian Grönroos

Service firms have always been relationship oriented. The nature of service businesses is relationship based. A service is a process or performance where the customer is involved, sometimes for a long period of time, sometimes only for a short moment, and sometimes on a regular basis, sometimes only as a one-time encounter. There is always a direct contact between a customer and the service firm. This contact makes it possible to create a relationship with the customer, if both parties are interested in such a way of doing business. As service firms, like banks, insurance firms, transportation companies, and retailers, have grown, the masses of customers have made the establishment of true relationships more difficult. In growing service businesses, the customer was turned from a relationship partner into market share statistics.

There are two obvious reasons for this. First, the difficulty to administer a relationship-oriented customer contact when the number of customers is increasing. Second, the growing influence from popular consumer goods-based, nonrelational marketing approaches. The marketing mix management paradigm and its flagship, the 4P model, established itself as the dominating marketing paradigm. At that time, especially during the 1960s and 1970s, this approach to marketing made sense for producers of consumer goods with their nonrelational customer contact. To a considerable degree it makes sense still today, although even in goods marketing a relational approach is called for (e.g., McKenna 1991; Rapp and Collins 1990). The nonmarketing approach did not meet the needs of service firms seeking relational customer contacts. Instead of focusing on the customer contacts, marketing became preoccupied with campaigns and other short-term activities where the interest in getting new customers dominated the task of keeping customers. Marketing was almost totally in the hands of marketing specialists organized in marketing departments. The people in the rest of the organization who in fact took care of the customers by producing and delivering the service to them more and more were forced to pay attention to other aspects of their job than satisfying customers. The relational-based service businesses became mass marketing oriented.

It is quite natural that the seeds of modern relationship marketing first started to grow in service marketing research. In fact, service marketing started to develop as a discipline because the marketing mix management paradigm and some of its key models fitted service firms' customer relations badly (see, for example, Rathmell 1974). The notion of the need to *market services internally* to the personnel first (Eiglier and Langeard 1976; George 1977; Grönroos 1978; Berry 1981), the *interactive marketing* concept (Grönroos 1979), the *customer relationship life cycle* concept (Grönroos 1982/1983), and *the part-time marketer* notion (Gummesson 1987) are relationship marketing notions and concepts that are derived from the relational customer interface of service firms. Many of these concepts were early developed within what has been called the *Nordic School of Services* (Grönroos and Gummesson 1985; see also Berry and Parasuraman 1993). In a 1983 conference paper, Berry (1983) finally introduced the concept *relationship marketing*.

However, even if the customer contacts of service firms are relational in nature, some contacts are such that no relationships could be established. A traveler who decides to stay at a hotel in a town where he never has been before and does not expect to return is not a profitable target for a relationship approach. Instead, transaction marketing that aims at getting the traveler to choose this particular hotel is probably a good marketing strategy in this case. Moreover, some customers do not wish to get involved in a relational association with a service firm (see Barnes 1994). Clearly there are situations where an orientation toward getting customers or a transaction marketing approach makes more sense than a relationship marketing approach.

A relationship marketing strategy is well applicable in service businesses, whereas a transaction marketing strategy often fits the marketing situation of a consumer goods company. However, there are situations where both types of firms benefit from taking another marketing approach. Of course, there are a number of mixed strategies where the relationship elements or the transaction elements, respectively, dominate. As I in another context (Grönroos 1991) have observed, the marketing strategies available can be seen as a continuum with a relationship-oriented strategy on one end and a transaction-oriented strategy on the other end. In the next section, we shall take a closer look at the implications of this continuum.

The Marketing Strategy Continuum

A relationship type of approach is long term in nature, whereas transaction marketing is more oriented toward short-term goals. One can say that the goal of transaction marketing is to get customers, whereas the goal of relationship marketing is to get *and keep* customers. Keeping customers becomes more important (although getting customers of course is the basis for having any customers to keep) because it is normally less expensive to make a satisfied existing customer buy more compared to what it costs to get a new customer. The economic consequences of reducing the customer defection rate are considerable (Reichheld and Sasser 1990).

The marketing implications across the strategy continuum (relationship versus transaction) are substantially different concerning the dominating marketing orientation, dominating quality function, customer information system, interdependency between business functions, and the role of internal marketing (Grönroos 1991).

Dominating marketing orientation. First of all, a relationship strategy requires that marketing is not restricted to the marketing mix activities. The interactive marketing effect of the production and delivery processes have a profound effect on the inclination of a customer to return. The "part-time marketers" of an organization (Gummesson 1987), who are not part of the marketing department and not reporting to a marketing manager, are the key marketing resources in a relationship marketing strategy. When the part-time marketers, with their dual responsibilities, do their job correctly and in an efficient manner and while doing so make a favorable marketing impact on the customer, they often either make or break the relationship. Of course, they are supported by back-office functions and physical resources, such as information systems and ATMs, but their role in the relationship is paramount. In transaction marketing, their role is more or less negligible. Instead, marketing mix activities, such as advertising campaigns and price offers, form the core of marketing. Such activities are of course not without importance in relationship marketing either, but they should more be seen as supporting interactive marketing and the part-time marketers. Interactive marketing and the part-time marketers are at the heart of relationship marketing.

Dominating quality dimension. Customers' considerations of quality will typically differ depending on what type of strategy the firm uses. In a transaction marketing strategy, it is normally enough if the output has an acceptable quality. The benefits sought by the customers are embedded in the technical solution provided by the core product. *What* the customer gets as the end result of the production process, which in service contexts is called output quality or technical quality, determines the level of satisfaction with quality. However, in order to start developing an ongoing relationship with a customer, the firm must be able to offer a good interaction process as well. All the interactions with the firm, with its contact personnel, information systems, and physical resources, have to support the quality perception of the customer. The *functional quality* or the impact of the interaction process, *how* the service production and delivery process itself is perceived, grows in importance, and in many cases becomes dominating. Of course, the technical quality has to be on an acceptable level, but it is no longer the only quality dimension of importance, and its part of the total perception of quality may even be marginal as long as it remains acceptable. If the part-time marketers are doing a good job and the interactive marketing effect is good, the functional quality impact will be favorable as well. Hence there is an obvious connection between functional quality and interactive marketing.

Customer information system. A firm pursuing a transaction marketing strategy normally has no or limited direct customer contacts. It relies on ad hoc customer satisfaction surveys and market share statistics to get information about the behavior and satisfaction of its customers. The customer base is managed indirectly through information systems that treat customers as numbers. Of course market share measures give important information about the relative number of customers a given firm has, but the firm does not know how satisfied its customers are or the defection rate of its customer base. Ad hoc studies may give additional information about these issues, but a real touch with the customer base is lacking. Market share and ad hoc surveys give a faceless proxy indication of satisfaction or dissatisfaction. Service firms, however, have natural direct contacts with their customers, and hence they can develop direct ways of managing their customer information systems. Customer satisfaction can be monitored by directly managing the customer base. The firm has at least some kind of direct knowledge of how satisfied its customers are. Instead of thinking in anonymous numbers, or market share, it thinks in terms of people with personal reactions and opinions. This of course gives quicker and much more accurate information about how customer satisfaction or dissatisfaction is developing. A firm that applies a relationship marketing strategy should monitor customer satisfaction by directly managing its customer base.

Interdependency between marketing, operations, and human resources. The level of interdependency between functions and departments in an organization depends on whether the firm has chosen a transaction-type strategy or a relationship-type strategy. In transaction marketing where the marketing mix activities dominate and constitute all or most of the elements of the customer relationship, the marketing department can take care of the marketing function. People in other functions and departments do not have to act as part-time marketers. Therefore, the interface between marketing and other functions have limited or no strategic importance to the firm. The situation is quite different for a firm that applies a relationship marketing strategy. There the interactive marketing function becomes critical to success, which requires a good cooperation between marketing and operations. And in order to ensure that the part-time marketers of the operations function accept their marketing role, the human resources function gets involved as well. Hence the interface between at least these three functions becomes important to the success of the firm.

Internal marketing. Preparing the part-time marketers for their marketing tasks is of course a paramount part of a relationship marketing strategy. The firm has to take an active approach to get the commitment to a marketing-like behavior of the personnel and to develop service and communication skills in the organization. The more persons in the firm who are involved in the marketing function as part-time marketers, the greater the need for active internal marketing. Hence it can be concluded that there is limited need for internal marketing in connection with a transaction marketing strategy, whereas a relationship marketing strategy requires a thorough and ongoing internal marketing process.

Conclusion

Few service firms will apply a pure transaction marketing strategy. Even highly standardized service operations include direct contacts with customers, and the customers do perceive the production and delivery process. Hence there are part-time marketers and functional quality effects, so we cannot talk about a pure transaction marketing situation. However, the more standardized the process is, the more dominating is the core service and the technical quality of the outcome of the production and delivery process and the less difficult it is to manage the personnel from a marketing point of view. Firms can position their strategic approach along the strategy continuum, and the more a relationship-type strategy is called for, the more has to be invested in interactive marketing, the functional quality impact, and internal marketing. In such a situation, it is at the same time more important to create information systems where the firm is managing its customer base directly and not relying on market share statistics and ad hoc customer surveys.

References

Barnes, James G 1994. "The Issues of Establishing Relationships With Customers in Service Companies. When are Relationships Feasible and What Form Should They Take?" Paper presented at the Third Frontiers in Services Conference, American Marketing Association and Vanderbilt University, Nashville, TN, October.

Berry, Leonard L 1981. "The Employee as Customer" *Journal of Retail Banking* (March): 33-40.

———. 1983. "Relationship Marketing." In *Emerging Perspectives on Services Marketing* Eds. Leonard L. Berry, G. Lynn Shostack, and Gregory Upah Chicago, IL: American Marketing Association, 25-8.

Berry, Leonard L. and A Parasuraman. 1993 "Building a New Academic Field—The Case of Services Marketing." *Journal of Retailing* 69 (Spring): 13-60.

Eiglier, Pierre and Eric Langeard. 1976 *Principes de politique marketing pour les enterprises de service* [Principles of Marketing Policy for Service Firms] Research report. I A E. Université d'Aix-Marseille, France, December.

George, William R. 1977. "The Retailing of Services. A Challenging Future." *Journal of Retailing* 53 (Fall). 85-98.

Grönroos, Christian 1978. "A Service-Oriented Approach to the Marketing of Services" *European Journal of Marketing* 8 (12). 588-602.

———. 1979. *Marknadsförnng av tjänster En studie av marknadsforingsfunktionen i tjänsteforetag* [The Marketing of Services A Study of the Marketing Function in Service Firms] Stockholm, Sweden Akademilitteratur/Marknadstekniskt centrum.

Grönroos, Christian 1983. *Strategic Management and Marketing in the Service Sector.* Cambridge, MA. Marketing Science Institute (Original work published 1982, Swedish School of Economics and Business Administration, Helsingfors, Finland).

———. 1991 "The Marketing Strategy Continuum. Toward a Marketing Concept for the 1990s" *Management Decision* 29 (1) 7-13.

Grönroos, Christian and Evert Gummesson 1985 *Service Marketing—A Nordic School Perspective* Research report Stockholm, Sweden Stockholm University.

Gummesson, Evert 1987 "The New Marketing—Developing Long-Term Interactive Relationships." *Long Range Planning* 20 (4) 10-20.

McKenna, Regis 1991 *Relationship Marketing Successful Strategies for the Age of the Customer* Reading, MA Addison-Wesley.

Rapp, Stan and Tom Collins. 1990 *The Great Marketing Turnaround* Englewood Cliffs, NJ Prentice Hall.

Rathmell, John M 1974 *Marketing in the Service Sector* Cambridge, MA Winthrop.

Reichheld, Frederick F and Earl W Sasser, Jr 1990 "Zero Defections Quality Comes to Service." *Harvard Business Review* 68 (September-October) 105-11.

12

From Marketing Mix to Relationship Marketing: Towards a Paradigm Shift in Marketing

Management Decision (Lead article)
Vol. 32, No. 2, 1994, pp. 4–20 (MCB University Press Award for Literary Excellence 1994; republished in 1997); also published in *Asia/Australia Journal of Marketing* Vol. 2, No. 1, 1994, pp. 9–30

Christian Grönroos

Has today's dominant marketing mix paradigm become a strait-jacket? A relationship building and management approach may be the answer

The marketing mix management paradigm has dominated marketing thought, research and practice since it was introduced almost 40 years ago. Today, this paradigm is beginning to lose its position[1-3]. New approaches have been emerging in marketing research. The globalization of business and the evolving recognition of the importance of customer retention and market economies and of customer relationship economics, among other trends, reinforce the change in mainstream marketing.

Relationship building and management, or what has been labelled *relationship marketing*, is one leading new approach to marketing which eventually has entered the marketing literature[2, 4-14]. A paradigm shift is clearly under way. In services marketing, especially in Europe and Australia but to some extent also in North America, and in industrial marketing, especially in Europe, this paradigm shift has already taken place. Books published on services marketing[15-17] and on industrial marketing[18-20] as well as major research reports published are based on the relationship marketing paradigm.

A major shift in the perception of the fundamentals of marketing is taking place. The shift is so dramatic that it can, no doubt, be described as a paradigm shift[21]. Marketing researchers have been passionately convinced about the paradigmatic nature of marketing mix management and the Four P model[22]. To challenge marketing mix management as the basic foundation for all marketing thinking has been as heretic as it was for Copernicus to proclaim that the earth moved[23, 24].

The purpose of this report is to discuss the nature and consequences of the dominating marketing paradigm of today, marketing mix management of the managerial school (cf.[25]) and how evolving trends in business and modern research into, for example, industrial marketing, services marketing and customer relationship economics demand a relationship-oriented approach to marketing. Relationship building and management are found to be an underlying facet in the research into these areas. Relationship marketing is suggested as one new marketing paradigm, and a number of consequences for marketing and management of a relationship-type marketing strategy is discussed based on the notion of a marketing strategy continuum. Finally, the possibility of building a general theory of marketing based on the relationship approach is examined. A further discussion of the nature of the relationship marketing paradigm is, however, beyond the scope of this report.

Marketing Mix and the Four Ps

Marketing the way most textbooks treat it today was introduced around 1960. The concept of the marketing mix and the Four Ps of marketing—product, price, place and promotion—entered the marketing textbooks at that time[26]. Quickly they also became treated as the unchallenged basic model of marketing, so totally overpowering previous models and approaches, such as, for example, the organic functionalist approach advocated by Wroe Alderson[27,28] as well as other systems-oriented approaches (e.g.[29,30]) and parameter theory developed by the Copenhagen School in Europe (e.g.[31,32]) that these are hardly remembered, even with a footnote in most textbooks of today. Earlier approaches, such as the commodity (e.g.[33]), functional (e.g.[34]), geography-related regional (e.g.[35]) and institutional schools (e.g.[36]) have suffered a similar fate. Only a few models from these approaches have survived. American Marketing Association, in its most recent definition, states that "marketing is the process of planning and executing the conception, pricing, promotion and distribution of ideas, goods and services to create exchange and satisfy individual and organizational objectives" (emphasis added)[37].

Eventually the Four Ps of the marketing mix became an indisputable paradigm in academic research, the validity of which was taken for granted[10,16,38]. For most marketing researchers in large parts of the academic world it seems to remain the marketing truth even today. Kent[38] refers to the Four Ps of the marketing mix as "the holy quadruple...of the marketing faith...written in tablets of stone" (p. 146). For an academic researcher looking for tenure and promotion, to question it has been to stick out his or her neck too far. Prospective authors of textbooks, who suggest another organization than the Four P solution for their books, are quickly corrected by most publishers. As a result, empirical studies of what the key marketing variables are, and how they are perceived and used by marketing managers, have been neglected. Moreover, structure has been vastly favoured over process considerations[38]. In marketing education, teaching students how to use a toolbox has become the totally dominating task instead of discussing the meaning and consequences of the marketing concept and the process nature of market relationships. Marketing in practice has to a large extent been turned into managing this toolbox instead of truly exploring the nature of the firm's market relationships and genuinely catering to the real needs and desires of customers.

How Did the Marketing Mix Emerge?

A paradigm like this has to be well founded by theoretical deduction and empirical research; otherwise much of marketing research is based on a loose foundation and the results of it questionable. The marketing mix developed from a notion of the marketer as a "mixer of ingredients"[39]. The marketer plans various means of competition and blends them into a "marketing mix" so that a profit function is optimized, or rather satisfied. The "marketing mix", concept was introduced by Neil Borden in the 1950s (e.g.[40]), and the mix of different means of competitions was soon labelled the Four Ps[26].

The marketing mix is actually a list of categories of marketing variables and, to begin with, this way of defining or describing a phenomenon can never be considered a very valid one. A list never includes all relevant elements, it does not fit every situation, and it becomes obsolete. And indeed, marketing academics every now and then offer additional Ps to the list, since they have found the standard "tablet of faith" too limited[41-54]. It is, by the way, interesting to notice that since the Four Ps were definitely canonized sometime in the early 1970s, new items to the list almost exclusively have been in the form of Ps[55, 56]. Advocators of the marketing mix management paradigm have sometimes suggested that *service* should be added to the list of Ps (e.g.[53,57]). This would be disastrous, because it would isolate customer service as a marketing variable from the rest of the organization, just as has happened with the Four P marketing mix variables. It would effectively counteract all attempts to make customer service the responsibility of everyone and not of a separate department only.

In fact, the Four Ps represent a significant oversimplification of Borden's original concept, which was a list of 12 elements not intended to be a definition at all. Moreover, the elements of this list would probably have to be reconsidered in any given situation. McCarthy either misunderstood the meaning of Borden's marketing mix, when he reformulated the original list in the shape of the rigid mnemonic of the Four Ps where no blending of the Ps is explicitly included, or his followers misinterpreted McCarthy's intentions. In many marketing textbooks organized around the marketing mix, such as Philip Kotler's well-known *Marketing Management* [58], the blending aspect and the need for integration of the Four Ps are discussed, even in depth, but such discussions are always limited owing to the fact that the model does not explicitly include an integrative dimension.

In the 1950s in Europe, researchers within the so-called Copenhagen School approached marketing in a similar way to the notion of the marketing mix, based on the idea of *action parameters* presented in the 1930s by von Stackelberg[59]. Arne Rasmussen[31] and Gösta Mickwitz[32] developed what became known as *parameter theory*, which was a dynamic marketing mix approach linked to the product life cycle and where the parameters were integrated by means of varying market elasticities. Moreover, Mickwitz also stated that the demand side has to be connected to the supply side in a managerial marketing theory. This was done using an economic approach rather than a behavioural approach. Parameter theory was a much more developed model than the Four P version of the marketing mix notion. Unfortunately, it never received enough international attention, and eventually it was overwhelmed by the Four Ps that were much easier to comprehend and teach. Today, the key aspects of parameter theory, dynamism and an integration of consumer behaviour and managerial decision making are pointed out as important research topics (cf.[3]).

Probably Borden's original idea of a list of a large number of marketing mix ingredients that have to be reconsidered in every given situation was shortened for pedagogical reasons and because a more limited number of marketing variables seemed to fit typical situations observed in the late 1950s and in the 1960s by the initiators of the short list of four standardized Ps. These typical situations can be described as involving consumer packaged goods in a North American environment with huge mass markets, a highly competitive distribution system and very commercial mass media. However, in other markets the infrastructure is to varying degrees different and the products are only partly consumer packaged goods. Nevertheless the four Ps of the marketing mix have become the universal marketing model or even theory and an almost totally dominating paradigm for most academics, and they have had a tremendous impact on the practice of marketing as well. Is there any justification for this?

The Nature of the Marketing Mix

Any marketing paradigm should be well set to fulfil the *marketing concept*, i.e. the notion that the firm is best off by designing and directing its activities according to the needs and desires of customers in chosen target markets. How well is the marketing mix fit to do that?

One can easily argue that the four Ps of the marketing mix are not well able to fulfil the requirements of the marketing concept. As Dixon and Blois[60] put it, "... indeed it would not be unfair to suggest that far from being concerned with a customer's interests (i.e. somebody *for whom* something is done) the views implicit in the Four P approach is that the customer is somebody *to whom* something is done!" (emphasis added) (p. 4). To use a marketing metaphor, the marketing mix and its four Ps constitute a *production*-oriented definition of marketing, and not a market-oriented or customer-oriented one (see[10,16]). Moreover, although McCarthy[26] recognizes the interactive nature of the Ps, the model itself does not explicitly include any interactive elements. Furthermore, it does not indicate the nature and scope of such interactions.

The problems with the marketing mix management paradigm are not the number or conceptualization of the decision variables, the Ps, as American Marketing Association as well as the authors of most publications criticizing the marketing mix management paradigm argue. Rather, the problem is of a theoretical nature. The Four Ps and the whole marketing mix management paradigm are, theoretically, based on a loose foundation, which in a recent *Journal of Marketing* article was also demonstrated by van Waterschoot and Van den Bulte[61]. They conclude: "To our knowledge, the classification property(-ies) or rationale for distinguishing four categories labelled 'product', 'price', 'place' and 'promotion' have never been explicated...Though casual observation of practitioners, students, and textbooks suggest a general consensus to classify marketing mix elements in the same categories, the lack of any formal and precise specification of the properties or characteristics according to which marketing mix elements should be classified is a major flaw". Van Waterschoot and Van den Bulte[61] recognize three flaws in the Four P model: "The properties or characteristics that are the basis for classification have not been identified. The categories are not mutually exclusive. There is a catch-all subcategory that is continually growing" (p. 85) (see also[38,62]). Many marketing-related phenomena are not included[63]. Moreover, as Johan Arndt[64,65] has concluded, marketing research remains narrow in scope and even myopic, and methodological issues become more important than substance matters. "Research in marketing gives the impression of being based on a conceptually sterile and unimaginative positivism...The consequence...is that most of the resources are directed toward less significant issues, overexplaining what we already know, and toward supporting and legitimizing the status quo"[64, p. 399]. Unfortunately, far too little has changed in mainstream marketing research since this was written over a decade ago.

The usefulness of the Four Ps as a general marketing theory for practical purposes is, to say the least, highly questionable. Originally, although they were largely based on empirical induction and earlier lists of marketing functions of the functional school of marketing (cf.[66]), they were probably developed under the influence of microeconomic theory and especially the theory of monopolistic competition of the 1930s (e.g. [67]), in order to add more realism to that theory. However, very soon the connection to microeconomic theory was cut off and subsequently totally forgotten. Theoretically, the marketing mix became just a list of Ps without roots.

Even in the area of consumer goods marketing in North America some doubts concerning marketing mix management has been expressed. Regis McKenna[68], a respected marketing consultant and writer, concludes in a discussion about the decline in North America of advertising, the flagship of traditional marketing, that "the underlying reason behind...(this decline)...is advertising's dirty little secret: it serves no useful purpose. In today's market, advertising simply misses the fundamental point of marketing—adaptability, flexibility, and responsiveness" (p. 13). Undoubtedly, this is to take it a little bit to the extreme, but the point is well taken. An interest in turning anonymous masses of potential and existing customers into interactive relationships with well-defined customers is becoming increasingly important (see e.g. [68-70]).

Consequences of the Marketing Mix

Managing the marketing mix makes marketing seem to easy to handle and organize. Marketing is separated from other activities of the firm and delegated to specialists who take care of the analysis, planning and implementation of various marketing tasks, such as market analysis, marketing planning, advertising, sales promotion, sales, pricing, distribution and product packaging. Marketing departments are created to take responsibility for the marketing function of the firm, sometimes together with outside specialists on, for example, market analysis and advertising. Both in the marketing literature and in everyday marketing vocabulary the expression "marketing department", and organization unit, is used as a synonym for marketing function, which is the process of taking care of the fulfilment of customer needs and desires. However, the organizational approach inherent in the marketing mix management paradigm is not very useful either (see e.g.[15,16,71-73]). The psychological effect on the rest of the organization of a separate marketing department is, in the long run, often devastating to the development of a customer orientation or market orientation in a firm. A *marketing orientation* with, for example, high-budget advertising campaigns may be developed, but this does not necessarily have much to do with true *market orientation* and a real appreciation for the needs and desires of the customers. The existence or introduction of such a department may be a trigger that makes everybody else lose whatever little interest in the customers they may have had[15]. The marketing department approach to organizing the marketing function has isolated marketing from design, production, deliveries, technical service, complaints handling, invoicing and other activities of the firm. As a consequence, the rest of the organization has been alienated from marketing. Therefore, it has made it difficult, often even impossible, to turn marketing into the "integrative function" that would provide other departments with the market-related input needed in order to make the organization truly market oriented and reach a stage of "co-ordinated marketing" (cf.[72, pp. 19-24]).

Furthermore, the marketing specialists organized in a marketing department may get alienated from the customers. Managing the marketing mix means relying on mass marketing. Customers become numbers for the marketing specialists, whose actions, therefore, typically are based on surface information obtained from market research reports and market share statistics. Frequently such marketers act without ever having encountered a real customer.

The marketing department concept is obsolete and has to be replaced by some other way of organizing the marketing function, so that the organization will have a chance to become market-oriented. A traditional marketing department will always, in the final analysis, stand in the way of spreading market orientation and an interest in the customer throughout the organization (cf.[15,16,71,72]).

Sometimes the term marketing has become a burden for the marketing function. Managers as well as their subordinates in other departments and functions do not want to take part in the marketing function. But according to the relationship marketing approach and contemporary models of industrial marketing and service marketing they do undoubtedly belong to this function. The use of the marketing mix management paradigm and the Four Ps has made it very difficult for the marketing function to earn credibility. Some firms have solved this problem not only by down-scaling or altogether terminating their marketing departments but also by banning the use of the term marketing for the marketing function (cf.[15]). Perhaps we even need this kind of semantics.

Contemporary Theories of Marketing

In most marketing textbooks the marketing mix management paradigm and its Four Ps are still considered *the* theory of marketing. Indeed, this is the case in much of the academic research into marketing, especially in North America but also to a considerable extent in other parts of the world as well. However, since the 1960s alternative theories of marketing have been developed. As Möller[63] observes in a recent overview of research traditions in marketing, "from the functional view of marketing 'mix' management our focus has extended to the strategic role of marketing, aspects of service marketing, political dimensions of channel management, interactions in industrial networks; to mention just a few evolving trends" (p. 197). Some of these theories have been based on studies of the market relationships of firms in specific types of industries. In this section the emerging theories and models of the *interaction/network approach to industrial marketing* and the *marketing of services* will be discussed. The growing interest in focusing on *customer relationship economics* and the long-term profitability of customer retention and market economies will also be touched on.

The Interaction and Network Approach to Industrial Marketing

The *interaction/network* approach to industrial marketing was originated in Sweden at Uppsala University during the 1960s[74] and has since spread to a large number of countries. Between the parties in a network various interactions take place, where exchanges and adaptations to each other occur. A flow of goods and information as well as financial and social exchanges takes place in the network[18,75,76]. In such a network the role and forms of marketing are not very clear. All exchanges, all sorts of interactions have an impact on the position of the parties in the network. The interactions are not necessarily initiated by the seller—the marketer according to the marketing mix management paradigm—and they may continue over a long period of time, for example, for several years.

The seller, who at the same time may be the buyer in a reciprocal setting, may of course employ marketing specialists, such as sales representatives, market communication people and market analysts but in addition to them a large number of persons in functions which according to the marketing mix management paradigm are non-marketing, such as research and development, design, deliveries, customer training, invoicing and credit management, has a decisive impact on the marketing success of the "seller" in the network. Gummesson[5-7] has coined the term *part-time marketers* for such employees of a firm. He observes that in industrial markets and in service businesses, the part-time marketers typically outnumber several times the full-time marketers, i.e. the marketing specialists of the marketing and sales departments. Furthermore, he concludes that "marketing and sales departments (the full-time marketers) are not able to handle more than a limited portion of the marketing as *its staff cannot be at the right place at the right time with the right customer contacts*" [7, p. 13]. Hence, the part-time marketers do not only outnumber the full-time marketers, the specialists; often they are the only marketers around.

The Marketing of Services

In the early 1970s the *marketing of services* started to emerge as a separate area of marketing with concepts and models of its own geared to typical characteristics of services. In Scandinavia and Finland, the Nordic School of Services, more than researchers into this field elsewhere, looked at the marketing of services as something that cannot be separated from overall management[77]. In North America, research into service marketing has to a much greater extent remained within the boundaries of the marketing mix management paradigm, although it has produced some creative results[17,78]. Grönroos brought quality back into a marketing context[79-81] by introducing the *perceived service quality* concept in 1982[15]. He introduced the concept of the *interactive marketing function*[15,82] to cover the marketing impact on the customer during the consumption of usage process, where the consumer of a service typically interacts with systems, physical resources and employees of the service provider. In France, Langeard and Eiglier[83] developed the *servuction* concept to describe this system of interactions. These interactions occur between the customer and employees who normally are not considered marketing people, either by themselves or by their managers, and who do not belong to a marketing or sales department. Nevertheless, they are part-time marketers.

   In many situations long-lasting relationships between service providers and their customers may develop. Grönroos[15,84] developed the *customer relationship life-cycle* model, originally called the "marketing circle", to cover the long-term nature of the establishment and evolution of the relationship between a firm and its customers. Managing this life-cycle is a relationship marketing task, although the term itself was not used at that time. Again, the marketing success of a firm is only partly determined by the "full-time marketers". In fact, the "part-time marketers" of a service provider may often have a much more important impact on the future purchasing decisions of a customer than, for example, professional sales people or advertising campaigns (e.g.[5,16]).

The Interest in Customer Relationship Economics

During the last few years there has been a growing interest in studying the economics of long-lasting customer relationships. Heskett[85] introduced the concept of *market economies*, by which he means achieving results by understanding the customers instead of by concentrating on developing scale economies. Reichheld[86] gives an example of this: "At MBNA (in the credit card business in the US), a 5 per cent increase in retention grows the company's profit by 60 per cent by the fifth year" (p. 65). More similar results from other industries are reported in a study by Reichheld and Sasser[87]. Long-term relationships where both parties over time learn how to best interact with each other lead to decreasing *relationship costs* for the customer as well as for the supplier or service provider. The relationship cost theory which is based on literature on, for example, quality costs (cf.[88]) and transaction costs (cf.[89]) has been suggested by Grönroos[90]. A mutually satisfactory relationship makes it possible for customers to avoid significant *transaction costs* involved in shifting supplier or service provider and for suppliers to avoid suffering unnecessary *quality costs*.

However, customer retention is not enough. Some long-lasting customer relationships, where the customers are obviously satisfied with what they get, are not profitable even in the long run, as Storbacka[91] demonstrates in a recent study in the retail banking industry (cf. also[92]). Therefore, segmentation based on *customer relationship profitability* analysis is a prerequisite for customer retention decisions. To conclude, there is clear evidence that from a profitability point of view intelligent relationship building and management make sense.

Relationship Building as a Cornerstone of Marketing

The interaction and network approach of industrial marketing and modern service marketing approaches, especially the one by the Nordic School, clearly views marketing as an interactive process in a social context where *relationship building* and *management* are a vital cornerstone[93-95]. They are in some respects clearly related to the systems-based approaches to marketing of the 1950s (cf. e.g.[29]). The marketing mix management paradigm with its Four Ps, on the other hand, is a much more clinical approach, which makes the seller the active part and the buyer and consumer passive. No personalized relationship with the producer and marketer of a product is supposed to exist, other than with professional sales representatives in some cases. Obviously, this latter view of marketing does not fit the reality of industrial marketing and the marketing of services very well.

The concept relationship marketing[96-98] has emerged within the fields of service marketing and industrial marketing[4-8,10-14,16,78,99,100]. The phenomenon described by this concept is strongly supported by on-going trends in modern business (cf.[95]). Grönroos defines relationship marketing[101,102] in the following way: "Marketing is to establish, maintain, and enhance relationships with customers and other partners, at a profit, so that the objectives of the parties involved are met. This is achieved by a mutual exchange and fulfilment of promises" ([16, p. 138]). Such relationships are usually but not necessarily always long term. Establishing a relationship, for example with a customer, can be divided into two parts: to *attract* the customer and to *build* the relationship with that customer so that the economic goals of that relationship are achieved.

An integral element of the relationship marketing approach is the *promise concept* which has been strongly emphasized by Henrik Calonius[103]. According to him the responsibilities of marketing do not only, or predominantly, include giving promises and thus persuading customers as passive counterparts on the marketplace to act in a given way. A firm that is preoccupied with giving promises may *attract* new customers and initially *build* relationships. However, if promises are not kept, the evolving relationship cannot be *maintained* and *enhanced*. Fulfilling promises that have been given is equally important as means of achieving customer satisfaction, retention of the customer base, and long-term profitability (cf. also [87]). Calonius also stresses the fact that promises are mutually given and fulfilled.

Another key element is *trust*. "The resources of the seller—personnel, technology and systems—have to be used in such a manner that the customer's trust in the resources involved and, thus, in the firm itself is maintained and strengthened"[99, p. 5] (c.f. e.g.[104]). In a recent study of relationships on the market for one industrial service, Moorman *et al.*[105] define trust as "...a willingness to rely on an exchange partner in whom one has confidence" (p. 3). This definition means, first of all, that there has to be a *belief* in the other partner's trustworthiness that results from the expertise, reliability or intentionality of that partner. Second, it views trust as a behavioural *intention* or behaviour that reflects reliance on the other partner and involves uncertainty and vulnerability on the part of the trustor. If there is no vulnerability and uncertainty trust is unnecessary, because the trustor can control the other partner's actions[105] (see also[106]). One should, however, bear in mind that in many relationship marketing situations it is not clear who is the trustor and who is the trustee; more likely, for example in a simple two-partner relationship, both partners are in both positions. Also, the relationships are often more complex than mere exchange relationships.

Relationship marketing is still in its infancy as a mainstream marketing concept, although it has established itself as an underlying paradigm in modern industrial marketing and services marketing. Its importance is recognized to a growing extent, however. Philip Kotler[107] concludes in a recent article that "companies must move from a short-term *transaction-oriented* goal to a long-term *relationship-building* goal" (p. 1). In an interview in the *Marketing Science Institute Review* in 1991, Philip Kotler[108] states that "A paradigm shift, as used by Thomas Kuhn..., occurs when a field's practitioners are not satisfied with the field's explanatory variables or breadth...What I think we are witnessing today is a movement away from a focus on exchange—in the narrow sense of transaction—and toward a focus on building value-laden relationships and marketing networks...We start thinking mostly about how to hold on to our existing customers...Our thinking therefore is moving from a marketing mix focus to a relationship focus". (pp. 1,4). Frederick Webster[95], another prominent American opinion leader in marketing, comes to a similar conclusion in a recent analysis of the current developments in business and in marketing: "There has been a shift from a transactions to a relationship focus" (p. 14), and "from an academic or theoretical perspective, the relatively narrow conceptualization of marketing as a profit-maximization problem, focused on market transactions or series of transactions, seems increasingly out of touch with an emphasis on long-term customer relationships and the formation and management of strategic alliances" (p. 10). In his analysis he does not, however, include what has been published on relationship marketing issues in Europe.

So far, there seem to be only two books for textbook purposes based on this emerging paradigm (Christopher, *et al.*[13] in English and Blomqvist *et al.*[14] in Swedish). However, relationship marketing is clearly the underlying approach in several books on services marketing(e.g.[16, 17]) and industrial marketing (e.g.[18-20, 109,110]). In a growing number of articles relationship issues are addressed (e.g.[4, 5,9,10,12,58,95,99,102,111-114]). The importance of relationship building is advancing even into books from the world of consumer goods marketing. There the existence of mass markets without any natural direct customer contacts for the firm causes certain consequences of their own. Market communication is a central means of reaching customers, and the focus on relationship building leads to an interest in emphasizing *dialogues* and creating, for example, advertising campaigns that facilitate various types of dialogues with identified customers (see, e.g.[69]). In the future, this marketing paradigm most certainly will be a focal point of marketing research, thus positioning itself as a leading marketing paradigm not only in services marketing and industrial marketing but in most or all marketing situations. In the rest of this article, some marketing and management consequences of a relationship-building and management approach will be discussed.

The Marketing Strategy Continuum

The major problem with the marketing mix and its Four Ps has been their position as the major, and in many situations as the only, acceptable marketing paradigm. Relationship marketing must not become such a strait-jacket. However, developing enduring customer relationships and achieving exchanges in such relationships through a relationship marketing approach (cf.[115]) is not only another addendum to marketing mix management. Rather, it is a different approach as compared to achieving exchanges in isolated transactions through the use of the Four Ps of the marketing mix. As Reichheld observes, "building a highly loyal customer base cannot be done as an add-on. It must be integral to a company's basic business strategy"[86, p. 64]. Hence, it should be useful to think about possible marketing approaches or strategies along a *marketing strategy continuum*[116]. *Relationship marketing* is placed at one end of the continuum. Here the general focus is on building relationships with customers (and other parties as well, although only customers are discussed in this context). At the other end of the continuum is *transaction marketing* where the focus of marketing is on one transaction at a time (cf.[4]). Thus marketing revolves around creating single transactions or exchanges at a time and not around building long-term relationships. The continuum and some marketing and management implications are illustrated in Figure 1.

Various types of goods and services can be placed along the continuum as indicated by the bottom part of Figure 1. The exact place and corresponding marketing approach cannot, of course, be located. This is indicated by the arrows. Marketers of consumer packaged goods will probably benefit most from a transaction-type strategy. Service firms, on the other hand, would normally, but probably not always, be better off by applying a relationship-type strategy. Manufacturers of consumer packaged goods have mass markets but no immediate contacts with their ultimate customers, while service firms almost always have such contacts, sometimes on a regular basis, sometimes only at discrete points in time. Therefore, the interface between the firm and its customers is expanded far outside the marketing department of marketing and sales specialists.

In consumer durables the customer interface is broader than for consumer packaged goods, and a pure transaction-type strategy is not the only naturally available option. Industrial goods, ranging from mass-produced components to complex

The strategy continuum	Transaction marketing	Relationship marketing
Time perspective	Short-term focus	Long-term focus
Dominating marketing function	Marketing mix	Interactive marketing (supported by marketing mix activities)
Price elasticity	Customers tend to be more sensitive to price	Customers tend to be less sensitive to price
Dominating quality dimension	Quality of output (technical quality dimension) is dominating	Quality of interactions (functional quality dimension) grows in importance and may become dominating
Measurement of customer satisfaction	Monitoring market share (indirect approach)	Managing the customer base (direct approach)
Customer information system	*Ad hoc* customer satisfaction surveys	Real-time customer feedback system
Interdependency between marketing, operations and personnel	Interface of no or limited strategic importance	Interface of substantial strategic importance
The role of internal marketing	Internal marketing of no or limited importance to success	Internal marketing of substantial strategic importance to success
The product continuum	Consumer packaged → ← Consumer → ← Industrial → ← Services goods durables goods	

Figure 1. The Marketing Strategy Continuum: Some Implications

Source: [12].

machines and projects, would probably fit best between consumer durables and services. However, in many industrial marketing situations the customer relationships are similar to many service situations, and here no distinctions between the industrial marketer and service marketer can be made on the continuum.

The time perspective of marketing differs depending on where on the continuum a firm is. As transaction marketing means that the firm focuses on single exchanges or transactions at a time, the time perspective is rather short. The unit of analysis is a single market transaction. Profits are expected to follow from today's exchanges, although sometimes some long-term image development occurs. In relationship marketing the time perspective is much longer. The marketer does not plan primarily for short-term results. His objective is to create results in the long run through enduring and profitable relationships with customers. In some cases single exchanges may even be unprofitable as such. Thus, relationships as such are equally the units of analysis.

Marketing Focus

Because of the lack of personal contacts with their customers and their focus on mass markets, firms pursuing a transaction-type strategy will probably benefit most from a traditional *marketing mix* approach. The Four P model will give guidance in most cases; and this model was indeed originally developed for consumer packaged goods marketing where transaction marketing is most appropriate.

For a firm applying a relationship strategy the marketing mix often becomes too restrictive. The most important customer contacts from a marketing success point of view are the ones outside the realm of the marketing mix and the marketing specialists. The marketing impact of the customer's contacts with people, technology and systems of operations and other non-marketing functions determines whether he or she (or the organizational buyer as a unit) will continue doing business with a given firm or not. All these customer contacts are more or less interactive. As has been said earlier, in services marketing literature, the marketing effects of these interactions are called the *interactive marketing function*. This marketing function can also be described as *the marketing activities outside the marketing mix*. It involves people who thus have dual responsibilities. Their main duties are in operations or some other non-marketing tasks. However, they also perform a crucial marketing task, because of their vital customer contacts. They have responsibilities as "part-time marketers". In relationship marketing interactive marketing becomes the dominating part of the marketing function. Of course, elements of the marketing mix are important here as well, but to a much lesser degree and merely supporting interactive marketing activities.

In transaction marketing there is not much more than the core product, and sometimes the image of the firm or its brands, which keeps the customer attached to the seller. When a competitor introduces a similar product, which is quite easily done in most markets today, advertising and image may help in keeping the customers, at least for some time, but price usually becomes an issue. A firm that offers a lower price or better terms is a dangerous competitor, because in transaction marketing the price sensitivity of customers is often high. A firm pursuing a relationship marketing strategy, on the other hand, has created more value for its customers than that which is provided by the core product alone. Such a firm develops over time more and tighter ties with its customers. Such ties may, for example, be technological, knowledge-related or information-related, or social in nature. If they are well handled they provide customers with added value, something that is not provided by the core product itself. Of course, price is not unimportant but is often much less an issue here. Thus, *relationship marketing makes customers less price sensitive.*

Customer Perceived Quality

The quality customers perceive will typically differ, depending on what strategy a firm uses. According to the model of total perceived (quality developed within the Nordic School of Services[15,117,118]) the *customer perceived quality* is basically a function of the customer perceptions of two dimensions: the impact of the outcome or the technical solution (*what* the customer receives), and an additional impact based on the customer's perception of the various interactions with the firm (*how* the so-called "moments of truth"[119] are perceived). The former quality dimension is sometimes called the *technical quality* of the outcome or solution, whereas the latter dimension is called the *functional quality* of the interaction process[15].

A transaction marketing approach includes no or minimal customer contacts outside the product and other marketing mix variables. The benefits sought by the customers are embedded in the technical solution provided by the product. The customer will not receive much else that will provide him with added value, other than perhaps the corporate or brand image in some cases. Hence, the technical quality of the product, or what the customer gets as an outcome, is the dominating quality-creating source in transaction marketing.

In relationship marketing the situation is different. The customer interface is broader, and the firm has opportunities to provide its customers with added value of various types (technological, information, knowledge, social, etc.). Hence, the second quality dimension, how the interaction process is perceived, grows in importance. When several firms can provide a similar technical quality, managing the interaction processes becomes imperative also from a quality perception perspective. Thus, *in relationship marketing the functional quality dimension grows in importance and often becomes the dominating one.* Of course, this does not mean that the technical quality can be neglected, but it is no longer the only quality dimension to be considered as one of strategic importance.

Monitoring Customer Satisfaction

A normal way of monitoring customer satisfaction and success is to look at market share and to undertake *ad hoc* customer satisfaction surveys. A stable or rising share of the market is considered a measure of success and, thus, indirectly, of customer satisfaction. When the customer base remains stable, market share is a good measurement of satisfaction. However, very often one does not know whether it in fact is stable, or whether the firm is losing a fair share of its customers, who are replaced by new customers by means of aggressive marketing and sales. In such situations following market share statistics only may easily give a false impression of success, when in fact the number of unsatisfied customers and ex-customers is growing and the image of the firm is deteriorating.

For a consumer packaged goods marketing firm, which typically would apply a transaction marketing strategy, there are no ways of continuously measuring market success other than monitoring market share. A service firm and many industrial marketers, on the other hand, who more easily could pursue a relationship marketing strategy, have at least some kind of interactions with almost every single customer, even if they serve mass markets. Thus, customer satisfaction can be monitored directly. A firm that applies a relationship-type strategy can *monitor customer satisfaction by directly managing its customer base*[16]. *Managing the customer base* means that the firm has at least some kind of direct knowledge of how satisfied its customers are. Instead of thinking in anonymous numbers, or market share, management thinks in terms of people with personal reactions and opinions. This requires a means of gathering the various types of data about customer feedback that are constantly, every day, obtained by a large number of employees in large numbers of customer contacts. In combination with market share statistics, such an intelligence system focusing on customer satisfaction and customer needs and desires forms a valuable source of information for decision making.

Consequently, in a relationship marketing situation the firm can build up an on-line, real-time information system. This system will provide management with a continuously updated database of its customers and continuous information about the degree of satisfaction and dissatisfaction among customers. This can serve as a powerful management instrument. In a transaction marketing situation it is impossible, or at least very difficult and expensive, to build up such a database.

The Strategic Importance of Intraorganizational Collaboration

The level of interdependency between functions and departments in an organization depends on whether the firm has chosen a transaction-type strategy or a relationship-type strategy. In transaction marketing, most or all of the firm's customer contacts are related to the product itself and to traditional marketing mix activities. Marketing and sales specialists are responsible for the total marketing function; no part-time marketers are involved. Thus, the internal interface between functions has no or very limited strategic importance to the firm.

In relationship marketing the situation is different. The customer interface is much broader involving often even a large number of part-time marketers in several different functions. This is the case, for example, in most industrial marketing and services marketing situations. A successfully implemented interactive marketing performance requires that all parts of the firm that are involved in taking care of customers can collaborate and support each other in order to provide customers with a good total perceived quality and make them satisfied. Thus, for a firm pursuing a relationship marketing strategy *the internal interface between marketing, operations, personnel and other functions is of strategic importance to success.*

Internal Marketing as a Prerequisite for External Marketing

The part-time marketers have to be prepared for their marketing tasks. *Internal marketing* is needed to ensure the support of traditional non-marketing people[15,16,99,120-122]. They have to be committed, prepared and informed, and motivated to perform as part-time marketers. As Jan Carlzon of SAS noticed, "only committed and informed people perform" [123]. This does not go for the back-office and frontline employees only. It is, of course, equally important that supervisors and middle-level and top-level managers are equally committed and prepared[124]. The *internal marketing concept* states that "the internal market of employees is best motivated for service mindedness and customer-oriented performance by an active, marketing-like approach, where a variety of activities are used internally in an active, marketinglike and coordinated way"[16, p. 223] (first introduced in English in[15]).

Internal marketing as a process has to be integrated with the total marketing function. External marketing, both the traditional parts of it and interactive marketing performance, starts from within the organization. As compared to transaction marketing situations, *a thorough and on-going internal marketing process is required to make relationship marketing successful.* If internal marketing is neglected, external marketing suffers or fails.

Service Competition

The more a firm moves to the right on the marketing strategy continuum away from a transaction-type situation, the more the market offer expands beyond the core product. Installing goods, technical service, advice about how to use a physical good or a service, just-in-time logistics, customer-adapted invoicing, technical know-how, information, social contacts and a host of other elements of bigger or smaller magnitude are added to the relationship, so that it becomes more attractive and indeed profitable for the customer (and other parties as well) to engage in an on-going relationship with a given partner on the marketplace. All such elements are different types of services. The more the firm adopts a relationship marketing strategy, the more it has to understand how to manage these service elements of its market offer. As we have concluded in earlier contexts (cf.[16]; see also[119]), managing services is to a substantial degree, although of course not totally, different from traditional management of manufactured goods: "...every firm, irrespective of whether it is a service firm by today's definition or a manufacturer of goods, has to learn how to cope with the *new competition of the service economy*"[16, p. 7]. We have coined the term *service competition* for this new competitive situation[16]. In conclusion, relationship marketing demands a deeper understanding of how to manage service competition than what is required of firms pursuing a transaction-type strategy.

The Relationship Approach as a Foundation for a Theory of Marketing

Marketing has never had a general theory, although the managerial school based on the marketing mix management paradigm is frequently treated as one. However, would it be possible to develop a general theory of marketing, or middle-range theories[125], based on the relationship marketing approach? In fact, notably in Europe, relationship-based theories of the middle range, far beyond isolated empirical findings or theoretical deductions, have already been developed in industrial marketing and services marketing. As far as a general theory is concerned, it is controversial whether such an overall theory can be created. Referring to Shelby Hunt's[126,127] criteria of a general theory, Sheth *et. al*[3] in their overview of the evolution of marketing schools argue that such a master theory indeed can exist. What is the potential of the relationship marketing perspective to serve as a foundation for such a theory?

Relationship marketing is systems-oriented, yet it includes managerial aspects. A systems approach is well suited as a basis for a general theory of marketing, because it makes it possible to include all relevant actors, environmental influence, and even the process nature of marketing (cf.[25]). The managerial facets facilitate actionable and normative elements that also are needed in such a theory. Furthermore, Sheth *et al.* express the following views about the scope of marketing and the dominant perspective in marketing: "...we need to expand our understanding of marketing to incorporate the basic tenets of marketing, that is, market behaviour, market transactions as the unit of analysis, marketing as a dynamic process of relationships between buyers and sellers, and the exogenous variables that influence market behaviour...What is needed is a perspective that reflects the *raison d'être* of marketing, a perspective that is the common cause that no stakeholder (consumer, seller, government, or social critic) can question. Indeed, that perspective should really reflect what marketing is all about"[3, p. 195]. Although we do not agree with the statement that single market transactions are the units of analysis, but rather the relationships themselves and their economic and noneconomic elements[93], we believe that this is a useful way of stating what marketing should be and what a theory of marketing should encompass.

According to the Grönroos definition of relationship marketing[10,16], marketing is a process including several parties or actors, the objectives of which have to be met. This is done by a mutual exchange and fulfilment of promises, a fact that makes *trust* an important aspect of marketing (cf.[99]). Inherent in this definition is a view of the suppliers or service providers interacting in a network with, among others, customers, suppliers, intermediaries, and environmental actors. It is possible to include the behaviour of the actors on the marketplace and in the nonmarket environment and to analyse the interactions and processes of the relationships in this system. Furthermore, managerial decisions and actions in the relationships are included. Relationship marketing is also dynamic, because of its process nature. Compare, for example, the dynamism of Howard's[128] managerial theory of marketing which also includes consumer behaviour ingredients. In conclusion, we think it is not unfair to say that the relationship building and management approach to marketing, relationship marketing, has the necessary ingredients for the development of a general theory of marketing. In such a theory the managerial approach with the notion of the marketing mix and other concepts and models become one facet.

Is There a Paradigm Shift in Marketing?

From a management point of view the Four Ps may have been helpful at one time, at least for marketers of consumer packaged goods. The use of various means of competition became more organized. However, the Four Ps were never applicable to all markets and to all types of marketing situations. The development of alternative marketing theories discussed in previous sections of this article demonstrates that even from a management perspective, the marketing mix and its Four Ps became a problem.

However, in the bulk of textbooks and in much of the on-going marketing research this paradigm is still strong today. In a standard marketing text, services marketing, industrial marketing and international marketing, for example, are touched on in a few paragraphs or they may be presented in a chapter of their own. However, they are always occurring as add-ons, never integrated into the whole text. "Books become compilations of fragmented aspects, like services marketing is being piled on top of the original structure or relationship marketing getting a small paragraph or footnote"[129, p. 257]. Why has the marketing mix management paradigm and the Four P model become such a strait-jacket for marketers? The main reason for this is probably the pedagogical virtues of the Four Ps that makes teaching marketing so easy and straightforward. The simplicity of the model seduces teachers to toolbox thinking instead of constantly reminding them of the fact that marketing is a social process with far more facets than that. As a consequence of this, researchers and marketing managers are also constrained by the simplistic nature of the Four Ps. The victims are marketing theory and customers.

On the other hand, marketing is more and more developing in a direction where the toolbox thinking of the marketing mix fits less well. In industrial marketing, services marketing, managing distribution channels and even consumer packaged goods marketing itself, a shift is clearly taking place from marketing to anonymous masses of customer to developing and managing relationships with more or less well-known or at least somehow identified customers. In marketing research new approaches have been emerging over the last decades, although they have not yet been able to over-throw the paradigmatic position of the marketing mix. As has been advocated in this article, an underlying dimension in these types of research is relationship building and management with customers and other parties.

Marketing mix management with its four Ps is reaching the end of the road as a universal marketing approach. However, even if marketing mix management is dying as the dominating marketing paradigm and the Four P model needs to be replaced, this does not mean that the Ps themselves, and other concepts of the managerial approach such as market segmentation and indeed the marketing concept[130-33], would be less valuable than before. Relationships do not function by themselves. As McInnes[134] said already three decades ago, "the existence of a market relation is the foundation of exchange not a substitute for it" (p. 56). Only in extreme situations, for example when the computer systems of a buyer and a materials provider are con-nected to each other in order to initiate and execute purchase decisions automatically, the relationship, at least for some time, may function by itself. In such situations one comes close to what Johan Arndt[135] called "domesticated markets", where "transac-tions... are usually handled by administrative processes on the basis of negotiated rules of exchange" (p. 56). Normally, advertising, distribution and product branding, for example, will still be needed, but along with a host of other activities and resources. However, what marketing deserves is new perspectives, which are more market-oriented and less manipulative, and where the customer indeed is the focal point as suggested by the marketing concept.

Most certainly relationship marketing will develop into such a new approach to managing marketing problems, to organizing the firm for marketing, and to other areas as well. Today it is still an exotic phenomenon on the outskirts of the marketing map. In the future this will change. In fact, this change has already started. Market-ing mix as a general perspective evolved because at one time it was an effective way of describing and managing many marketing situations. Before the marketing mix there were other approaches. Now time has made this approach less helpful other than in specific situations. New paradigms have to come. After all, we live in the 1990s, and we cannot for ever continue to live with a paradigm from the 1950s and 1960s. However, bearing in mind the long-term damages of the marketing mix as the univer-sal truth, we are going to need several approaches or paradigms (compare, however, Kuhn's[24] discussion of the possibility of simultaneously existing paradigms). Rela-tionship marketing will be one of them.

Notes and References

1. The marketing mix management paradigm with its most central model, the Four P model, is fre-quently treated as if it always has existed and as if there have not been any other approaches to marketing. In a chapter named "Quo Vadis, Marketing?"[2] of an anthology we have discussed the background of the marketing mix and other theoretical approaches to marketing which existed at the time when the marketing mix was introduced. Sheth et al.[3] provide an extensive overview of the evolution of marketing thought. However, as they only observe the development in North

America (out of well over 500 publications in their very elaborate reference list only six are published outside North America, and five of these are written by Americans), some important contributions are missing.

2.   Grönroos, C., "Quo Vadis, Marketing? Towards a Neo-Classical Marketing Theory", in Blomqvist, H.C., Grönroos, C. and Lindqvist, L.J. (Eds), *Economics and Marketing, Essays in Honour of Gösta Mickwitz*, Economy and Society, No. 48. Swedish School of Economics and Business Administration, Helsingfors, Finland, 1992, pp. 109-24.

3.   Sheth, J.N., Gardner, D.M. and Garrett, D.E., *Marketing Theory: Evolution and Evaluation*, Wiley, New York, NY, 1988.

4.   Jackson, B.B., "Build Customer Relationships That Last", *Harvard Business Review*, Vol. 63, November-December 1985, pp. 120-8.

5.   Gummesson, E., "The New Marketing—Developing Long-term Interactive Relationships", *Long Range Planning*, Vol. 20 No. 4, 1987, pp. 10-20.

6.   Gummesson, E., *Marketing—A Long-Term Interactive Relationship. Contribution to a New Marketing Theory*, Marketing Technique Center, Stockholm, Sweden, 1987.

7.   Gummesson, E., *The Part-time Marketer*, Center for Service Research, Karlstad, Sweden, 1990.

8.   Gummesson, E., *Relationsmarknadsföring, Från 4 P till 30 R* (Relationship Marketing. From 4 Ps to 30 Rs), Stockholm University, Sweden, 1993.

9.   Dwyer, F.R, Shurr, P.H. and Oh, S., "Developing Buyer and Seller Relationships", *Journal of Marketing*, Vol. 51, April 1987, pp. 11-27.

10. Grönroos, C., "Defining Marketing: A Market-oriented Approach", *European Journal of Marketing*, Vol. 23 No. 1, 1989, pp. 52-60.

11. Grönroos, C., "A Relationship Approach to Marketing: The Need for a New Paradigm", Working Paper 190, Swedish School of Economics and Business Administration, Helsingfors, Finland, 1989.

12. Grönroos, C., "The Marketing Strategy Continuum: A Marketing Concept for the 1990s", *Management Decision*, Vol. 29 No. 1, 1991, pp. 7-13.

13. Christopher, M., Payne, A. and Ballantyne, D., *Relationship Marketing: Bringing Quality, Customer Service and Marketing Together*, Butterworth, London, 1991.

14. Blomqvist, R., Dahl, J. and Haeger, T., *Relationsmarknadsföring, Strategi och metod för servicekonkurren* (Relationship marketing. Strategy and methods for service competition), IHM Förlag, Göteborg, Sweden, 1993.

15. Grönroos, C., *Strategic Management and Marketing in the Service Sector*, Swedish School of Economics and Business Administration, Helsingfors, Finland, (published in 1983 in the US by Marketing Science Institute and in the UK by Studentliteratur/Chartwell-Bratt), 1982.

16. Grönroos, C., *Service Management and Marketing, Managing the Moments of Truth in Service Competition*, Free Press/Lexington Books, Lexington, MA, 1990.

17. Berry, L.L. and Parasuraman, A, *Marketing Services, Competing through Quality*, Free Press/Lexington Books, Lexington, MA, 1991.

18. Håkansson, H., (Ed.) *International Marketing and Purchasing of Industrial Goods*, Wiley, New York, NY, 1982.

19. Turnbull, P.W., and Valla, J-P. (Ed.), *Strategies for International Industrial Marketing*, Groom Helm, London, 1986.

20. Ford, D., (Ed.), *Understanding Business Markets: Interactions, Relationships and Networks*, Academic Press, London, 1990.

21. Kuhn, T.S., *The Structure of Scientific Revolutions*, University of Chicago Press, Chicago, IL, 1962.

22. A typical example of this paradigmatic position was expressed by a US professor at a services marketing conference in the late 1980s. When in a panel discussion the dominating role of marketing mix management and its four Ps were questioned, he responded by stating that he was a student of McCarthy and nothing could convince him that there could be anything wrong with the four Ps and the marketing mix.

23. As Kuhn[24] puts it: "Consider...the men who called Copernicus mad because he proclaimed that the earth moved...Part of what they meant by 'earth' was fixed position. Their earth, at least, could not be moved. Correspondingly, Copernicus's innovation was not simply to move the earth. Rather, it was a whole new way of regarding the problems of physics and astronomy, one that necessarily changed the meaning of both 'earth' and 'motion'. Without these changes the concept of a moving earth was mad" (pp. 149-50). See also Kuhn[25].

24. Kuhn, T.S., *The Structure of Scientific Revolutions*, 2nd ed., University of Chicago Press, Chicago, IL, 1970.

25. Kuhn, T.S., *The Copernican Revolution*, Cambridge, MA, 1957.

26. McCarthy, E.J., *Basic Marketing*, Irwin, Homewood, IL, 1960.

27. Alderson, W., "Survival and Adjustment in Organized Behavior Systems", in Cox, R., and Alderson, W. (Eds), *Theory in Marketing*, Irwin, Homewood, IL, 1950, pp. 65-88.

28. Alderson, W., *Marketing Behavior and Executive Action*, Irwin, Homewood, IL, 1957.

29. Fisk, G., *Marketing Systems*, Harper & Row, New York, NY, 1967.

30. Fisk, G. and Dixon, D.F., *Theories of Marketing Systems*, Harper & Row, New York, NY, 1967.

31. Rasmussen, A., *Pristeori eller parameterteori—studier omkring virksomhedens afsaetning* (Price theory or parameter theory—studies of the sales of the firm, Erhvervsokonomisk Forlag, Copenhagen, Denmark, 1955.

32. Mickwitz, G., *Marketing and Competition*, Societas Scientarium Fennica, Helsingfors, Finland (available from University Microfilms, Ann Arbor, MI), 1959.

33. Copeland, M.T., "The Relation of Consumers' Buying Habits to Marketing Methods", *Harvard Business Review*, Vol. 1, April 1923, pp. 282-9.

34. Weld, L.D.H., "Marketing Functions and Mercantile Organizations", *American Economic Review*, Vol. 7, June 1917, pp. 306-18.

35. Reilly, W.J., *The Law of Retail Gravitation*, University of Texas, Austin, TX, 1931.

36. Duddy, E.A. and Revzan, D.A., *Marketing. An Institutional Approach*, McGraw-Hill, New York, NY, 1947.

37. "AMA Board Approves New Marketing Definition", *Marketing News*, 1 March 1985.

38. Kent, R.A. "Faith in Four Ps: An Alternative", *Journal of Marketing Management*, Vol. 2 No. 2, 1986, pp. 145-54.

39. Culliton, J.W, *The Management of Marketing Costs*, Harvard University Press, Boston, MA, 1948.

40. Borden, N.H. "The Concept of the Marketing Mix", *Journal of Advertising Research*, Vol. 4, June 1964, pp. 2-7.

41. Kotler[42] has, in the context of *megamarketing*, added *public relations* and *politics*, thus expanding the list to six Ps. In service marketing, Booms and Bitner[43] have suggested three additional Ps, *people, physical evidence* and *process*. Judd[44], among others, has argued for just one new P, *people*. The way of challenging the Four Ps has always been to use the same clinical approach, i.e. to simplify the market relationship by developing a list of decision-making variables. No real innovativeness or challenge to the foundation of the underlying paradigm, have been presented. In the 1960s and early 1970s, categories which did not begin with the letter P were suggested; e.g. Staudt and Taylor, Lipson and Darling and Kelly and Lazer[45-47] (three categories each), whereas the letter P almost always has been present in lists of categories put forward in the 1980s and 1990s; e.g. Traynor[48] (five categories), Johnson[49] (12), Keely[50] (four Cs), Berry[51] and Mason and Mayer[52] (six), Collier[53] (seven) and LeDoux[54] (five).

42. Kotler, P. "Megamarketing", *Harvard Business Review*, Vol. 64, March-April 1986, pp. 117-24.

43. Booms, B.H., and Bitner, M.J., "Marketing Strategies and Organization Structures for Service Firms", in Donnelly, J.H. and George, W.R. (Eds), *Marketing of Services*, American Marketing Association, Chicago, IL, 1982, pp. 47-51.

44. Judd, V.C., "Differentiate with the 5th P: People", *Industrial Marketing Management*, Vol. 16, November 1987, pp. 241-7.

45. Staudt, T.A. and Taylor, D.A., *Marketing. A Managerial Approach*, Irwin, Homewood, IL, 1965.

46. Lipson, H.A., and Darling, J.R., *Introduction to Marketing: An Administrative Approach*, Wiley, New York, NY, 1971.

47. Kelly, E.J. and Lazer, W., *Managerial Marketing*, Irwin, Homewood, IL, 1973.

48. Traynor, K., "Research Deserves Status as Marketing's Fifth P", *Marketing News* (Special marketing manager's issue), 8 November, 1985.

49. Johnson, A.A., "Adding More Ps to the Pod or—12 Essential Elements of Marketing", *Marketing News*, 11 April 1986, p. 2.

50. Keely, A. "The 'New Marketing' Has Its Own Set of Ps", *Marketing News*, Vol. 21, 6 November, 1987, pp. 10-1.

51. Berry, D, "Marketing Mix for the 90s Adds an S and 2 Cs to the 4 Ps", *Marketing News*, 24 December 1990, p. 10.

52. Mason, N. and Mayer, M.L., *Modern Retailing Theory and Practice*, Irwin, Homewood, IL, 1990.

53. Collier, D.A. "New Marketing Mix Stresses Service", *The Journal of Business Strategy*, Vol. 12, March-April 1991, pp. 42-5.

54. LeDoux, L. "Is Preservation the Fifth 'P' or Just Another Microenvironmental Factor?", in McKinnon, G.F. and Kelley, C.A., (Eds), *Challenges of a New Decade in Marketing Education*, Western Marketing Educators' Association, 1991, pp. 82-6.

55. In spite of all the additional categories of marketing variables that have been offered by various authors, there is only one textbook that is thoroughly based on anything else than the Four Ps: Donald Cowell's[56] book on the marketing of services which is organized around the Seven P framework.

56. Cowell, D., *The Marketing of Services*, Heineman, London, 1984.

57. Lambert, D.D. and Harrington, T.C., "Establishing Customer Service Strategies within the Marketing Mix: More Empirical Evidence", *Journal of Business Logistics*, Vol. 10 No. 2, 1989, pp. 44-60.

58. Kotler, P., *Marketing Management. Analysis, Planning, and Control*, 7th ed., Prentice-Hall, Englewood Cliffs, NJ, 1991.

59. von Stackelberg, H., "Theorie der Vertriebspolitik und der Qualitätsvariation", *Smollers Jahrbuch*, Vol. 63 No. 1, 1939.

60. Dixon, D.F. and Blois, K.J., *Some Limitations of the 4Ps as a Paradigm for Marketing*, Marketing Education Group Annual Conference, Cranfield Institute of Technology, UK, July, 1983.

61. van Waterschoot, W. and Van den Bulte, C., "The 4P Classification of the Marketing Mix Revisited", *Journal of Marketing*, Vol. 56, October 1992, pp. 83-93.

62. Van den Bulte, C., "The Concept of Marketing Mix Revisited: A Case Analysis of Metaphor in Marketing Theory and Management", Working Paper, State University of Ghent, Belgium, 1991.

63. Möller, K., "Research Traditions in Marketing: Theoretical Notes", in Blomqvist, H.C., Grönroos, C. and Lindqvist, L.J. (Eds), *Economics and Marketing Essays in Honour of Gösta Mickwitz*, Economy and Society, No. 48, Swedish School of Economics and Business Administration, Helsingfors, Finland, 1992, pp. 197-218.

64. Arndt, J., "Perspectives for a Theory in Marketing", *Journal of Business Research*, Vol. 9 No. 3, 1980, pp. 389-402.

65. Arndt, J., "On Making Marketing Science More Scientific: Role of Orientations, Paradigms, Metaphors, and Puzzle Solving", *Journal of Marketing*, Vol. 49, Summer 1985, pp. 11-23.

66. McGarry, E.D., "Some Functions of Marketing Reconsidered", in Cox, R. and Alderson, W. (Eds), *Theory in Marketing*, Richard D. Irwin, Homewood, IL, 1950, pp. 263-79.

67. Chamberlin, E.H., *The Theory of Monopolistic Competition*, Harvard University Press, Cambridge, MA, 1933.

68. McKenna, R., *Relationship Marketing. Successful Strategies for the Age of the Customer*, Addison-Wesley, Reading, MA, 1991.

69. Rapp, S. and Collins, T., *The Great Marketing Turnaround*, Prentice-Hall, Englewood Cliffs, NJ, 1990.

70. Clancy, K.J. and Shulman, R.S., *The Marketing Revolution. A Radical Manifesto for Dominating the Marketplace*, Harper Business, New York, NY, 1991.

71. Piercy, N., *Marketing Organization. An Analysis of Information Processing, Power and Politics*, George Allen & Unwin, London, 1985.

72. Piercy, N., *Marketing-led Strategic Change*, Butterworth Heinemann, Oxford, 1992.

73. Webster, Jr, F.E., "The Rediscovery of the Marketing Concept", *Business Horizons*, Vol. 31, May-June 1988, pp. 29-39.

74. Blankenburg, D. and Holm, U. "Centrala steg i utvecklingen av nätverkssynsättet inom Uppsalaskolan", in Gunnarsson, E. and Wallerstedt, E., (Eds), *Uppsalaskolan och dess rötter* (The Uppsala school and its roots), Uppsala University, Sweden, 1990, pp. 16-35.

75. Johanson, J. and Mattsson, L.-G., "Marketing Investments and Market Investments in Industrial Networks", *International Journal of Research in Marketing*, No. 4, 1985, pp. 185-95.

76. Kock, S., *A Strategic Process for Gaining External Resources through Long-lasting Relationships*, Swedish School of Economics and Business Administration, Helsingfors/Vasa, Finland, 1991.

77. Grönroos, C. and Gummesson, E., "The Nordic School of Service Marketing", in Grönroos, C. and Gummerson, E., (Eds), *Service Marketing—Nordic School Perspectives*, Stockholm University, Sweden, 1985, pp. 6-11.

78. Berry, L.L., "Relationship Marketing", in Berry, L.L., Shostack, G.L. and Upah, G.D. (Eds), *Emerging Perspectives of Services Marketing*, American Marketing Association, Chicago, IL, 1983, pp. 25-8.

79. It is interesting to notice that in the 1950s economists, such as Abbott[80], Brems[81] and Mickwitz[32], who tried to add more marketing-oriented realism to microeconomic price theory, introduce *quality* as one of their key parameters. Especially for Abbott, quality was the focal parameter. His definition of quality was astonishingly modern, very close to the ones of perceived service quality and TQM: "The term 'quality' will be used...in its broadest sense, to include all the qualitative elements in the competitive exchange process—materials, design, services provided, location, and so forth" [80, p. 4]. Quality was one of the marketing variables explicitly included in *parameter theory* (cf.[32]).

80. Abbott, L., *Quality and Competition*, New York, NY, 1955.

81. Brems, H., *Product Equilibrium under Monopolistic Competition*, Harvard University Press, Cambridge, MA, 1951.

82. Grönroos, C., *Marknadsföring av tjänster. En studie av marknadsföringsfunktionen i tjänsteföretag* (Marketing of services. A study of the marketing function of service firms), with an English summary (diss.; Swedish School of Economics and Business Administration Finland), Akademilitteratur/ Marketing Technique Center, Stockholm, 1979.

83. Langeard, E. and Eiglier, P., *Servuction. Le marketing des Services*, Wiley, Paris, 1987.

84. Grönroos, C., "Designing a Long-range Marketing Strategy for Services", *Long Range Planning*, Vol. 13, April 1980, pp. 36-42.

85. Heskett, J.L., "Lessons in the Service Sector", *Harvard Business Review*, Vol. 65, March-April 1987, pp. 118-26.

86. Reichheld, F.E., "Loyalty-based Management", *Harvard Business Review*, Vol. 71, March-April 1993, pp. 64-73.

87. Reichheld, F.E. and Sasser, Jr, W.E., "Zero Defections: Quality Comes to Service", *Harvard Business Review*, Vol. 68, September-October, 1990 pp. 105-11.

88. Crosby, P.B., *Quality is Free*, McGraw-Hill, New York, NY, 1979.

89. Williamson, O., *Markets and Hierarchies: Analysis and Antitrust Implications*, Free Press, New York, NY, 1975.

90. Grönroos, C., "Facing the Challenge of Service Competition: The Economies of Service", in Kunst, P. and Lemmink, J. (Eds), *Quality Management in Services*, Van Gorcum, Assen, Maastricht, The Netherlands, 1992, pp. 129-40.

91. Storbacka, K., *Customer Relationship Profitability*, Swedish School of Economics and Business Administration, Helsingfors, Finland, 1993.

92. Barnes, J.G. and Cumby, J.A., "The Cost of Quality in Service-oriented Companies: Making Better Customer Service Decisions through Improved Cost Information", Research Paper, ASB Conference 1993, University of New Brunswick, Canada, 1993.

93. In their overview of schools of marketing thought, Sheth *et al.*[3] observe research into services marketing, but they do not see any new lines of thought in it. However, as they have studied North American research only, they do not recognize the new approaches to services marketing inherent, for example, in the Nordic school of services. Industrial marketing research goes without much comment, mainly because the authors do not include the European interaction/ network approach in their discussion. In the last chapter of their book, the authors conclude that interactions which are market transactions should be the unit of analysis in marketing (p. 193). However, they add that instead of studying single transactions only (cf. [94]) a time dimension has to be included: "Consequently, it is very likely that the domain of marketing will be defined around, not only the market, but also the concept of *repeated market transactions* or what is more popularly called 'relationship marketing'. This should strongly suggest that the focus is not on a single market transaction or on selling, but on a continued relationship between the buyer and the seller" (p. 194). According to the authors, relationship marketing is viewed as a range of repeated market transactions between the same seller and buyer where the fundamental unit of analysis is the single market transaction (pp. 200-1). This is, however, still a transaction marketing-oriented view of relationship marketing. In the relationship marketing concept which has evolved within services marketing and industrial marketing the relationships themselves, as well as elements involved in the establishment and management of relationships, are considered the focal issue and the "unit of analysis". Single transactions, or interactions, are only part of it. Furthermore, interactions may also be noneconomic in nature, and not only economic. In his analysis of the current change in marketing focus, Webster[95] concludes that "the focus shifts from products and firms as units to people, organizations, and the social processes that bind actors together in ongoing relationships" (p. 10). According to him, subjects that have been the study of psychologists, organizational behaviourists, political economists and sociologists have to be considered fundamental areas of interest to marketing.

94. Bagozzi, R., "Marketing as Exchange", *Journal of Marketing*, Vol. 39, October 1975, pp. 32-9.

95. Webster, Jr, F.E., "The Changing Role of Marketing in the Corporations", *Journal of Marketing*, Vol. 56, October 1992, pp. 1-17.

96. The term "relationship marketing" was first introduced by Berry in a services marketing context[78]. Managing relationships is, however, nothing new in business. Many entrepreneurs do business by building and managing relationships and always have, but without using the term relationship marketing. In a historical perspective, relationships were of utmost importance in ancient trade. An old proverb from the Middle East says that "as a merchant, you'd better have a friend in every town". However, in growing companies the focus was shifted away from relationships by the occurrence of scientific management. This development goes even further back to Adam Smith's *The Wealth of Nations*. Smith[97] advocated, among other things, that one should pursue the division of labour, so that the capability of a person to perform one given task in an organization would improve and the time it would take to take care of this task would decrease. The ideas of Adam Smith and later of *scientific management* (cf. [98]) were, among other things, specialization and division of labour, whereas relationship building and management require cross-functional teamwork and close collaboration within a firm. However, as Webster[95] points out, even during the times of scientific

management influential industrialists such as Henry Ford and others emphasized the importance of relationship building.

97. Smith, A., *The Wealth of Nations. An Inquiry into the Nature and Cause of the Wealth of Nations*, Methuen, London, 1950 (the original published 1776).

98. Taylor, F.W., *Scientific Management*, Harper & Row, London, 1947, (a volume of two papers originally published in 1903 and 1911 and a written testimony for a Special House Committee in the US in 1912).

99. Grönroos, C., "Relationship Approach to the Marketing Function in Service Contexts: The Marketing and Organizational Behavior Interface", *Journal of Business Research*, Vol. 20 No. 1, 1990, pp. 3-12.

100. Gummesson, E., "Marketing Revisited: The Crucial Role of the Part-time Marketers", *European Journal of Marketing*, Vol. 25 No. 2, 1991, pp. 60-7.

101. This definition is slightly developed from earlier ones in Grönroos[10,11]. Normally, formal definitions cannot be found in the literature. Instead authors offer descriptions, some of which are more informative than others. In his discussion of marketing for multi-service organizations, Berry[78] views relationship marketing as a strategy to attract, maintain and enhance customer relationships. Rapp and Collins[69] say that the goals of relationship marketing are to create and maintain lasting relationships between the firm and its customers that are rewarding for both sides. Christopher *et al.* [13] consider relationship marketing an approach that aligns marketing, customer service and quality, with an emphasis on a focus on customer retention, an orientation on product benefit, a long time-scale, a high customer service orientation, a high customer commitment and a high customer contact as well as on the notion that quality is the concern of all. Blomqvist *et al.*[14] offer the following key characteristics of relationship marketing: every customer is considered an individual person or unit, activities of the firm are predominantly directed towards existing customers, it is based on interactions and dialogues, and the firm is trying to achieve profitability through the decrease of customer turnover and the strengthening of customer relationships. Gummesson[8] concludes that relationship marketing is a strategy where the management of interactions, relationships and networks are fundamental issues. There are also some more practice-oriented descriptions of relationship marketing: for example, the one by Copulinsky and Wolf[102] that states that relationship marketing is a process where the main activities are to create a database including existing and potential customers, to approach these customers using differentiated and customer-specific information about them, and to evaluate the life-term value of very single customer relationship and the costs of creating and maintaining them. In most of these descriptions, only the relationship between a supplier and its customers are included. This seems to be too narrow a view of relationship marketing.

102. Copulinsky, J.R. and Wolf, M.J., "Relationship Marketing: Positioning for the Future", *Journal of Business Strategy*, Vol. 11, July-August 1990, pp. 16-20.

103. Calonius, H., "A Buying Process Model", in Blois, K., and Parkinson, S. (Eds), *Innovative Marketing—A European Perspective*, proceedings from the XVIIth Annual Conference of the European Marketing Academy, University of Bradford, 1988, pp. 86-103.

104. Swan, J.E., Trawick, F. and Silva, D.W., "How Industrial Salespeople Gain Customer Trust", *Industrial Marketing Management*, Vol. 13, August 1985, pp. 203-11.

105. Moorman, C., Deshpandé, R. and Zaltman, G., "Relationships between Providers and Users of Market Research: The Role of Personal Trust", Working Paper No. 93-111, Marketing Science Institute, Cambridge, MA, 1993.

106. Zaltman, G. and Moorman, C., "The Role of Personal Trust in the Use of Research", *Journal of Advertising Research*, Vol. 28, October-November 1988, pp. 16-24.

107. Kotler, P., "It's Time for Total Marketing", *Business Week ADVANCE Executive Brief*, Vol. 2, 1992.

108. "Philip Kotler Explores the New Marketing Paradigm", *Marketing Science Institute Review*, Spring 1991, pp. 1, 4-5.

109. Jackson, B.B., *Winning and Keeping Industrial Customers. The Dynamics of Customer Relationships*, Lexington Books, Lexington, MA, 1985.

110. Vavara, T.G., *Aftermarketing: How to Keep Customers for Life through Relationship Marketing*, Business One Irwin, Homewood, IL, 1992.

111. Sonnenberg, F.K., "Relationship Management Is More Than Wining and Dining", *Journal of Business Strategy*, Vol. 9, May-June 1988, pp. 60-3.

112. Czepiel, J.A., "Managing Relationships with Customers: A Differentiating Philosophy of Marketing", in Bowen, D.E. and Chase, R.D. (Eds), *Service Management Effectiveness*, Jossey-Bass, San Francisco, CA, 1990, pp. 299-323.

113. Congram. C.A., "Building Relationships That Last", in Congram, C.A., and Friedman, M.L. (Eds), *Handbook of Marketing for the Service Industries*, AMACOM, New York, NY, 1991, pp. 263-79.

114. Ferguson, J.M. and Brown, S.W., "Relationship Marketing and Association Management", *Journal of Professional Services Marketing*, Vol. 2 No. 2, 1991, pp. 137-47.

115. Houston, F.S. and Gassenheimer, J.B., "Marketing and Exchange", *Journal of Marketing*, Vol. 51, October 1987, pp. 3-18.

116. We first introduced the concept of the *marketing strategy continuum* with relationship marketing at one end and transaction marketing at the other in 1991 in an article "The Marketing Strategy Continuum: A Marketing Concept for the 1990s" in *Management Decision*[12]. A previous version mainly focusing on services was published in 1990 in *Service Management and Marketing*[16].

117. Lehtinen, J., *Quality-oriented Services Marketing*, University of Tampere, Tampere, Finland, 1986.

118. Gummesson, E. *Quality Management in Service Organizations*, ISQA (International Service Quality Association), New York, NY, 1993.

119. Normann, R., *Service Management*, Wiley, New York, NY, 1984.

120. George, W.R., "Internal Marketing for Retailers. The Junior Executive Employee", in Lindqvist, J.D. (Ed.), *Developments in Marketing Science*, Academy of Marketing Science, 1984.

121. Compton, F., George, W.R., Grönroos, C. and Karvinen, M., "Internal Marketing", in Czepiel, J.A., Congram, C.A. and Shanahan, J. (Eds), *The Service Challenge: Integrated for Competitive Advantage*, American Marketing Association, Chicago, IL, 1987, pp. 7-12.

122. Barnes, J.G., "The Role of Internal Marketing: If the Staff Won't Buy It, Why Should the Customer", *Irish Marketing Review*, Vol. 4 No. 2, 1989, pp. 11-21.

123. Carlzon, J., *Moments of Truth*, Harper & Row, New York, NY, 1987.

124. It is interesting to notice that Taylor in his testimony about scientific management in 1912 explicitly states that "... in its essence, scientific management involves a complete *mental revolution* on the part of the working men engaged in any particular establishment or industry... And it involves the equally complete mental revolution on the part of those on the management's side... And without this complete mental revolution on both sides scientific management does not exist"[98, testimony, p. 27] (emphasis added). Relationship marketing can be successfully implemented only if such a "mental revolution" or cultural change through "attitude management"[16] takes place in the organization.

125. Merton, R.K., *Social Theory and Social Structure*, Free Press, New York, NY, 1957.

126. Hunt, S.D., "The Morphology of Theory and the General Theory of Marketing", *Journal of Marketing*, Vol. 35, April 1971, pp. 65-8.

127. Hunt, S.D., "The Nature and Scope of Marketing", *Journal of Marketing*, Vol. 40, July 1976, pp. 17-28.

128. Howard, J.A., "Marketing Theory of the Firm", *Journal of Marketing*, Vol. 47, Fall 1983, pp. 90-100.

129. Gummesson, E. "Marketing According to Textbooks: Six Objections", in Brownlie, D., Saren, M., Wensley, R. and Whittington, R. (Eds), *Rethinking Marketing: New Perspectives on the Discipline and Profession*, Warwick Business School, Coventry, 1993, pp. 248-58.

130. The marketing concept is attributed to McKitterick[131] and to Keith[132] and the Pillsbury Company. However, this customer-oriented approach to doing business is, of course, nothing new. For example, in a book on advertising and market communication published in 1916 in Norway, the author, Romilla (Robert Milars), gives the following piece of advice: "Førsøk at se paa tingen fra kundens side av disken (Try to look at the situation from the customer's side of the counter)"[133, p. 35]. And according to an old Chinese saying, "customers are the precious things; goods are only grass". The industrial revolution and scientific management, among other reasons, made managers and researchers lose sight of it.

131. McKitterick, J.B., "What Is the Marketing Management Concept", in Bass, F. (Ed.), *The Frontiers of Marketing Thought in Action*, American Marketing Association, Chicago, IL, 1957, pp. 71-82.

132. Keith, R.J., "The Marketing Revolution", *Journal of Marketing*. Vol. 24, January 1960, pp. 35-8.

133. Romilla, *Reklame-laere* (Advertising), Aktietrykkeriet, Trondhjem, 1916.

134. Mclnnes, W., "A Conceptual Approach to Marketing", in Cox, R., Alderson, W. and Shapiro, S.J. (Eds), *Theory in Marketing*, Richard D. Irwin, Homewood, IL, 1964, pp. 51-67.

135. Arndt, J., "Towards a Concept of Domesticated Markets", *Journal of Marketing*, Vol. 43, Fall 1979, pp. 69-75.

Application Questions

(1) Compare the author's point that "the marketing department is obsolete" with parallel organization structural initiatives in the management of quality. How would marketing organize itself without a department?

(2) How does your organization enact its relationships with its customers? Think particularly about "moments of truth".

(3) Is the marketing mix paradigm dead—or dying? What might such a paradigm shift mean in organizations of the future?

13

Relationship Approach to Marketing in Service Contexts: The Marketing and Organizational Behavior Interface

Journal of Business Research
Vol. 20, No. 1, 1990
pp. 3–11

Christian Grönroos

A relationship approach to marketing is described. Marketing in a service context, i.e., concerning both service firms and service operations of manufacturers, is considered especially. The traditional view of marketing as a function for specialists planning and executing a marketing mix may not be altogether true when services are concerned. Instead, marketing can be considered as revolving around relationships, some of which are like single transactions, narrow in scope and not involving much or any social relationship (e.g., marketing soap or breakfast cereals). Other relationships, on the other hand, are broader in scope and may involve even substantial social contacts and be continuous and enduring in nature (e.g., marketing financial or hospitality services). The nature of a relationship marketing strategy is explored. Two interfaces between marketing and organizational behavior, both as business functions and as academic disciplines, which follow from this approach to marketing are discussed, viz., the need for a service culture, and internal marketing. These areas represent a major challenge for marketing and organizational behavior, practitioners and academic alike, to remove traditional borderlines and work together.

Introduction

The purpose of this article is to describe the nature and contents of the marketing function in a service organization and how this function is related to other business functions and academic disciplines, especially to personnel and organizational behavior. The approach is that of what internationally has been called the *Nordic School of Services*, originating in Scandinavia/Northern Europe (see, e.g., Gronroos, 1983; and Gronroos and Gummesson, 1985). The expression *service contexts* implies all types of service activities, irrespective of whether they occur in so-called service firms or in public institutions, not-for-profit organizations, or manufacturers of goods.

The Traditional Role of Marketing

Traditionally, marketing is viewed as an intermediate function, where the specialists of the marketing department are the only persons who have an impact on the customers' views of the firm and on their buying behavior. Employees in other departments are neither recruited nor trained to think marketing, nor are they supervised so that they would feel any marketing responsibilities. In this approach, the core of marketing is the marketing mix. In many consumer packaged goods situations, this conceptualization of marketing functions sufficiently well. If the product is a preproduced item with no needs for service or other contacts between the firm and its customers, marketing specialists are clearly capable of taking care of the customer relationships. Good market research, packaging, promotion, pricing, and distribution decisions by the marketing specialists lead to good results.

As a general framework, the 4 P's of the marketing mix (introduced by McCarthy [1960] based on Borden's [e.g., 1965] and Culliton's [1948] notions of the marketer as a "mixer of ingredients"), in spite of its pedagogical virtues, is far too simplistic and may easily misguide both academics and practitioners; and it has never been empirically tested (compare Cowell, 1984; Gronroos 1989; Kent, 1986). Particularly in services marketing, and also in industrial marketing, the marketing mix approach frequently does not cover all resources and activities that appear in the customer relationships at various stages of the customer relationship life cycle (see Gronroos, in press, 1983, 1989; Gronroos and Gummesson, 1986; Gummesson, 1987a,b; as well as Hakansson, 1982; Hakansson and Snehota, 1976; Kent, 1986; Webster, 1982). Especially during the consumption process, there is a range of contacts between the service firm and its customer, which are outside the traditional marketing function as defined by the P's of the marketing mix (compare Rathmell, 1974). Managing and operating these contacts (e.g., with bank and hotel facilities, automatic teller machines, waiters, air stewardesses, telephone receptionists and bus drivers, R&D people, design engineers, maintenance people, etc.) are the responsibilities of operations and other nonmarketing departments only. However, these buyer–seller interactions or interfaces, or the service encounter, have an immense impact on the future buying behavior of the customers as well as on word of mouth, and, therefore, they should be considered marketing resources and activities. The marketing function is spread throughout the entire organization (Gummesson, 1987a), and the customers take an active part in the production process.

A Relationship Approach to the Buyer–Seller Interface

Far too often, customers are seen in terms of numbers. When someone stops being a customer, there are new potential customers to take the empty place. Customers, individuals, and organizations alike are numbers only. In reality, this is, of course, not true. Every single customer forms a customer relationship with the seller that is broad or narrow in scope, continuous or discrete, short or lasting in nature, which the firm has to develop and maintain. Customer relationships are not just there; they have to be earned. According to an alternative approach to defining marketing, this function is considered to revolve around customer relationships, where the objectives of the parties involved are met through various kinds of exchanges, which take place in order to establish and maintain such relationships.

Especially long-term relationships with customers are important (Gummesson, 1987b). In services, as in general, short-term relationships, where the customers come and go, are normally more expensive to develop. The marketing budget needed to create an interest in the firm's offerings and make potential customers accept the firm's promises are often very high. As Berry (1983) observes, "clearly, marketing to protect the customer base is becoming exceedingly important to a variety of service industries" (p. 25). This holds true for industrial marketing as well (see Hakansson, 1982; Jackson, 1985). This is not to say that new customers who perhaps make one purchase only would not be desirable, but it means, however, that the emphasis should be on developing and maintaining enduring, long-term customer relationships. Berry (1983) introduced the concept of relationship marketing, as opposed to transaction marketing, to describe such a long-term approach to marketing strategy (see also Crosby et al., 1988; Gummesson, 1987b; Rosenberg and Czepiel, 1984). If close and long-term relationships can be achieved, the possibility is high that this will lead to continuing exchanges requiring, lower marketing costs per customer.

A Relationship Definition of Marketing

The marketing concept as the basic philosophy guiding marketing in practice still holds. The marketing mix approach to transferring this concept to marketing in practice is, however, considered too simplistic and too narrow in scope to be more than partly useful in most service situations. In conclusion to this discussion we formulate a relationship definition of marketing (Gronroos, in press, 1989; also compare Gummesson 1987a,b; Berry, 1983). This definition states that

> Marketing is to establish, maintain, enhance and commercialize customer relationships (often but not necessarily always long term relationships) so that the objectives of the parties involved are met. This is done by a mutual exchange and fulfillment of promises.

Furthermore, this definition can be accompanied by the following supplement: The resources of the seller—personnel, technology and systems—have to be used in such a manner that the customer's trust in the resources involved and, thus, in the firm itself is maintained and strengthened. The various resources the customer encounters in the relation may be of any kind and part of any business function. However, these resources and activities cannot be totally predetermined and explicitly categorized in a general definition.

The concept of promises as an integral part of marketing vocabulary has been stressed by the Finnish researcher Calonious (1986, 1988). In establishing and maintaining customer relationships, the seller gives a set of promises concerning, e.g., goods, services or systems of goods and services, financial solutions, materials administration, transfer of information, social contacts, and a range of future commitments. On the other hand, the buyer gives another set of promises concerning his commitments in the relationship. Then, the promises have to be kept on both sides, if the relationship is expected to be maintained and enhanced for the mutual benefits of the parties involved.

Long-term customer relationships mean that the objective of marketing is mainly to go for enduring relationships with the customers. Of course, in some situations, short-term sales—what sometimes is called transaction marketing—may be profitable (see, e.g., Jackson, 1985). However, generally speaking, the long-term scope is vital to profitable marketing. Thus, commercializing the customer relationships means that the cost–benefit ratio of transactions of goods, services, or systems of goods and services is positive at least in the long run.

Establishing, maintaining and enhancing customer relationships, respectively, implies that the marketing situation is different depending on how far the customer relationships have developed. From the service provider's point of view, 1) establishing a relationship involves giving promises; 2) maintaining a relationship is based on fulfillment of promises; and, finally, 3) enhancing a relationship means that a new set of promises are given with the fulfillment of earlier promises as a prerequisite.

This relationship definition of marketing does not say that the traditional elements of the marketing mix, such as advertising, personal selling, pricing, and conceptualizing of the product, are less important than earlier. However, it demonstrates that so much else may be of importance to marketing than the means of competition of the marketing mix. It is based on how to develop and execute good marketing performance, rather than just on what decisions to make to do marketing.

Implications of the Relationship Approach to Marketing

A distinct difference exists between handling the moments of truth (to use an expression introduced in the service management literature by Normann, 1984) of the buyer–seller interactions as a marketing task and executing traditional marketing activities, such as advertising, personal selling, and sales promotion. Normally, the latter are planned and implemented by marketing and sales specialists. On the other hand, the former tasks are implemented by persons who are specialists in other fields. More-over, how the moments of truth are carried out is frequently planned and managed by nonmarketing managers and supervisors. To put it bluntly, the moments of truth with their tremendous marketing impacts are frequently both managed and executed by people who neither are aware of their marketing responsibilities nor are interested in customers and marketing.

The employees involved in marketing as nonspecialists have been called "part-time marketers" by Gummesson (1981, 1987a; compare also Gronroos, 1988). They are, of course, specialists in their areas, and they are supposed to remain so. At the same time, however, they will have to learn to perform their tasks in a marketinglike manner so that the customers will want to return, and the customer relationships are strengthened. Hence, they, and their bosses as well, will have to learn to think in terms of marketing and customer impact.

The marketing aspect of the moments of truth is related to interactive processes, and, therefore, this part of marketing is called the Interactive Marketing Function (see, e.g., Gronroos, 1980, 1983). The impact of the "part-time marketers" as well as the customer orientation of systems, technology, and physical resources is paramount to the success of interactive marketing. Hence, the interactive marketing function recognizes that every component—human as well as other—in producing a service, every production resource used and every stage in the service production and delivery process, should be the concern of marketing as well, and not considered operations or personnel problems only. The marketing consequences of every resource and activity involved in interactive marketing situations have to be acknowledged in the planning process, so that the production resources and operations support and enhance the organization's attempts to develop and maintain relationships with its customers.

As Gummesson (in press) observes, "there is extreme interdependence between the traditional departments of a service firm—production, delivery, personnel, ad-ministration, finance, etc.—and marketing." For example, marketing, personnel, op-erations, and technological development have to go hand in hand. These functions are linked together by the common objective of providing customers with good service. As Schneider and Rentsch (1987) formulate it, service has to become an "organiza-tional imperative." Here, we shall only focus upon one interrelationship between busi-ness functions, the one between marketing and personnel/organizational behavior. Because the marketing impact of the "part-time marketers" is crucial, efforts have to be made to secure service orientation and marketing-oriented attitudes and corre-sponding skills among the personnel. Next, we are going to discuss, very briefly, two important and interrelated aspects of human resources development that emerge from a service-oriented and relationship-oriented approach to marketing.

The Need for a Service Culture

In a service context a strong and well-established corporate culture, which enhances an appreciation for good service and customer orientation, is extremely important (e.g., Bowen and Schneider, 1988, George and Gronroos, in press; Gronroos, in press; Schneider, 1986). This follows from the nature of services. Normally, service production cannot be standardized as completely as an assembly line, because of the human impact on the buyer–seller interface. Customers and their behavior cannot be standardized and totally predetermined. The situations vary, and, therefore, a distinct service-oriented culture is needed that tells employees how to respond to new, unforeseen and even awkward situations (Schneider, 1986). The culture has a vital impact on how service-oriented its employees are and, thus, how well they act as "part-time marketers" (Bowen and Schneider, 1988).

Internal projects or activities, such as service or marketing training programs, probably have no significant impact on the thinking and behavior of, e.g., employees of firms where goods-oriented standards are regarded highly. Moreover, Schneider and Bowen (1985) have found that when employees identify with the norms and values of an organization, they are less inclined to quit, and, furthermore, customers seem to be more satisfied with the service. In addition to this, "... when employee turnover is minimized, service values and norms are more transmitted to newcomers and successive generations of service employees" (Bowen and Schneider, 1988, p. 63).

Developing a service culture is clearly a means of creating and enhancing good interactive marketing performance needed for implementing a relationship marketing strategy. The corporate culture issue is closely linked to another personnel-related issue that has emerged from the research into services marketing. This is internal marketing.

The Need for Internal Marketing

During the past 10 years or so, the concept of internal marketing has emerged first in the literature on services marketing (see, e.g., Berry, 1981; Compton et al., 1987; George et al., 1987; George and Gronroos, in press; Gronroos, 1978, 1981, 1985; see also Eiglier and Langeard, 1976), and then was adopted by the service management literature (see, e.g., Carlzon, 1987; Normann, 1984), and also found to be valuable in industrial marketing (Gronroos and Gummesson, 1985). Heskett (1987) recently touches upon this phenomenon as well observing that "... high-performing service companies have gained their status in large measure by turning the strategic service vision inward..." (pp. 120–121). An increasing number of firms have recognized the need for internal marketing programs. Maybe the most spectacular internal marketing process is the one implemented by Scandinavian Airline System (SAS) (Carlzon, 1987). Today, internal marketing is considered a prerequisite for successful external marketing (see, e.g., Compton et al., 1987; Gronroos, 1985).

First of all, internal marketing is a management philosophy. Management should create, continuously encourage, and enhance an understanding of and an appreciation for the roles of the employees in the organization. Employees should have holistic views of their jobs. This is illustrated by an anecdote told by Jan Carlzon, president and CEO of SAS, about two stonecutters who were chipping square blocks out of granite: "A visitor to the quarry asked what they were doing. The first stone cutter, looking rather sour, grumbled, 'I'm cutting this damned stone into a block.' The second, who looked pleased with his work, replied proudly, 'I'm on this team that's building a cathedral.'" (Carlzon, 1987, p. 135). (It is interesting to notice that in slightly different words, this anecdote is also told by Michail Gorbatjov in his book on the perestroika in the Soviet Union [Gorbatjov, 1987].)

The focus of internal marketing is on how to get and retain customer-conscious employees. It is also a means of developing and maintaining a service culture, although internal marketing alone is not sufficient (see George and Gronroos, in press; Gronroos, 1989). Goods and services as well as specific external marketing campaigns, new technology, and new systems of functioning have to be marketed to employees before these goods and services are marketed externally. Every organization has an internal market of employees, which first has to be successfully taken care of. Unless this is done properly, the success of the organization's operations on its ultimate, external markets will be jeopardized. To put it in the words of Heskett (1987), "Effective service requires people who understand the idea" (p. 124).

Conclusions

Joint Challenges for Marketing and Organizational Behavior

Clearly, the tasks of developing and maintaining a service culture and of internal marketing offer an important interface between marketing and organizational behavior. Hence, they also offer an arena where marketing practitioners and academics on one hand, and personnel and human resources development people and academics from the field of organizational behavior on the other hand, are challenged to work together.

This, of course, requires that among other things, the traditional borderlines that far too often have become insurmountable walls between marketing and personnel as business functions and as academic disciplines are challenged and, if necessary, torn down.

References

Berry, Leonard L., Relationship Marketing, in *Emerging Perspectives on Services Marketing*. L. L. Berry et al., eds., American Marketing Association, Chicago, 1983, pp. 25–28.

Berry, Leonard L., The Employee as Customer, *Journal of Retail Banking* 3 (March 1981): 33–40.

Borden, Neil H., The Concept of the Marketing Mix, in *Science in Marketing*. G. Schwartz, ed., Wiley, New York, 1965.

Bowen, David E., and Schneider, Benjamin, Services Marketing and Management: Implications for Organizational Behavior, in *Research in Organizational Behavior*. B. Stow and L. L. Cummings, eds., JAI Press, Greenwich, CT, Vol. 10, 1988.

Calonius, Henrik, A Buying Process Model, in *Innovative Marketing—A European Perspective*. K. Blois and S. Parkinson, eds., Proceedings from the XVII Annual Conference of the European Marketing Academy, University of Bradford, England, 1988.

Calonius, Henrik, A Market Behaviour Framework, in *Contemporary Research in Marketing*. K. Moller and M. Paltschik, eds., Proceedings from the XV Annual Conference of the European Marketing Academy, Helsinki, Finland, 1986.

Carlzon, Jan, *Moments of Truth*, Ballinger, New York, 1987.

Compton, Fran, George, William R., Gronroos, Christian, and Karvinen, Matti, Internal Marketing, in *The Service Challenge: Integrating for Competitive Advantage*. J. A. Czepiel et al., eds., American Marketing Association, Chicago, 1987, pp. 7–12.

Cowell, Donald, *The Marketing of Services*, Heineman, London, 1984.

Crosby, Lawrence A., Evans, Ken R., and Cowles, Deborah, *Relationship Quality in Service Selling: An Interpersonal Influence Perspective*, Working Paper No. 5, First Interstate Center for Services Marketing, Arizona State University, 1988.

Culliton, John W., *The Management of Marketing Costs*, The Andover Press, Andover, MA, 1948.

Deshpande, R., and Webster, Jr., Frederick E., *Organizational Culture and Marketing: Defining the Research Agenda*. Report No. 87-106. Marketing Science Institute, Cambridge, MA, 1987.

Eiglier, Pierre, and Langeard, Eric, *Principles Politique Marketing pour les Enterprises des Service*, Working Paper, Institute d'Administration des Enterprises, Aix-en-Provence, France, 1976.

George, William, R., Internal Communications Programs as a Mechanism for Doing Internal Marketing, in *Creativity in Services Marketing*. V. Venkatesan et al., eds., American Marketing Association, Chicago, 1986, pp. 83–84.

George, William R., Internal Marketing for Retailers. The Junior Executive Employee, in *Developments in Marketing Science*. J. D. Lindqvist, ed., Academy of Marketing Science, 1984, Vol. VII, pp. 322–325.

George, William R., and Gronroos, Christian, Developing Customer-Conscious Employees at Every Level: Internal Marketing, in *Handbook of Services Marketing*, C. A. Congram and M. L. Friedman, eds., AMACON, in press.

Gorbatjov, Mikhail, *Perestroika—New Thinking for our Country and the World*, Harper & Row, New York, 1987.

Gronroos, Christian, Defining Marketing: A Market-Oriented Approach, *European Journal of Marketing* 23 (1989): 52–60.

Gronroos, Christian, New Competition of the Service Economy: The Five Rules of Service, *International Journal of Operations & Production Management* 8 (1988): 9–19,

Gronroos, Christian, Internal Marketing—Theory and Practice, in *Services Marketing in a Changing Environment*. T. M. Bloch et al., ed., American Marketing Association, Chicago, 1985, pp. 41–47.

Gronroos, Christian, *Strategic Management and Marketing in the Service Sector*, Marketing Science Institute, Cambridge, MA, 1983.

Gronroos, Christian, Internal Marketing—An Integral Part of Marketing Theory, in *Marketing of Services*. J. H. Donnelly and W. R. George, eds., American Marketing Association, Chicago, 1981, pp. 236–238.

Gronroos, Christian, Designing a Long Range Marketing Strategy for Services, *Long Range Planning* 13 (April 1980): 36–42.

Gronroos, Christian, A Service-Oriented Approach to Marketing of Services, *European Journal of Marketing* 12 (1978): 588–601.

Gronroos, Christian, *Service Management and Marketing. Managing the Moments of Truth in Service Competition*. Lexington, MA: D.C. Heath Lexington Books, in press.

Gronroos, Christian, and Gummesson, Evert, Service Orientation in Industrial Marketing, in *Creativity in Services Marketing. What's New, What Works, What's Developing*, American Marketing Association, Chicago, 1986, pp. 23–26.

Gronroos, Christian, and Gummesson, Evert, eds. *Service Marketing—Nordic School Perspectives*, Stockholm University, Sweden, 1985.

Gummesson, Evert, The New Marketing—Developing Long-Term Interactive Relationships, *Long Range Planning* 20 (1987a): 10–20.

Gummesson, Evert, *Marketing—A Long Term Interactive Relationship. Contribution to a New Marketing Theory*, Marketing Technique Center, Stockholm, Sweden, 1987b.

Gummesson, Evert, Marketing Cost Concept in Service Firms, *Industrial Marketing Management* 10 (1981): 175–182.

Gummesson, Evert, Organizing for Marketing and Marketing Organizations, in *Handbook on Services Marketing*. C. A. Congram and M. L. Friedman, eds., Amacon, New York, in press.

Hakansson, Hakan, ed. *International Marketing and Purchasing of Industrial Goods*, Wiley, New York, 1982.

Hakansson, Hakan, and Snehota, Ivan, *Marknadsplanering. Ett satt att skapa nya problem?* (Marketing Planning. A Way of Creating New Problems?), Studentlitteratur, Malmo, Sweden, 1976.

Heskett, James L., Lessons in the Service Sector, *Harvard Business Review* 65 (March–April 1987): 118–126.

Jackson, Barbara B., Build Customer Relationships That Last, *Harvard Business Review* 63 (November–December 1985): 120–128.

Kent, Ray A., Faith in Four Ps: An Alternative, *Journal of Marketing Management* 2 (1986): 145–154.

Kotler, Philip, *Marketing Management, Analysis, Planning, and Control*. Prentice-Hall, Englewood Cliffs, NJ, 1984.

Levitt, Theodore, After the Sale is Over, *Harvard Business Review* 61 (September–October 1983): 87–93.

McCarthy, E. Jerome, *Basic Marketing*, Irwin, Homewood, IL, 1960.

Normann, Richard, *Service Management*, Wiley, New York, 1984.

Rathmell, John R, *Marketing in the Service Sector*, Winthrop, Cambridge, MA, 1974.

Rosenberg, Larry J., and Czepiel, John A., A Marketing Approach for Customer Retention, *The Journal of Consumer Marketing* 1 (1984): 45–51.

Schneider, Benjamin, Notes on Climate and Culture, in *Creativity in Services Marketing, What's New, What Works, What's Developing*, F. Venkatesan et al., eds., American Marketing Association, Chicago, IL, 1986, pp. 63–67.

Schneider, Benjamin, and Bowen, David E., Employee and Customer Perceptions of Service in Banks: Replication and Extension, *Journal of Applied Psychology* 70 (1985): 423–433.

Schneider, Benjamin, and Rentsch, J., The Management of Climate and Culture: A Futures Perspective, in *Futures of Organizations*. J. Hage, ed., D.C. Heath Lexington Books, Lexington, MA, 1987.

Webster, Jr., Fredrick E., Management Science in Industrial Marketing, *Journal of Marketing* 1 (January 1978): 21–27.

14

Marketing Redefined

Management Decision
Vol. 28, No. 8, 1990
pp. 5–9

Christian Grönroos

Do the universalities of the "4Ps" apply to all industries? One of the senior exponents of the "Nordic School" of marketing challenges the dominant product-led consumer concepts of marketing.

Marketing management through the Western world has traditionally been based on definitions agreed in the US and presented in American textbooks. But are these definitions really right for Europe and the rest of the world? This article puts forward a new definition of marketing which is geared to the nature of modern marketing research and practice in Northern Europe. This new definition is more truly market orientated than the standard textbook definitions.

The Marketing Concept

The marketing concept which defines marketing as a philosophy states that a firm should base its activities on customers' needs and wants in selected target markets. Obviously, restrictions imposed by society (laws, industry agreements, norms, etc) must be recognised. But if the basic concept is applied by the firm, its operations should be successful and profitable. This is also called a market-orientated view in contrast to production orientation, where the firm's activities are geared to existing technology, products or production processes.

It is easy to use the marketing concept as a basis for marketing planning. But it is much harder to devise satisfactory ways of implementing the marketing concept. Indeed, its conventional application to practical business situations has been less than satisfactory—the theories simply do not fit the realities of the business environment.

The Marketing Mix

Dozens of textbooks develop and describe models for translating the marketing concept into practical marketing. At the heart of these is the model of the marketing mix, often known as the 4Ps (product, price, promotion, place). According to this model the marketer, sitting in the marketing department, blends the 4Ps into an appropriate mix so as to make the greatest profit.

The limitations of this model have become increasingly obvious; other Ps have been added (e.g. politics, public relations) in attempts to stretch the model to make it fit new marketing perspectives. This is not, however, the best way to deal with the model's inadequacies. It would be much better to appraise the marketing activity afresh, and from this to create a more relevant definition.

Background to the Model

Academics as well as practising marketers still base their thoughts on the model of the marketing mix. Despite its evident limitations, it is still widely considered and used as the general marketing model throughout the Western world. Yet its limitations are not surprising when the specific facts about its development are remembered:

(1) It was developed from empirical research on consumer-packaged goods and durables.
(2) It was developed in North America, in a marketing environment which in many aspects is quite specific—having, for example:

- a huge domestic market;
- a unique media structure;
- a highly competitive distribution system.

This marketing model may indeed cover many marketing situations in North America, but its general validity has been more taken for granted than formally proved. The widespread use of the model is perhaps understandable. Marketing management was first developed systematically in the US, and the new marketing thinking swept over Europe. The model of the marketing mix was considered to be valid academically (though no formal validation has been presented), and has been used unchanged in the European business environment. But it is not valid in European marketing practice, yet we have developed no marketing theory or model geared to European conditions—for which we Europeans have only ourselves to blame. Furthermore the model has been applied to products for which it was never intended, even in the US, and for which it is inappropriate—e.g. in marketing services and industrial marketing.

The American Definition

In 1985, the American Marketing Association (AMA) produced an updated definition of marketing:

Marketing is the process of planning and executing the conception, pricing, promotion and distribution of ideas, goods and services to create exchange and satisfy individual and organizational objectives[1].

Note that the definition still consists of a list of activities

- conception
- pricing
- promotion
- distribution

not so very different from the old definition of the 4Ps. No real shift has occurred in the view of what marketing is. And the logical consequence of such a list is that anything not on it is, by definition, not marketing.

The AMA definition is based on convenience—those activities that are easily defined and separated from other activities in the firm, and can thus be called "marketing", and made into a specialist function. The definition does not take the customer's wishes into account—other than possibly indirectly. Market research is conducted in order to discover what the market wants, but these pieces of research fit more or less into the existing marketing model.

As a marketing philosophy, the marketing concept is still valid: i.e. that a company should base its activities on the customers' needs and wants in selected target markets. However, the standard way of transforming this concept into marketing in practice is production-orientated, because it starts from the firm and not from the market. What is needed is a truly market-orientated definition of marketing.

Marketing Research in Northern Europe

With this in mind, a new research approach has been developed in Northern Europe—particularly in Scandinavia and Finland—over the past decade. Researchers working in the areas of industrial and services marketing have aimed at developing a deeper understanding of the marketing function based on:

(1) customer relationships;
(2) real marketing situations.

Their research can be characterised as:

- highly empirical;
- reliant upon close contact between researchers and the market;
- case-study based;
- using quantitative methods when appropriate.

These results of research in the two areas of industrial and services marketing support each other. They conclude that the most important issue in marketing is to establish, strengthen and develop customer relationships:

— where this can be done at a profit, and
— where individual and organisational objectives are met.

But before customer relationships can become the keystone of marketing, a truly market-orientated management is required.

Marketing-Orientated Management

The view of the marketing function is a key issue in modern European research. This is NOT the same as the function of the marketing department, which is a purely organisational matter. The marketing function itself depends on the nature of customer relationships, and is spread over a large part of the organisation—from the switchboard operator to the chief executive. It is not solely the responsibility of the marketing department, but concerns all of the organisation's activities which have an impact on buyer-behaviour.

In consequence of this new understanding of the total marketing function, many firms have decreased the size and importance of their marketing departments; in some cases the department has been closed down altogether. Increased responsibility for initiating and implementing marketing activities has been delegated to the line managers in other specialist functions—e.g. production, service, deliveries. Thus these firms have attempted to integrate marketing and operations.

But it is not only operations that are affected by marketing—many staff and support functions also include a marketing element. A large number of employees may be in direct contact with the customer, for example:

- counter staff in banks
- check-in and in-flight services of airlines
- joint R&D projects with customers
- technical services
- deliveries
- customer training
- telephone reception.

Furthermore, many employees who have no direct customer-contact are indirectly involved: they supply backup services which enable other functions and employees to serve the customer. These indirectly involved staff should be encouraged to see their colleagues as 'internal customers' who have to be served—and served well—as part of the service to the ultimate, external customer.

Part-time Marketers

There is frequently only a limited number of marketing (and sales) specialists engaged in direct marketing activities such as:

- advertising
- personal selling
- mass communication

- market research
- marketing planning.

Employees involved in marketing-like contacts with customers greatly outnumber the marketing specialists. The former are often called "part-time marketers"[2], since their main job is something other than marketing—e.g. production, technical services, deliveries, invoicing, claims handling, R&D. In their own work, they have to demonstrate job skills and provide a level of service whereby the customers' trust in them is maintained and strengthened. As a result these employees are true part-time marketers, fulfilling their responsibilities as members of the total marketing function of the firm.

Management thus has a duty:

(1) to understand the dual responsibilities of many groups of employees;
(2) to ensure that all the part-time marketers in the company realise that they have a marketing role.

As marketing spreads throughout the organisation, it is evident that it cannot be the total responsibility of a specialist function. Instead marketing becomes an integral part of top management, with marketing specialists providing support in direct marketing activities: e.g. market research, advertising, telemarketing, personal selling. It is therefore much more accurate, in terms of practical marketing, to view marketing as market-orientated management than as a separate function only.

Customer Relationships: The Cornerstone of Marketing

Marketing, then, is not the same as the marketing department, which is supposed to be responsible for initiating, planning, executing and controlling the marketing activities of a company. Marketing itself is a management concern rather than a specialist function, allowing for differences between industries, customers and even specific situations. And at the heart of this general management concern lie customer relationships.

According to the research carried out both in Finland and Scandinavia, and also in a wider European context, marketing revolves around customer relationships whereby the objectives of the parties involved are achieved through various kinds of exchanges. Moreover, exchanges take place in order to establish and maintain these relationships—long-term relationships are especially stressed in the research that has been carried out[3]. And interestingly, the same approach is also emerging in American marketing literature[4].

A key to understanding this approach is the acceptance that the first customer-contact may not pay off. That is establishing contact with a customer, and achieving the first sales, often cost so much that the net return on the deal is minimal or even negative. But as the relationship continues, leading to more business, the customer becomes profitable to the seller. It is almost always more profitable in the medium and long term to develop enduring customer relationships.

Close and long-term customer relationships can be achieved through:

- exchange of information
- exchange of goods
- exchange of services
- social contacts

—and in their turn these will lead to profit.

Furthermore, it should be noted that the relationship can involve the buyer and seller in a network consisting of several parties, e.g.

- other suppliers
- other customers
- customers customers
- financial organisations
- political decision makers

This whole network is part of the customer relationship and has an impact on the development of that relationship.

The Importance of Promises

The concept of the promise is another aspect of a market-orientated, European framework of marketing[5]. This is as important to customer relationships as the exchange concept. Just as goods and/or services are exchanged for money, so promises are exchanged between buyer and seller. The seller gives a set of promises relating to, e.g.

- goods
- services
- financial solutions
- materials administration
- transfer of information
- social contacts
- future commitments.

On the other hand, the buyer gives a set of promises concerning his/her commitments to the relationship. Obviously, the promises must be kept on both sides if the relationship is to flourish.

A European Definition of Marketing

A new definition of marketing has been developed as a result of the research in Scandinavia. This definition starts with the customers' views of the marketing function, and is geared to the prevailing conditions in the marketplace. It takes account of the following:

(1)   Management Responsibility

In today's competitive environment, marketing is more of an overall management responsibility than a specialist function.

(2)   Part-time Marketers

The marketing function is spread all over the firm. Because of this, there are a large number of part-time marketers whose main duties are concerned with other tasks and functions.

(3)   Customer Relationships

Customer relationships lie at the core of marketing. Marketing is not simply the planning and implementation of a set of variables in a marketing mix. It is rather the establishment and development of customer relationships so that individual and organisational objectives are met.

(4)   Promises

Promises are mutually exchanged and kept in the relationship between buyer and seller. As a result, the customer relationship is established, strengthened and developed for commercial profit.

Marketing Redefined

Arising from the foregoing, this new definition of marketing has emerged:

> Marketing is to establish, maintain and enhance long-term customer relationships at a profit, so that the objectives of the parties involved are met. This is done by a mutual exchange and fulfilment of promises.[6]

This brief statement can be supplemented as follows. The resources of the firm—personnel, technological and systems—have to be used in such a manner that the customer's trust in them, and hence in the firm itself, is maintained and strengthened. The exchange of promises indicated in the definition may be of any kind, involving any type of thing or activity. In the same way the various resources—personnel, technological and systems—representing the customer, whether a household or another organisation, cannot be predetermined or explicitly categorised.

The main objective of marketing, then, is to go for enduring relationships with the customers. Of course sometimes, and for some firms, short-term sales may be profitable. But generally speaking the longer-term approach is vital to profitable marketing.

This new definition does not diminish the value of traditional elements of the marketing mix, such as advertising, personal selling, pricing and distribution. However, it does demonstrate that marketing is a wider function involving all those elements of a firm's activities that establish and develop long-term customer relations.

In both services and industrial marketing, the concept of interactive marketing has been found to be important—i.e. the marketing impact of the customer's interactions with the seller's resources outside the marketing/sales department: e.g. production, technical services, claims handling, deliveries. This concept demonstrates the significance of part-time marketers in marketing. In most situations the impact of interactive marketing on the customer could be considered the most vital part of a firm's total marketing effort. Outstanding interactive marketing may create the competitive edge.

Conclusion

The marketing concept as a basic philosophy guiding marketing in practice still holds—a firm should base its activities on the needs, wants and expectations of customers in selected target markets. There has been no debate over the concept itself. But the definition of marketing in practice and the marketing management model has been found wanting.

Emerging from this is a new definition of marketing which is truly market-orientated. It is based on conceptual and empirical research within the areas of industrial and services marketing. Much of the empirical work has been done in Northern Europe, although the approach is spreading elsewhere. More research is now needed concerning the application of this market-orientated approach, considering:

- various types of products and customers;
- different geographical areas.

On a practical level, however, all managers can use these insights as a basis for considering their own firm's marketing efforts: how important are customer relationships, and how much do you value and train all the part-time marketers in your company (internal marketing)? The answers to these questions may prove vital to your business survival and growth.

References

1. "AMA Board Approves New Marketing Definition", *Marketing News*, No. 5, 1 March 1985.
2. Gummesson, E., *The Part-time Marketer*, research report 90:3, Service Research Center, University of Karlstad, Sweden, 1990.

3.   Gummesson, E., "The New Marketing—Developing Long Term Interactive Relationships", *Long Range Planning*, No. 4, 1987.
4.   Jackson, B.B., "Build Customer Relationships that Last", *Harvard Business Review*, November-December 1985.
5.   Calonius, H., *The Promise Concept*, research report, Swedish School of Economics and Business Administration, Helsinki, Finland, 1987.
6.   Grönroos, C., *Service Management and Marketing: Managing the Moments of Truth in Service Competition*, Lexington Books, Lexington, Mass., 1990, p. 138.

Application Questions

(1)   Is your firm's marketing effort production orientated or market orientated?

(2)   How important are long-term customer relationships to your organisation? What practical steps could be taken to improve them?

(3)   How many of your firm's employees could be defined as part-time marketers? Are all of them aware of this role and its importance? Are their supervisors aware of it?

(4)   What contribution do you think the part-time marketers currently make to your firm's total marketing effort? How could you best activate/educate/motivate them to improve your marketing performance?

(5)   What emphasis does your organisation place on the keeping of promises?

(6)   Could the size and importance of your marketing department be reduced? What would be the implications for managing marketing activities within the organisation?

Action Points

•   *Consider* carefully the ways in which your organisation uses the model of the marketing mix. Look at the practical realities of your total marketing effort and see how well these relate to the model.

•   *List* the practical changes in your own managerial strategy and role resulting from:

    (a)   your staff being seen as part-time marketers, as well as having their own particular area of expertise;

    (b)   marketing becoming part of overall management responsibility rather than a specialist function;

    (c)   your organisation's marketing effort being directed mainly towards long-term customer relationships.

Perspectives of Other Scholars

15

Relationship Marketing: A Review of the Scholarly Contribution of Christian Grönroos

Adrian Payne

Christian Grönroos is a pioneer in the field of both services marketing and relationship marketing. His work in the area of relationship marketing has made a significant and sustained contribution to the discipline. This collection of 14 articles demonstrates both the quality and breadth of Christian's contribution to the field.

Christian's early work focused on service management and marketing. I became closely aware of his work in late 1980s when I moved to Cranfield University in the United Kingdom to take up an appointment as Britain's first professor of services marketing. Shortly afterwards, Christian published one of the first substantial books in this area (Grönroos, 1990a). An important feature of his early work was a recognition that marketing extended beyond the restrictive tyranny of the marketing mix and that marketing, in a services context, needs to be more closely aligned with management. Since then, Christian has continued his research on services and service and this work has had an important influence on his subsequent contribution to the emerging discipline of relationship marketing.

The decade of the 1980s represented one in which services marketing became an area of major academic focus (Christopher et al., 1991). Whilst recent academic interest in relationship marketing can be traced to the early 1980s, it was not until the 1990s that the topic of relationship marketing started to develop into a major field of academic research. This more recent focus on relationship marketing commenced with articles by academics such as Berry (1983), Levitt (1983), and Jackson (1985). As an innovator in conceptual research in the area of services, Christian Grönroos was already considering the importance of relational approaches and he was quick to see the importance of the broader relationship context. While some hailed relationship marketing as a new discovery, Grönroos (1994) and others (e.g., Sheth and Parvatiyar,

1995) pointed to its much earlier manifestations. These early articles were influential in emphasizing the need to understand the types of relationships and the extent to which relationship approaches are appropriate to different forms of enterprise.

In 1993, I met Christian for the first time when he was one of a small number of pioneering international scholars who were invited to attend the first *International Colloquium in Relationship Marketing (ICRM)* organized by David Ballantyne, held at Monash University in Australia. Since then, over a period of two decades, I have had the opportunity to interact with him regularly, especially at *ICRM* events. In common with many academics and practitioners, I have learned much from his insightful research and practical approach to relationship building and I have greatly valued our professional and personal relationship. It is a great pleasure to be able to comment on Christian's contribution to the field of relationship marketing.

In this brief review, I discuss three aspects of Christian Grönroos's contribution: his early work in relationship marketing and its impact; the scope of his research in relationship marketing, including a commentary on three particular contributions in this volume; and his broader academic accomplishments.

Christian Grönroos's Early Work in Relationship Marketing

In this section I consider Christian's first three chronological articles in this volume. Grönroos's earliest of these contributions is an article (Grönroos, 1990b) published in the *Journal of Business Research*. This article, "Relationship Approach to Marketing in Service Contexts: The Marketing and Organizational Behavior Interface," is important as it extends Berry's (1983) definition of relationship marketing to include: (1) meeting the objectives of all parties involved; and, (2) achieving these objectives through the mutual exchange and fulfillment of promises. The topic of promises management is developed further in a much later article in this volume (Grönroos, 2009). This 1990 article also examines the implications of the relationship marketing approach to marketing. He emphasizes the importance of involving a whole range of business functions in marketing-related tasks. This discussion predates much of the more recent focus on cross-functional management of marketing activities. The article also focuses on the relationship marketing interface between marketing and organizational behavior and points to the need for a both a service culture and strong internal marketing in order to make a relationship-based approach successful.

Christian's second chronological article in this volume, "From Marketing Mix to Relationship Marketing: Towards a Paradigm Shift in Marketing," was presented as a paper at the first *ICRM* in 1993. This was the start of Christian's long-term association and deep involvement with the *ICRM* series, which celebrated its 20th year in 2012. This paper was subsequently published in both the *Asia-Australia Journal of Marketing* and as a lead article in *Management Decision* (Grönroos, 1994) and has had a major impact on the relationship marketing discipline. In this article he provides a scholarly review of how the marketing mix concept developed, and identifies its drawbacks as well. Challengingly, he argues that: "The marketing department concept is obsolete and has to be replaced by some other way of organizing the marketing function, so that the organization will have a chance to become market oriented" (1994: 7). Drawing on the network approach to industrial marketing and his own work on the marketing of services, Grönroos identifies relationship building as a "cornerstone of marketing" (1994: 8). He discusses a marketing strategy continuum that contrasts transaction marketing with relationship marketing and explains how different forms of goods and services relate to different positions on this continuum.

This article (Grönroos, 1994), later republished for the third time in 1997 in *Management Decision*, has had a huge impact on marketing scholars interested in relationship marketing. This impact is evidenced by more than 1,500 academic citations in the literature. This work is amongst the most influential arguing that relationship marketing represents a move towards a new paradigm for marketing. Grönroos points out that the major problem with the marketing mix is that, in many instances, it appears as the only acceptable marketing paradigm. He argues convincingly that relationship marketing represents a fundamentally different approach compared with viewing exchanges as isolated marketplace transactions. Relationship marketing, by contrast, focuses on building relationships. He concludes:

> The simplicity of the [marketing mix] model seduces teachers to toolbox thinking instead of constantly reminding them of the fact that marketing is a social process with far more facets than that. As a consequence of this, researchers and marketing managers are also constrained by the simplistic nature of the Four Ps. The victims are marketing theory and customers.... Marketing mix management with its four Ps is reaching the end of the road as a universal marketing approach. (Grönroos, 1994: 14)

This article has acted as a catalyst, inspiring many marketing scholars to accept relationship marketing as a new paradigm and motivating them to become involved in undertaking research in relationship marketing.

By 1994, it was clear that several distinctive approaches to relationship marketing were developing. At a research conference on relationship marketing convened by Jagdish Sheth and Atul Parvatiyar at Emory University, Coote (1994) identified three broad approaches to relationship marketing, all of which had different emphases and scope. He termed these: the "Nordic approach," based on the work of Christian and his colleagues (e.g., Grönroos, 1994; Gummesson, 1994); the "Anglo-Australian approach," based on work by Martin Christopher, David Ballantyne, and myself (e.g., Christopher et al., 1991) and the "North American approach," based on the work of a number of US scholars (e.g., Berry, 1983; Levitt, 1983; Jackson, 1985; Sheth and Parvatiyar, 1995). Coote's work sought to identify the foundational theories, concepts, and research emphases associated with each of these three approaches. Whilst Coote's typology is not complete, it serves to graphically illustrate the alternative approaches to relationship marketing that developed in different geographic regions.

The Nordic approach and the Anglo-Australian shared much common ground and viewed relationship marketing from a broader and more holistic perspective. The North American approach, at this time, viewed relationship marketing from a much narrower firm–customer dyad perspective. The Anglo-Australian approach recognized the importance of relationships in six key stakeholder groupings or market domains (Christopher et al., 1991), and the Nordic approach also recognized the importance of other stakeholders beyond the firm–customer dyad (e.g., Gummesson, 1994). Although Grönroos's work during this period focused principally on the relationships between firms and their customers, he explicitly noted the importance of relationships with "other parties as well" (Grönroos, 1994: 10). More specifically, he also emphasized the importance of the internal market domain (Grönroos, 1990a, 1990b).

Grönroos's third chronological contribution in this volume, "Relationship Marketing: The Strategy Continuum" was published in 1995 in the *Journal of the Academy of Marketing Science*. In 1986, Jagdish Sheth argued for the need to develop a high profile for relationship marketing through publication in high-quality journals and the involvement of respected scholars. These activities represent two key steps in moving relationship marketing toward the status of a discipline (Sheth, 1996). This latter article by Grönroos (1995) is of particular significance as it appears this is the first example of an article with the title "relationship marketing" appearing in one of the top five US academic marketing journals. This article extends earlier contributions (Grönroos, 1991, 1994). It discusses how the relationship approach was substantially different to a transaction marketing approach in terms of the dominating marketing orientation, the dominating quality function, customer information systems, interdependency between business functions and the role of internal marketing. He argues that firms should position their strategic approach along this "relationship to transaction" strategy continuum and that the more a relationship type of strategy is called for, the more emphasis needs to be placed on interactive marketing, the impact of functional quality, and internal marketing.

The Scope of Christian Grönroos's Subsequent Research in Relationship Marketing

The 14 articles in this volume collectively represent a good cross-section of Christian Grönroos's academic output in the field of relationship marketing. However, they represent only a proportion of his prolific work in this area. His other work includes academic articles, book chapters and a large number of conference papers. The remaining contributions in this volume, published between 1997 and 2012, address a range of specific issues within the relationship marketing domain. These include value-driven considerations in relationship marketing (Grönroos, 1997); relationship marketing challenges for the organization (Grönroos, 1999a); an overview of the Nordic perspective on relationship marketing (Grönroos, 1999b); the importance of dialog in relationship marketing (Grönroos, 2000); bringing customer focus into the board room (Grönroos, 2003); relationship levels as predictors of customer commitment (Sääksjärvi et al., 2007); relationship marketing as promises management (Grönroos, 2009); the interface between value creation interaction and marketing (Grönroos, 2011); and a detailed exploration of the concept of return on relationships (Grönroos and Helle, 2012).

Most of these contributions in this volume are conceptual (for two exceptions, see Sääksjärvi et al., 2007; Grönroos and Helle, 2012). This conceptual emphasis is, in my opinion, a key strength of Christian's work. The importance of conceptual research is now increasingly recognized by marketing scholars, as reflected by recent calls in the *Journal of Marketing* for more conceptual research in marketing (MacInnis, 2011; Yadav, 2010). Each reader will find different topics that are of particular interest to them in this volume. Space for this commentary does not permit a discussion of all these contributions, so I comment briefly on three contributions that resonate strongly with me.

The first contribution I select in this section is a chapter published in Sheth and Parvatiyar's (1999) seminal *Handbook of Relationship Marketing*. This edited compilation provides a review of key work by leading scholars in the relationship marketing field that was undertaken in the 1980s and 1990s. It also provides a detailed summary of alternative approaches and emerging "schools" (e.g., Coote, 1994) of relationship marketing. Christian Grönroos's chapter in this compilation will be of especial interest to those less familiar with his work. The chapter explains how the Nordic School of marketing grew out of a substantial research into services marketing undertaken in the Scandinavian and Finnish regions and how this research in services marketing evolved into a relationship marketing school of thought. It makes explicit the strong synergies between the relational nature of Grönroos's early services research and his subsequent work in relationship marketing. It also explains the linkages the Nordic School has with other research originating in Scandinavia. This latter research, by the Industrial Marketing and Purchasing (IMP) Group, focuses on the interaction and network approach to the management of business-to-business relationships (e.g., Håkansson, 1982; Håkansson and Snehota, 1995).

This chapter draws together much of Grönroos's earlier work. It also provides a succinct summary of Christian's work on the value process in relationship marketing, and in particular draws on his thinking on the nature of customer perceived value (e.g., Ravald and Grönroos, 1996). This chapter provides clear guidelines as to what is necessary for the successful execution of relationship marketing strategy. Grönroos identifies three key implementation areas that include: (1) an *interaction process* as being central to relationship marketing; (2) a *dialog process* which supports the development and enhancement of relationships; and (3) a *value process* which is an outcome of relationship marketing. The chapter also identifies a useful research agenda for future work in relationship marketing, including a number of the items that have not yet been satisfactorily addressed by extant research.

A very short, but important, contribution in this volume, published in *Marketing Theory*, is titled "Taking a Customer Focus Back into the Boardroom: Can Relationship

Marketing do It?" (Grönroos, 2003). As Christian notes in this 2003 article, both the marketing function and marketing executives are becoming increasingly marginalized in many enterprises. This view is as current today, a decade later, as it was when this article was published. This pithy article points to two of the potential key reasons why marketing has been marginalized: (1) much of the marketing budget is spent on activities that often have too limited an impact on customers; and, (2) marketing has become a cost issue instead of a balance sheet investment issue. He points out: "The relationship paradigm has an opportunity to make marketing relevant for shareholders, top management, customers and the management of customers again" (2003: 172). It remains for many companies today to shift from viewing marketing as a "spending a budget function" to viewing marketing as the process of investment in customers and customer segments with the objective of obtaining a future return on that investment.

This concept of obtaining a return on the relationship marketing investment is echoed, in much greater detail, in the most recent article in this volume titled "Return on Relationships: Conceptual Understanding and Measurement of Mutual Gains from Relational Business Engagements" (Grönroos and Helle, 2012). The concept of gaining a "return on relationships" appears to have been first addressed substantively by Gummesson (2004). The related issue of gaining an "ROI on CRM" has also been considered by Ang and Buttle (2002).

As Grönroos and Helle point out, the area of marketing accountability has recently become an important focus for research in marketing. They develop a framework that conceptualizes mutual value creation as a key driver of return on relationships (ROR). Interestingly, they argue that gaining a "return on relationships" involves the actors' relational competences, rather than the actors' ability to advance each others' separate strategies. Their framework proposes that return on the relationships (ROR) is driven by three factors: "the cost associated with each party's relational investment following from a 'practice' matching process, the capacity of the actors to create joint productivity gains, as well as their ability to negotiate a share of the joint productivity gain through price as value" (Grönroos and Helle, 2012: 17). This article also identifies metrics for a developing reciprocal return on relationships, based on the concept of mutual value creation. It illustrates the concept of return on relationships using a case study of an industrial organization. As the authors note, this study provides a shift in perspective from *viewing customers as assets*, to understanding and measuring the *relationships between actors as assets*. This article addresses an especially important contemporary issue and I believe it will have an important influence on future relationship marketing research and practice.

Christian Grönroos's Other Academic Accomplishments

The previous discussion has focused on Christian's research output, with a particular focus on his relationship marketing work published in academic journals and scholarly books. In this concluding section, I comment briefly on some other aspects of his academic accomplishments.

Christian Grönroos has pursued most of his academic career at the Hanken School of Economics in Helsinki, Finland. Whilst this institution has been his primary academic base, he has been highly actively globally and has built a reputation as a truly international scholar. In addition to his position as Professor of Service Management and Relationship Marketing, and Chairman of the Board of the research and knowledge center CERS—Centre for Relationship Marketing and Service Management at Hanken, he is an Honorary Professor at Nankai University and Tianjin Normal University in People's Republic of China (PRC), as well as at Oslo School of Management, Norway. He has also had visiting professor or visiting scholar associations with Arizona State and Stanford Universities in the United States of America, Lund, and Karlstad universities in Sweden, University of Auckland in New Zealand, and Thammasat University in Thailand. He is also a Distinguished Faculty member at Center for Services Leadership at Arizona State University in the United States of America. He is an honorary member of the Italian Marketing Association and a guest professor at Marketing Research Center of China. His work on both relationship and services marketing has been published in 14 languages.

Christian Grönroos has also been a major contributor to and influence on the *ICRM* series. These Colloquia have been highly influential in the ongoing development of the relationship marketing discipline. When David Ballantyne launched this series in 1993 he had the vision of a Colloquium which went beyond the bounds of a conventional conference, to one which would expand and sustain an international community of academics and researchers with an interest in relationship marketing. Since then, Colloquia have been held in many countries including the United Kingdom, Sweden, Finland, the United States of America, New Zealand, Canada, Germany, Argentina, and the Netherlands. As mentioned earlier, Christian was an invitee to the first *ICRM* in Australia in 1993 and in 1996 he acted as convenor of the fourth *ICRM* at the Hanken Business School in Helsinki. Over 20 years, Grönroos has been active in providing guidance to convenors on the content and structure of *ICRM* events.

Christian, through his involvement at CERS, has also made a great contribution in terms of engaging with his colleagues, his students, and with practicing managers. Whilst always listening to and reflecting on the views of others, Christian is passionate about defending his own ideas. He is a professor who "professes"! He has been especially active in supporting students' doctoral work and starting them on their academic publishing careers. Students working under him have been fortunate in receiving strong intellectual guidance; two of the contributions in this volume are co-authored with doctoral students. He has supported many Ph.D. students who have gone on to develop academic careers. In the relationship marketing area, two examples are Kaj Storbacka, a professor at the University of Auckland and David Ballantyne, an associate professor at the University of Otago. Many master's level students have also benefited from what they have learned on his courses.

Finally, a key feature of Christian's work has been its managerial relevance. He has adopted a practical perspective in his academic work, which is framed in a managerially useful context. This is reflected in his popularity with companies seeking to benefit from his knowledge and academic institutions running executive programs for managers seeking his services. In addition to his academic work, he frequently lectures on relationship marketing and service management in university-level executive programs and on in-company training programs. He has undertaken this work in Europe, North America, Latin America, China, and Australasia.

In sum, Christian Grönroos has played an important role in the development of relationship marketing as an academic discipline within marketing. As one of the leading European scholars in the field of marketing, Christian has provided high credibility and support for development of the field of relationship marketing. His colleagues, students, and reflective managerial practitioners have all substantially benefited from his contribution to relationship marketing.

References

Ang, L., and F.A. Buttle. 2002. "ROI on CRM: a Customer-Journey Approach," *Conference Proceedings of the IMP (Industrial Marketing and Purchasing*, December, in Perth, Australia.

Berry, L.L. 1983. "Relationship Marketing," in L.L. Berry, G.L. Shostack, and G.D. Upah (eds), *Emerging Perspective on Services Marketing*, pp. 25–28. Chicago: American Marketing Association.

Christopher, M., A. Payne, and D. Ballantyne. 1991. *Relationship Marketing: Bringing Quality, Customer Service and Marketing Together*. Oxford: Butterworth Heinemann.

Coote, L. 1994. "Implementation of Relationship Marketing in an Accounting Practice," in J.N. Sheth and A. Parvatiyar (eds), *Relationship Marketing: Theory, Methods and Applications*, Research Conference Proceedings. Atlanta, USA: Emory University.

Grönroos, C. 1990a. *Services Management and Marketing*. Lexington, MA: Lexington Books.

———. 1990b. "Relationship Approach to Marketing in Service Contexts: The Marketing and Organizational Behavior Interface," *Journal of Business Research*, 20 (1): 3–11.

———. 1991. "The Marketing Strategy Continuum," *Management Decision*, 29 (1): 7–13.

———. 1994. "From Marketing Mix to Relationship Marketing: Towards a Paradigm Shift in Marketing, *Management Decision*, 32 (2): 4–20. [Republished in 1997; also published in *Asia/Australia Journal of Marketing*, 1994, 2 (1): 9–30.]

———. 1995. "Relationship Marketing: The Strategy Continuum," *Journal of the Academy of Marketing Science*, 23 (4): 252–54.

———. 1996. "Relationship Marketing Logic," *Asia-Australia Marketing Journal*, 4: 7–18. [Republished in 1996 as "Relationship Marketing: Strategic and Tactical Implications," *Management Decision*, 34 (3): 5–14.]

———. 1997. "Value-Driven Relational Marketing: From Products to Resources and Competencies," *Journal of Marketing Management*, 13 (5): 407–19.

———. 1999a. "Relationship Marketing: Challenges for the Organization," *Journal of Business Research*, 46 (3): 327–35.

———. 1999b. "Relationship Marketing: The Nordic School Perspective," in J.N. Sheth and A. Parvatiyar (eds), *Handbook of Relationship Marketing*, pp. 95–118. Thousand Oaks, CA: SAGE Publications.

———. 2000. "Creating a Relationship Dialogue: Communication, Interaction and Value," *The Marketing Review*, 1 (1): 5–14.

———. 2003. "Taking a Customer Focus Back into the Boardroom: Can Relationship Marketing Do It?" *Marketing Theory*, 3 (1): 171–73.

Grönroos, C. 2009. "Relationship Marketing as Promise Management," in P. Maclaran, M. Saren, B. Stern, and M. Tadajewski (eds), *The SAGE Handbook of Marketing Theory*, pp. 397–412. Los Angeles, CA: SAGE Publications.

———. 2011. "A Service Perspective in Business Relationships: the Value Creation and Marketing Interface," *Industrial Marketing Management*, 40 (1): 240–47.

Grönroos, C., and P. Helle. 2012. "Return on Relationships: Conceptual Understanding and Measurement of Mutual Gains from Relational Business Engagements," *Journal of Business & Industrial Marketing*, 27 (5): 344–59.

Gummesson, E. 1994. *Relationship Marketing: From 4Ps to 30Rs*. Stockholm: Stockholm University.

———. 2004. "Return on Relationships (ROR): The Value of Relationship Marketing and CRM in Business-to-Business Contexts," *Journal of Business & Industrial Marketing*, 19 (2): 136–48.

Håkansson, H. (ed.). 1982. *International Marketing and Purchasing of Industrial Goods*. New York, NY: Wiley.

Håkansson, H., and I. Snehota. 1995. *Developing Relationships in Business Networks*. London: Routledge.

Jackson, B.B. 1985. *Winning and Keeping Industrial Customers: The Dynamics of Customer Relationships*. Lexington, MA: D.C. Heath.

Levitt, T. 1983. "After the Sale Is Over," *Harvard Business Review*, 62 (1): 87–93.

MacInnis, D.J. 2011. "A Framework for Conceptual Contributions in Marketing," *Journal of Marketing*, 75 (July): 136–54.

Ravald, A., and C. Grönroos. 1996. "The Value Concept and Relationship Marketing," *European Journal of Marketing*, 30 (2): 19–30.

Sääksjärvi, M., K. Hellén, J. Gummerus, and C. Grönroos. 2007. "Love at First Sight or a Long-Term Affair? Different Relationship Levels as Predictors of Customer Commitment," *Journal of Relationship Marketing*, 6 (1): 45–61.

Sheth, J.N. 1996. "Relationship Marketing: Paradigm Shift or Shaft?" Paper presented at the Annual Meeting of the Academy of Marketing Science, Miami, FL.

Sheth, J.N., and A. Parvatiyar. 1995. "The Evolution of Relationship Marketing," *International Business Review*, 4: 397–418.

——— (eds). 1999. *Handbook of Relationship Marketing*. Thousand Oaks, CA: SAGE Publications.

Yadav, M.S. 2010. "The Decline of Conceptual Articles and Implications for Knowledge Development," *Journal of Marketing*, 74 (1): 1–19.

16

Christian Grönroos: Architect of Truth

Michael Saren

The contribution of management academics to the credit crunch of 2007–08 has not received much attention in the press, despite their role as educators of business executives and guardians of the veracity of management knowledge. In 2009, however, no less a publication than the *Economist*—not regarded as a radical exponent of counter business culture—held business schools and their professors responsible for the lack of critique of questionable management theories and practices which contributed directly to the financial crisis:

> Business schools have done too little to reform themselves in the light of the credit crunch. You do not have to accept the idea that the business schools were "agents of the apocalypse" to believe that they need to change their ways, at least a little, in the light of recent events.… Professors are always inclined to puff the businesses that provide them, at the very least, with their raw materials and, if they are lucky, with lucrative consultancy work. HBS has produced fawning studies of almost every recent corporate villain from Enron (which was stuffed full of HBS alumni) to the Royal Bank of Scotland. A taste for cheerleading has been reinforced by the rise of a multi-million-dollar management-theory industry. Professors with dollar signs in their eyes are always announcing the birth of the latest revolutionary management technique.… Business schools need to make more room for people who are willing to bite the hands that feed them: to prick business bubbles, expose management fads and generally rough up the most feted managers. (*Economist*, 2009)

Business schools and universities in Europe and the United States of America have undergone a thorough marketization process during the last 15–20 years (Lowrie and Willmott, 2005). Students have been redefined as customers who demand the latest useful knowledge from their instructors, whose role has become that of the service providers of business techniques, models, and theories. Theories can certainly broaden people's minds, but there is a danger that they also tie them into particular ways of thinking, skewing their perspectives in ways that often go unquestioned and unrecognized. The building blocks of theory are its underlying concepts and definitions, the unstated assumptions that are often normative and shared amongst a particular group of individuals. That is why we also need academics who are able and willing to question, interrogate and, some argue, even to be suspicious of theory (Maclaran et al., 2009).

Although the authors of the *Economist's* column quoted above were no doubt thinking mainly of financial engineering and risk management disciplines, if a dean were to reorganize their business school according to this advice, then in my view the ideal and exceptional professor who would be able and willing to fulfill this role of critiquing management fads, questioning existing knowledge and interrogating the latest theories is none other than Christian Grönroos.

As the quotation suggests, this is not a role which comes naturally to business school professors, nor one which maximizes current or future earnings. The ancient Geeks called such a person a parrhesia, a fearless truth teller, whatever the danger, however unpopular (Foucault, 2001). Yet, this is what Grönroos has done on several occasions, by revealing the flaws in several powerful marketing shibboleths from the marketing mix to the 4Ps to the role of marketing management and the marketing function. But telling truth to power has always been risky, and as Machiavelli demonstrated, many a medieval confidante to princes and queens played the ultimate price, literally with their life, for voicing unacceptable truths.

Many of Grönroos's critiques of existing marketing models and theories are represented in the publications which are reprinted in this volume. Of course Grönroos does not just critique for its own sake. These articles are actually primarily concerned with building and promoting new ideas and theories with which to replace those which are lacking. In this commentary I will focus on one of these in particular; his 1994 *Management Decision* article, "From Marketing Mix to Relationship Marketing: Towards a Paradigm Shift in Marketing." I do not intend to reiterate or evaluate all the arguments against the mix or for the relationship approach which are also articulated in many others of his papers here—you can read these for yourself. My aim is to draw attention to the reasoning and evidence which is adduced in order to illustrate how Christian embodies many of the characteristics of the modern parrhesia and to reflect on his contribution to marketing in this respect. I will also consider to how Christian may be considered representative of the context, values, and approach of the Nordic school of marketing.

Critique of the Marketing Mix

Grönroos's 1994 Management Decision article is widely regarded as a seminal publication in the emergence of relationship marketing. Marion (2010) brackets it along with Keith's (1960) groundbreaking "Marketing Revolution" in *Journal of Marketing*. "From Marketing Mix to Relationship Marketing: Towards a Paradigm Shift in Marketing" has been republished three times and at the most recent count at the time of writing has more than 1,600 citations. The headline above the title asks, "Has today's dominant marketing mix paradigm become a strait-jacket?" Grönroos sets out the aims of his article with typical straightforwardness and clarity.

> Relationship marketing is suggested as *one new marketing paradigm*, and a number of consequences for marketing and management of a relationship-type marketing strategy is discussed based on the notion of a marketing *strategy continuum*. Finally, *the possibility of building a general theory* of marketing based on the relationship approach is examined. A further discussion of *the nature* of the relationship marketing paradigm is, however, *beyond the scope* of this report. (Grönroos, 1994, my italics)

I have highlighted particular phrases in this statement to illustrate the clarity and care with which Christian expresses his thoughts. Note that relationship marketing is one new paradigm, not a singular dominant one; strategy is a continuum, not a defined set of typologies; and further exploration of the nature of this paradigm is not within the scope of this article, thereby recognizing the complexity of the notion of paradigm, as distinct from a discussion of the possibility of building a general theory.

Of the many problems with the mix concept which Grönroos identifies in this paper, one which he comes back to at various points is its lack of an integrative dimension. As he points out, this absence is astonishing given the fact that Borden (1964) developed the notion of the mix in terms of the cooking analogy as "mixture of ingredients" which is blended together into a coherent, optimal, integrated whole. One would expect both practitioners and theorists to be concerned to develop means and processes in order to achieve this "blending" of the variables. A recipe consisting solely of a list of ingredients without instructions about preparation and how to mix and cook the "food." So for the marketing mix concept, and as Grönroos highlights, for many other things, process is as important as content.

Following Borden, however, all the attention shifted away from the integrative, mixing process. Subsequent marketing authors concentrated almost exclusively on the various "P" elements (even Borden had more than four) and mobilized the "toolkit" metaphor in place of that of a "recipe" of ingredients. Incidentally, I wonder whether it was the drive for scientism, professionalization, or gender bias which explains why mechanics somehow became a more suitable metaphor than cookery. In his paper though, Grönroos is not side-tracked by such speculation, concentrating instead on how the 4Ps model originated, why it became so dominant. And whether this was justified.

> Probably Borden's original idea of a list of a large number of marketing mix ingredients that have to be reconsidered in every given situation was shortened for pedagogical reasons and because a more limited number of marketing variables seemed to fit typical situations observed in the late 1950s and in the 1960s by the initiators of the short list of four standardized Ps.... Nevertheless the four Ps of the marketing mix have become the universal marketing model or even theory and an almost totally dominating paradigm for most academics, and they have had a tremendous impact on the practice of marketing as well. Is there any justification for this? (Grönroos, 1994: 6)

Dominance of the Marketing Mix

Grönroos observes that the concept of the marketing mix became unchallenged very quickly following its entry into the marketing textbooks in the early 1960s, totally superseding previous models and approaches. Along with the four Ps of marketing—product, price, place, and promotion—it completely overshadowed such that previous models and approaches "are hardly remembered, even with a footnote in most textbooks of today" (Grönroos, 1994: 4).

Of course this phenomenon of can be explained by Kuhn's (1962) notion of scientific progress through paradigmatic revolutions. We are not all Kuhnians, but it is the case that no discipline can simply comprise the summation of all prior theories, constantly competing with more and more models for explanatory power. New dominant theories must always drive out some of the old ones, but this "forgetting" process does appear to be exceptionally rapid and absolute in the marketing discipline. It is as if the academy's collective publication memory bank contains limited space and after a fairly short period of time the pressure for recency of citations supersedes the requirement to retain past knowledge (Baker, 2001); and far less for historical completeness (Herodotus, 1985).

One example of a "forgotten" approach that Grönroos (1994) cites, which along with the institutional, functional, and commodity schools of marketing was completely eclipsed by the marketing mix, is the early geography-related regional approach to marketing such as Reilly's (1931) Law of Retail Gravitation. Yet the early initiators of the mix themselves were strongly influenced in their development of what became the 4P variables by what they regarded as "typical situations" for marketing. As Grönroos points out, these typical situations were the geographically based characteristics of US markets:

> These can be described as involving consumer packaged goods in a North American environment with huge mass markets, a highly competitive distribution system and very commercial mass media. However, in other markets the infrastructure is to varying degrees different and the products are only partly consumer packaged goods. (Grönroos, 1994: 6)

So geography was an underlying influence on the development of the mix variables. Furthermore, the mix concept itself may be context specific, in other markets and territories the characteristics are significantly different in terms of market structure, transport, logistics, competition, infrastructure, products, etc. Grönroos (1989) points out that the North American marketing environment is quite specific in many respects with a huge domestic market, a unique media structure, and a non-oligopolistic, highly competitive distribution system.

"This marketing model may cover many marketing situations in North America, but its general validity has more been taken for granted than formally proved. In spite of this we have, for instance, no European marketing theory or model geared to European conditions" (Grönroos, 1989: 53).

The geographical site of the academic researchers partly explains the origination of the 4Ps marketing mix approach. It may also be important in explaining differences in relationships marketing and later developments, specifically the territorial origins of many of its early exponents like Grönroos in northern Europe, which became known as the Nordic School.

The Nordic School(s)

Grönroos envisaged the development of a distinct Nordic or Northern European approach to marketing theory emerging from their unique research approach in the areas industrial and services marketing (Grönroos, 1999). The research tradition in the Nordic School relies on a close contact between researchers and actors in the marketplace and on case study methodology. The term Nordic School has been used widely to distinguish the conceptualization and methods of scholars such as Grönroos and Gummesson (1985). The new ideas and approaches to marketing which have emanated from the Nordic approach are predicated on the conceptualization of relationship marketing as first and foremost a holistic organization-wide process. Therefore, the management of marketing activities extend beyond the functional department labeled "marketing" involving the entire organization, and because it is conceptualized as essentially a process there are no specified marketing variables (see Grönroos, 1997 in this volume).

That local environmental conditions affect marketing practices and relationships is one of the major contributions of the Nordic marketing tradition. Similarly, the importance of attention to local territorial conditions which affect architectural practice and design is one of the major contributions of the Nordic approach to architecture. Nordic architecture blends the social with the natural surroundings, emphasizing the buildings' relationships to their site. This is of course what we marketers would immediately identify as a highly relationship-oriented approach.

In architecture, Harris (1954) advocated the importance of "Regionalism of Liberation" which he defined as

> …the manifestation of a region that is especially in tune with the emerging thought of the time. We call such a manifestation "regional" only because it has not yet emerged elsewhere. It is the genius of this region to be more than ordinarily aware and more than ordinarily free. Its virtue is that its manifestation has significance for the world outside itself. To express this regionalism architecturally it is necessary that there be building, - preferably a lot of building-at one time. Only so can the expression be sufficiently general, sufficiently varied, sufficiently forceful to capture people's imaginations and provide a friendly climate long enough for a new school of design to develop. (Harris, 1954)

More specifically, Frampton (1983) argues that regionalism should relate to the surroundings, climate, light, colors, etc. When materials are able to be sourced, shipped, supplied, and built anywhere in the world they become separated from their natural surroundings. Such materials are no longer true to their region or area, and when used in buildings they are no longer personal to location and wrenched from their natural sources and surroundings, Frampton argues that they are reduced to the status of commodities. This philosophy led the Nordic approach to architectural design considerations such as how the materials used on the interior and exterior of buildings affect the user's experience; how the design and materials bring the user closer to the outside, or provide a significant barrier between indoors or outdoors; how the material and geometrical proportions impact the use of the space; and how they influence users' experience of the light and climactic conditions.

In Nordic architecture, we can see from this brief explanation that the key relationships for people are with buildings and surroundings, which allowing for differences in context is not dissimilar from the Nordic marketing researchers' focus on relationships between market actors. Learning from Nordic appreciation of space and place, in marketing—as in architecture—the key relationship of the future may not simply be between marketplace actors, but between marketing processes and the territories in which it occurs. Compared to the prior dominance of the 4Ps approach, Grönroos and the Nordic School of marketing also represent a "Regionalism of Liberation."

Continuing the Critique

For me, Grönroos's contribution to the demolition of the supremacy of the marketing mix provided a fantastic revelation and a boost for us to continue our work questioning the validity and efficacy of the marketing concept and its associated theories, which Douglas Brownlie and I had begun to do, somewhat timorously, on my part at any rate (Brownlie and Saren, 1992a, 1992b, 1995). We did so despite the fact that Christian did remind us starkly of the risks involved.

"For an academic researcher looking for tenure and promotion, to question [the mix] has been to stick out his or her neck too far" (Grönroos, 1994: 5).

One result of this disincentive to question the 4Ps which Grönroos highlights was a neglect of empirical studies of what the key marketing variables are and how they are used by marketing managers. And one might also observe the general absence of research into what marketing managers actually do and their efficacy. The question regarding academic's failure to question the marketing mix is why was there not more critique of the 4Ps at the time when Borden (1964) and McCarthy (1960) promulgated them? It is not as though there was an absence of contemporary critique of marketing as an activity and a profession outside the marketing academy, even in the United States of America. For example, Vance Packard's critical analysis of the methods and effects of the advertising industry in *The Hidden Persuaders* (1957) and J.K. Galbraith's economic analysis of *The Affluent Society* (1958).

It was another Nordic scholar, Johann Arndt, who may provide the answer as to why there was so little critique of the 4Ps at that time. He argued that marketing had been limited to one philosophical orientation which rendered it one-dimensional and unable to critique existing theories more widely and to develop alternative approaches. Arndt identified four alternative paradigms which contain different assumptions about the nature of the marketing discipline and the study of marketing phenomena (Arndt, 1985). Arndt's major contribution to the debate about marketing's philosophical approach and knowledge was that he introduced marketing scholars to a number of alternative paradigms from which they could engage in research.

Another possible barrier to academics engaging with more critique of marketing theories is the view that this has little perceived relevance for students to their future tasks as managers. They may well ask: "Who would employ me as a manager if I am critical towards business?" Despite the call from the *Economist* for more critique of business methods and ethos, the answer is probably "very few companies." Another illustration of a similar problem of widening the scope of marketing is the question asked by a group of international MBA students when the instructor was discussing the buying behavior of poor consumers. "Why do we need to know about marketing to the poor?" asked these future leaders of multinational business; "they don't have any money."

This issue represents a particularly restrictive view of marketing theory that equates marketing with those activities pursued by the individual firm, rather than with a broader, societal perspective (Wilkie and Moore, 1999). Marketing education should enable students to develop self-esteem, courage and intellectual strength, and a sense of agency in order to challenge the orthodox marketing management role, organizational *group thinking*, and the prevailing role of marketing in society. Marketing scholars must show them how to evaluate theories critically by scrutinizing their underlying concepts, definitions, and unstated assumptions. That is why we need top academics like Christian Grönroos, who is a fearless truth teller, a parrhesia, able and willing to question and interrogate the dominant theories as well as building new ones.

References

Arndt, J. 1985. "The Tyranny of Paradigms: The Case for Paradigmatic Pluralism in Marketing," in Nikhilkesh Dholakia and Johan Arndt (eds), *Changing the Course of Marketing: Alternative Paradigms for Widening Marketing Theory*, pp. 3–25. Greenwich: JAI Press.

Bagozzi, R.P. 1978. "Marketing as Exchange: A Theory of Transactions in the Marketplace," *American Behavioral Scientist*, 21 (March/April): 535–56.

Baker, M.J. 2001. "Introduction," in M.J. Baker (ed.), *Marketing: Critical Perspectives in Marketing*, Volume 1, pp. 1–25. London: Routledge.

Borden N.H. 1964. "The Concept of the Marketing Mix," *Journal of Advertising Research*, 4 (June): 2–7.

Brownlie, D., and M. Saren. 1992a. "The Four P's of the Marketing Concept: Prescriptive, Polemical, Permanent and Problematical," *European Journal of Marketing*, 26 (4): 34–47.

———. 1992b. "Developing the Marketing Concept as an Ideological Resource," *British Academy of Management Conference*, September, University of Bradford, England.

———. 1995. "The Commodification of Marketing Knowledge," *Journal of Marketing Management*, 11 (7): 619–28.

Economist. 2009. "The Pedagogy of the Privileged," September 24, *Economist*, London.

Foucault, M. 2001. *Fearless Speech*. Edited by Pearson J. Los Angeles: Semiotext(e).

Frampton, K. 1983. "Prospects for a Critical Regionalism," *Perspecta*, 20: 147–62.

Galbraith, J.K. 1958. *The Affluent Society*. London: Hamish Hamilton.

Grönroos, C. 1989. "Defining Marketing: A Market-Oriented Approach," *European Journal of Marketing*, 23(1): 52–60.

———. 1994. "From Marketing Mix to Relationship Marketing: Towards a Paradigm Shift in Marketing," *Management Decision*, 32 (2): 4–20.

———. 1995. "Relationship Marketing: The Strategy Continuum," *Journal of the Academy of Marketing Science*, 23 (4): 252–54.

———. 1999. "Relationship Marketing: The Nordic School Perspective," in Jagdish N. Sheth and Atul Parvatiyar (eds), *Handbook of Relationship Marketing*, pp. 95–118. Thousand Oaks, CA: SAGE Publications.

Grönroos, C. and E. Gummesson. 1985. *Service Marketing: Nordic School Perspectives*. Stockholm: Stockholm University.

Harris, H. 1954. "Regionalism and Nationalism," address to the *North West Regional Council of the Architectural Institute of America*, Eugene, Oregon.

Herodotus. 1985. *Herodotus: The History*. Translated by David Green. Chicago: University of Chicago Press.

Hill, R.P. 2002. "Consumer Culture and the Culture of Poverty: Implications for Marketing Theory and Practice," *Marketing Theory*, 2 (3): 273–93.

Jones, B., and D. Monieson. 1990. "Early Development of the Philosophy of Marketing Thought," *Journal of Marketing*, 54 (1): 102–13.

Keith, R.J. 1960. "The Marketing Revolution," *Journal of Marketing*, 24 (1): 35–38.

Kuhn, T. 1962. *The Structure of Scientific Revolution*. Chicago: University of Chicago Press.

Lowrie, A., and H. Willmott. 2005. "Marketing Higher Education: The Promotion of Relevance and the Relevance of Promotion," *4th International Critical Management Studies Conference*, July, University of Cambridge, England.

Maclaran, P., M. Saren, L. Stevens, and C. Goulding. 2009. "Rethinking Theory Building and Theorizing in Marketing," *38th European Marketing Academy Conference*, May, University of Nantes, France.

Marion, G. 2010. "Conformity around Dominant Cognitive Marketing Products," *Marketing Theory*, 10 (2): 192–209.

McCarthy, J.E. 1960. *Basic Marketing: A Managerial Approach*. Homewood, IL: Richard D. Irwin.

Morgan, R.M., and S.D. Hunt. 1994. "The Commitment-Trust Theory of Relationship Marketing," *Journal of Marketing*, 58 (3): 20–38.

Packard, V. 1957. *The Hidden Persuaders*. London: Longmans, Green & Co.

Reilly, W.J. 1931. *The Law of Retail Gravitation*. Austin, TX: University of Texas.

Svensson, Peter. 2007. "Producing Marketing: Towards a Social-Phenomenology of Marketing Work," *Marketing Theory*, 7 (3): 271–90.

Veloutsou, C., M. Saren, and N. Tzokas. 2002. "Relationship Marketing. What if...?" *European Journal of Marketing*, 36 (4): 433–39.

Webster, F. 1992. "The Changing Role of Marketing in the Corporation," *Journal of Marketing*, 56 (1): 1–17.

Wilkie, W.L., and E.S. Moore. 1999. "Marketing's Contributions to Society," *Journal of Marketing*, 63 (Special Issue): 198–218.

17

Christian Grönroos: A Personal Appreciation

Richard Varey

This is a personal appreciation of a body of work on "Relationship Marketing" that has been in my consciousness throughout my doctoral research project conducted in the early 1990s, and continuing in my work on understanding marketing as a social process. Christian Grönroos's writing has been an inspiration, because I agreed with his explanation and thus could quote his definitions, or because my differing understanding was illuminated. Thus, I have been influenced and inspired—I found an intellectual domain for my critical work and have remained engaged with the Nordic School for almost 20 years.

I am grateful for this impetus to re-read an extensive body of work together for the first time, and this has revealed a methodical progression which I can identify as largely the basis for my own style and motivation, even though I also recognize that my work is rather more eclectic and less focused and programmatic.

I've always found reading Christian's work pleasurable in both his writing style and the substantial insights, and I also find that I often smile at the occasional grammatical tangles and what seem to me to be somewhat eccentric choices of words and phrases, but then I'm a Yorkshire man, claiming to speak the Queen's English!

My introduction to Christian's work came when I was a member of a master's class on service marketing led by Dr Barbara Lewis at Manchester School of Management in about 1988. Among a range of readings recommended were articles and books by Evert Gummesson and Christian Grönroos, and the class was introduced to the idea of a Nordic School of thinking, as well as the obligatory North American managerial literature. Taken together, the Scandinavian books and articles were for me much more engaging than the managerial style of the North American writers (it's also interesting for me to realize that I've never fully engaged with the IMP program in spite of its contribution in the Nordic School, largely because my focal point has been the social person as citizen and not the firm). My Ph.D. project (begun in 1992 and completed in early 1996) was a thorough conceptual review of Internal Marketing, and of course this led to the growing literature on Relationship Marketing that was emerging at the time, just as Christian was taking a lead in the research literature from the early 1990s. By 2002, I had gone further and written and published critical books on marketing communication and relationship marketing. In these I was inspired, provoked, and motivated to try to re-humanize marketing in a kind of post-industrial as a more social/societal alternative to mechanistic rationality, necessarily treating communication and relationship with greater depth and reflection than was typically the case in marketing texts. Christian's then recent book on service management and marketing was a major catalyst. Since my marketing and customer service consulting experiences in the late 1980s, I had been pondering the theory of service quality, communication, and marketing—we'd probably now call all of this value creation, and I wasn't satisfied with the "technological" assertions and assumptions prevailing in textbooks. Christian's notion of "interactive communication" seemed consistent with my ambitions for bringing a liberated conception of communication to the fore in the discipline, and was thus a provocation to take the communication perspective in my writing and teaching. I even, for a time, moved into a Corporate Communication research unit, then an Information Systems group, broadening my philosophical and critical awareness, before returning to a marketing department in 2003 in a school with a "sustainable enterprise" purpose.

During my doctoral project readings, which were intentionally catholic and comprehensive (I read and cited over 500 publications in marketing management, service management, quality management, communication studies, and beyond), Barbara Lewis recommended that I read the then recently published special issue of the *Asia-Australia Marketing Journal* (which later was renamed the *Australasian Marketing Journal*) edited by David Ballantyne (Volume 2, 1994) which collected papers from the first *International Colloquium in Relationship Marketing* (hosted that year at Monash University in Australia). This was because Barbara wanted me to be aware of new thinking in service marketing. Christian's highly influential article in this issue was republished in *Management Decision* and I have been told it has now been cited over 1,600 times! After reading that issue's articles, I contacted David Ballantyne—another catalyst in my scholarship—and we have been in close collaboration since, having now co-authored 10 publications. Subsequently, we've both moved to New Zealand, so are now much closer in both mind and space.

In my Ph.D. thesis on "A Broadened Conception of Internal Marketing," I proposed broadening understanding and application beyond managerial limits of scientistic/mechanistic thinking, and this led me to Relationship Marketing—indeed my thesis conclusion suggested that Internal Marketing be termed internal relationship marketing to shift thinking from the limited transactional conception of marketing to a broader (and deeper) "relational" conception (see Varey, 1995, 1996). This led directly to me realizing that there was a potential (publishable) contribution in thinking beyond the orthodox. I'm currently revisiting both Internal Marketing and Relationship Marketing to elaborate the interaction and communication basis of the *service-dominant logic* framework of premises.

Relationship Marketing was understood by many managers, students, educators, and researchers as the alternative to transactional marketing, to be used in special cases (e.g., for competitively selling intangible product "services"). From the alternative "marketing as social process" perspective that I was pursuing, Relationship Marketing is understood as the general case (the norm), whereas transactional marketing had become the assumed norm in human relations in the work sphere and commerce (seen as *industrialized* relations!).

My subsequent "alternative" textbook on relationship marketing (Varey, 2002) was largely inspired by my reading of *Service Management and Marketing: A Customer Relationship Management Approach* (2000) in which service management was proposed as the purpose for marketing drawing on the integrated and integrative character and power of the marketing process. Hence when the service-dominant logic for marketing was made explicit in the mainstream literature (Vargo and Lusch, 2004), it resonated as well as surprised. It was apparently emanating from the US managerial school of scholarship, yet it opened up and integrated a much more comprehensive perspective. Steve Vargo and Bob Lusch also drew on Christian's focus on service, citing his 2000 book as well as his article on the "paradigm shift" to relationship marketing (Grönroos, 1994).

I've only met Christian once. This was in a conference session in New Orleans. I presented a paper on internal marketing co-authored with my colleague and former doctoral supervisor Barbara Lewis at the 1999 *AMA SERVSIG Conference on Services Marketing Research*. I wasn't aware that the famously erudite and prolific Professor Grönroos was in the room and I made several comments about his work, citing half a dozen of his writings. Our paper identified the then popular conception of internal marketing in a historical review. We highlighted themes to frame our examination of the concept. This analysis surfaced a management strategy focusing on the relationships of a purposive social system, not limited to the coordination of economic transactions. We revealed confusion over possible form, consequent role, and implementation. It was quite a critical discussion. Imagine my surprise when Christian came over to speak to me after the presentation and introduced himself, telling me that he was grateful that I had helped to resolve some issue he had with a student's research project! That's just the kind of confidence boost you need as an aspiring researcher with a freshly minted Ph.D. trying to make a mark in the academy.

In looking over the key works republished here as well as my engagement with Christian's work, I note that I have more than 50 of his publications listed in my expanding endnote bibliographic database (which I began compiling in 1991 and now extends to almost 20,000 references). Some 26 of the listed publications authored by Christian are focused on relationship marketing. In my Ph.D. thesis bibliography, I cited eight publications (1981–91) on internal marketing and service quality. In thinking of a possible synthesis in my appreciation of this body of work within a "big picture," it is most clear to me that communication and interaction were the attracting features in his writing on relationship marketing, then his highlighting of "dialog," and more recently an alternative "organic" and more "human" explanation of marketing that is less abstractly technological, albeit firm-centric.

Although I've kept up with most of Christian's work through his prolific journal article publications, it is his series of books that have been the foundation of my engagement with his work: In 1983, Christian published *Strategic Management and Marketing in the Service Sector* (Chartwell-Bratt) and I could see marketing's strategic character. In 1990 service management came to the fore in *Service Management and Marketing: Managing the Moments of Truth in Service Competition* (Lexington Books), and this was revised 10 years later in the 2000 book *Service Management and Marketing: A Customer Relationship Management Approach* (second edition, Wiley), bringing Relationship Marketing forward as market-based relationship management. The third edition in 2007 centered the whole understanding firmly back in service in *Service Management and Marketing: Customer Management in Service Competition* (third edition, Wiley). Also in 2007 Christian published his "career anthology" *In Search of a New Logic for Marketing: Foundations of Contemporary Theory* (Wiley). Each book has been an expansion, the extensions, elaborations, and refinements of what came before, so the evolutionary trajectory is clear to me, culminating in the overview in 2007 that shows Christian's alternative pathway to the notion of relationship marketing as the management of value formation in service.

In the articles collected here some highlights are worthy of highlighting. There's an (almost) complete framework for explaining marketing that is far more sophisticated than the "marketing mix," one that is necessary for the evolution of marketing's purpose and form for a sustainable society beyond wasteful and unsatisfying corporate-driven consumerism. In 1994, building and managing relationships with customers and others came firmly onto the marketing agenda, and this required recognition that the marketing mix is not the foundation for marketing. The discipline must align with sociocultural evolution in the post-industrial society, yet still the 4Ps framework persists as the easy road for "teaching" marketing!

In Christian's work (Grönroos, 1996), service had become the basis of relationship marketing; thus, service management is relationship-oriented management throughout the firm and a functional/department form of organization is inadequate and damaging to the core purpose of commerce. Relational thinking is refined (Grönroos, 1997), recognizing that relationship is always latent in a social system, but intents can differ, so mode of interaction is highlighted as a key consideration.

By 1999, experience of process is what constitutes value(-able) experience, and interaction, communication, and relationships are key concepts in explaining the marketing system (Grönroos, 1999). Service is highlighted, showing early signs of what would surface elsewhere under the rubric of a *service-dominant logic* for marketing. The concept of total communication is outlined, recognizing process integration beyond the communication program (advertising campaigns, etc.). However, communication and interaction are separated, with the former supporting the latter. This error was a catalyst for my later work with David Ballantyne on dialogue and interaction. In

2000, dialog practice is to the fore as the basis for explaining how value is known (Grönroos, 2000). Then in 2009, Christian conducts an overview of an assessment of the role of marketing as support for the formation of value through interaction. This is the fundamental concept for process-oriented management, and the promise management definition is central to understanding relationship marketing as service-oriented management. This remains a firm-centric view, of course, yet when marketing is understood to be a social process then there are particular and differing participant perspectives to be appreciated in a network picture.

My own work on Relationship Marketing draws on Christian's conceptualizations in a series of colloquium papers, books, and journal articles in the period from 2002 to 2009. I have convened a senior undergraduate class on Relationship Marketing each year since 2004, and we have drawn on key quotations, the relational marketing triangle, and a number of article readings to support student learning. The article from 1994 has remained at the heart of my reading list as we construct a critical examination of the meaning and implications of marketing relationships in contemporary society each time.

In the transition from goods-centered thinking to a service orientation, Relationship Marketing has remained for many practitioners a managerial tool, and has yet to become fully relational. Paraphrasing Christian's thinking in his 1997 article, there is as yet insufficient commitment to relational intent, and many so-called "relationships" are but simulated relationships, orchestrated by one party. I can see in the 2007 book conclusions on a "new logic for marketing" the strong shift toward humanistic marketing which comes in making service central rather than exchange. The functional, tactical, distributive, persuasive form of marketing is counterpointed with the ideological, strategic, and constructive form. Amazingly (at least to me!), I still meet a majority of senior marketing undergraduate students for whom the notion of a paradigm shift in marketing thought is something of a revelation. All are still fed a diet of marketing mix and service(s) as an impoverished intangible equivalent of goods, and only those who choose (perhaps mostly for instrumental reasons) the Relationship Marketing paper as part of their study program are challenged with the alternative conception of marketing.

So, in conclusion, what lessons can be learned from reading this selection of Christian's articles, and what have I learned from my review and reflection? How has Christian's work influenced and inspired my scholarship? Initially it has been his writing style, as well his incisive analysis and practical focus. But also, importantly, it has been the catalyst in his sometimes not quite getting it right! By this I'm thinking of the terminology that appears through his writings. Whereas Christian has coined terms for phenomena he discerned in his Scandinavian social philosophical analysis, always from within the practices of marketing, I've been motivated to adopt sociological, anthropological, and ecological concepts from a critical stance. Hence our differences in terminology for what appear to be the same concepts. His is a somewhat "managerial" terminology, e.g., "interactive marketing," "transaction marketing," "perceived quality," "customer perceived value," and "value perception." My discomfort with each of these has prompted me to inquire further on what is understood as communication and relationship, and in doing so I've come to the view that the instrumentality of managerial marketing is veiled by a narrowness in not understanding that interaction is the basic concept, and that differing forms of interaction are observable and necessary to the social purpose of marketing. Such forms are informative (monological) interaction and communicative (dialogical) interaction, and the distinctions explicated in Martin Buber's thinking on dialogue—of technical, genuine, and with monological disguised as dialogical—are very helpful but under-applied.

For me, in my early career, I wasn't comfortable with the orthodox view from within the marketing discipline, and could sense much more of the social/societal big picture that challenged assumptions and intentions. The heretical, unconventional style in Christian's writings were and still are inspirational, and he showed me that my apparent disposition towards "intellectual trespassing" (as a colleague once called my work) was the way to "go my own way." Social system thinker Sir Geoffrey Vickers once said that the dogs were the best fed at the medieval banquet since they could roam among the tables for a varied menu of scraps whereas the lords and ladies ate only what was placed in front of them. Eighteenth-century philosopher Arthur Schopenhauer is reputed to have observed that all truth passes through three stages. Firstly, it is ridiculed as irrelevant and plain stupid. Then it is violently opposed, and finally it is accepted as self-evident. I try to always be sensitive to those ideas that are just too sensible, and 20 years ago sensed that there was a long-term career ahead for me in bringing forth the alternative understandings, often by merely connecting ideas that were not popularly understood together. Back in 1999, I published a review of Marshall McLuhan's body of work because I believe that specialists can benefit from an appreciation of its significance to marketing thought and practice. I also strongly recommend that anyone seriously committed to understanding marketing's contemporary significance and future should re-read Christian Grönroos's published work as a corpus, beginning with some defining articles included in this volume. Everyone engaged with the marketing literature can learn much in clarity by a reading of this work.

I'm proud to have often been recognized (even accused) of being an idealist—I like the commitment to ideas! For me, Christian has been an intellectual pathbreaker—and I continue to follow in my own way.

References

Grönroos, C. 1994. "From Marketing Mix to Relationship Marketing: Towards a Paradigm Shift in Marketing," *Asia-Australia Journal of Marketing*, 2 (1): 9–30. Also published the same year in *Management Decision*, 32 (2): 4–20.

————. 1996. "Relationship Marketing Logic," *Asia-Australia Marketing Journal*, 4: 7–18, republished 1996 as Relationship Marketing: Strategic and Tactical Implications, *Management Decision*, 34 (3): 5–14.

————. 1997. "Value-Driven Relational Marketing: From Products to Resources and Competencies," *Journal of Marketing Management*, 13 (5): 407–19.

Grönroos, C. 1999. "Relationship Marketing: The Nordic School Perspective," in J.N. Sheth and A. Parvatiyar (eds), *Handbook of Relationship Marketing*, pp. 95–118. Thousand Oaks, CA: SAGE Publications.

———. 2000. "Creating a Relationship Dialogue: Communication, Interaction and Value," *The Marketing Review*, 1 (1): 5–14.

———. 2007. *In Search of a New Logic for Marketing: Foundations of a Contemporary Theory.* Chichester: John Wiley.

———. 2009. "Relationship Marketing as Promise Management," in P. Maclaran, M. Saren, B. Stern, and M. Tadajewski (eds), *The SAGE Handbook of Marketing Theory*, pp. 397–412. Los Angeles, CA: SAGE Publications.

———. 1995a. "Internal Marketing: A Review and Some Inter-Disciplinary Research Challenges," *International Journal of Service Industry Management*, 6 (1): 40–63.

———. 1995b. "A Model of Internal Marketing for Building and Sustaining a Competitive Service Advantage," *Journal of Marketing Management*, 11 (1–3): 25–40.

———. 1996. *A Broadened Conception of Internal Marketing.* Ph.D. diss., UMIST, Manchester.

———. 1999. "Marketing, Media, and McLuhan: Rereading the Prophet at Century's End," *Journal of Marketing*, 63 (3): 148–53.

———. 2002a. *Marketing Communication: Principles and Practice.* London: Routledge.

———. 2002b. *Relationship Marketing: Dialogue and Networks in the E-Commerce Era.* Chichester: John Wiley.

Varey, R.J., and B.R. Lewis. 1999. "Beyond the Popular Conception of Internal Marketing," paper presented at the Jazzing into the New Millennium, the *AMA SERVSIG Conference on Services Marketing Research*, New Orleans, USA.

David Ballantyne Interviews Christian Grönroos

18

Relationship Marketing Will Be Important for Businesses in Future

David Ballantyne: *The Nordic School of services has been important in the early development of relationship marketing insights. How did it come about that "service" became the basis for studies of "relationships" within the Nordic school?*

Christian Grönroos: Originally, Nordic School research was about marketing challenges and subsequently market-oriented, customer-centric management for service firms. Although this was not articulated explicitly, in the 1980s it developed into studies of service without making a distinction between service firms and goods manufacturers. It was this development that made relationships between firms and their customers a focal issue. Len Berry's (1983) conference paper on relationship marketing for services and Barbara Bund Jacksons's (1985) article and book on relationships in business used the word relationship, and we got a term for what we were studying. The starting point was service, and we observed that services are inherently relational. The finding that followed was that firms cannot develop relationships with customers without service. Supplying customers with goods or core services only is not enough to create the trust and commitment that is considered necessary for relationships to evolve. Additional resources have to be embedded in an ongoing business engagement, where customers are supported—serviced—and not just as objects of transactions.

DB: How does the Nordic School relationship perspective compare with that of the Industrial Marketing and Purchasing (IMP) group? There seem to be many shared perspectives. Are there differences as well?

CG: This is an interesting question. There are indeed many shared perspectives. For example, in Nordic School and in IMP studies the actors, interactions, and networks are central concepts. However, the two schools approach these topics in different ways and develop different concepts and models to describe them and their relation to other concepts. The resource heterogeneity notion which is a key issue in IMP research has not been emphasized in Nordic School research, probably because IMP studies are about business-to-business relationships, whereas Nordic School studies do not limit themselves to certain types of markets. Moreover, the starting point for knowledge development is different. Whereas Nordic School research takes service as the point of departure, in IMP research service is not a central phenomenon.

DB: *Customer Relationship Management (CRM) in many cases has departed from the mutually beneficial relationship concepts you and other thought leaders had proposed in the 1980s. How could this happen?*

CG: In my opinion, this is a sad story. To put it bluntly, the CRM notion—the very appealing concept of strategic management of customer relationships—was hijacked by the IT and database business, and as a consequence, from having been developed as a strategic approach, CRM was turned into a tactical support tool for firms interested in keeping track of their customer contacts and managing sales and marketing based on customer data systems. Marketed in this way by big and well-known vendors, the now mostly tactical CRM was considered appealing enough to catch the interest of big firms, and the grand idea of developing a strategic management approach to manage customer interactions from a relational perspective deteriorated into a tactical tool. CRM as a strategic management approach requires cross-functional management and implementation, which is difficult, whereas CRM as a tactical database management tool is much easier to manage in a traditional functionally organized firm. Of course, this has not worked out well. We know from a number of studies that most CRM projects fail, and buyers of so-called CRM tools and software suffer major losses. Some researchers try to advocate CRM as a strategic management approach, but it seems as if all sour tactical CRM investments made by firms have almost fatally hurt the CRM concept.

DB: *Would you say that your scholarly work tends to focus on the one-to-one management of customer relationships, or do you currently have a more holistic network view of markets and marketing?*

CG: In my research I have recognized the importance of networks in which firm–customer dyads exist and are managed, but I have tended to focus on dyads. In my view, networks add considerable complexity, and we have to understand the dyadic micro level before we move into a network context. Today I emphasize more than before the importance of considering the impact of the surrounding networks on the dyads within, but when studying relationships I still mainly hold a dyadic view of marketing.

DB: Internal marketing is an organizational strategy involving marketing, operations and HRM specialists working together. It seems obvious enough that its organizational-wide benefits depend on cooperation between these groups. Can you see any prospects of this developing in the future?

CG: Internal marketing is such a cross-disciplinary issue that academic researchers seem to be reluctant to pick it up. However, theoretically, I sense a growing interest in studying internal marketing again. After promising studies of internal marketing from a relational perspective, this research stream seems to have come to a standstill. This is a pity, because employees do work in relational contexts, and it would be natural to take a relationship approach. In practice, internal marketing seems to be considered too multi-functional to be adopted as a strategic issue. Far too often internal marketing is implemented as training programs only, and then the strength of the internal marketing idea is lost. Training requires follow-up actions by supervisors and managers, communication, and other supportive activities. Furthermore, in many firms employees do not seem to be considered a strategic resource, and this also restricts the use of internal marketing. Best results of internal marketing can be achieved when it is considered a strategic issue by top management, and when internal marketing is instilled as an ongoing process where tactical activities of many types are used.

DB: Do you think that digital social networks will be a platform suitable for businesses to develop new forms of relationship marketing?

CG: Yes, I do believe that social media and digital social networks can be helpful means of implementing relationship marketing. On the other hand, there is a risk that firms react in a reverse manner, reacting to customer activities in a transactional way. However, this is a field which I have not studied myself.

DB: What advice have you got for the next generation of marketing scholars?

CG: My major advice would be to believe in yourself and in your ideas, in spite of all the negative reactions one often gets, and to pursue your research avenue until you perhaps realize yourself that you should not. However, learn from criticism you get, but don't let others talk you out of your ideas. Relationship marketing is an important field, it will be important for businesses in the future. However, don't revert to viewing it as a tool only, but as strategic approach to managing business engagements, which of course requires the use of various activities. Don't look at relationship marketing as a set of tools and activities only, but put them into a strategic perspective.

About the Editors and Contributors

Jagdish N. Sheth is the Charles H. Kellstadt Professor of Marketing in the Goizueta Business School at Emory University, USA. Earlier, he has worked at the University of Southern California and Massachusetts Institute of Technology. He is well known for his scholarly contributions to the study of consumer behavior, relationship marketing, competitive strategy, and geopolitical analysis.

Professor Sheth has worked for numerous industries and companies in the United States, Europe, and Asia, both as an Advisor and as a Seminar Leader.

A prolific author, in 2000, Professor Sheth, along with Andrew Sobel, published *Clients for Life,* a bestseller. His book, *The Rule of Three* (2002), coauthored with Rajendra S. Sisodia, altered the current notions of the top-ten business books on Leadership in 2007.

David Ballantyne is Associate Professor of Marketing at the University of Otago, School of Business, New Zealand, and International Fellow at the Centre for Relationship Marketing and Service Management, Hanken School of Economics, in Helsinki, Finland. He is the coauthor of *Relationship Marketing: Bringing Quality, Customer Service and Marketing Together* (1991), the first international text published in this field of inquiry. He is a member of the editorial review boards of the *European Journal of Marketing, Journal of Business-to-Business Marketing, Industrial Marketing Management, Journal of Business Market Management*, and *International Marketing Review*. His current research interests are the service-dominant logic of marketing, relationship marketing, internal marketing, and dialogue as a co-creative knowledge generating mode in marketing.

Adrian Payne is Professor of Marketing at the Australian School of Business at the University of New South Wales, Australia, and a visiting professor at Cranfield University, UK. His main research interests are CRM, customer retention, service marketing, and relationship marketing. His publications have appeared in the *Journal of Marketing, Journal of the Academy of Marketing Science, Journal of Business Research, Industrial Marketing Management, Journal of International Business Studies, European Journal of Marketing, Long Range Planning, Human Relations*, and *Marketing Theory*.

His books include: *The Handbook of CRM: Excellence in Customer Management*; *Relationship Marketing: Creating Stakeholder Value*; and *Creating a Company for Customers*. He serves on the review board of a number of international journals.

Michael Saren is Professor of Marketing at the University of Leicester, UK. He has previously held chairs in marketing at the universities of Stirling and Strathclyde. He was awarded an Honorary Fellowship and Life Membership of the UK Academy of Marketing in July 2007. He was a convener of the marketing streams at the Critical Management Studies Conferences, 1999–2011; and one of the founding editors in 2001 of the journal *Marketing Theory* and continues as a member of the advisory board. Mike has co-edited books titled *Rethinking Marketing* (1999) and *Critical Marketing: Defining the Field* (2007). He has also authored an introductory marketing text, *Marketing Graffiti: The View from the Street* (2006). His research interests cover marketing theory, critical marketing, consumer research, technology and marketing.

Richard Varey is Professor of Marketing and former Chair of the Department of Marketing at the University of Waikato, New Zealand. Richard's research and teaching interests are in marketing and society, relationship marketing, and marketing interaction. He is a co-editor (Pacific Rim) of the *Journal of Business-to-Business Marketing*, an associate editor (Asia-Pacific) of the *Journal of Customer Behaviour*, and a founding member of the editorial advisory board and an associate editor, *Social Business*. He was also editor of the *Australasian Marketing Journal* in 2006–08. Richard has co-edited (with Professor Barbara Lewis) *Internal Marketing: Directions for Management* (2000), *Marketing Communication: Principles and Practice* (2001), and *Relationship Marketing: Dialogue and Networks in the E-Commerce Era* (2002). He is a member of several editorial boards including *Marketing Theory, European Journal of Marketing, Journal of Communication Management, Journal of Marketing Communications, Corporate Reputation Review*, and *PRism*.